C000258187

ESSENTIAL ENGLISH

SUSAN DAVIES

HEINEMANN
EDUCATIONAL

Heinemann Educational Books Ltd
Halley Court, Jordan Hill, Oxford OX2 8EJ

OXFORD LONDON EDINBURGH
MADRID ATHENS BOLOGNA PARIS
MELBOURNE SYDNEY AUCKLAND SINGAPORE TOKYO
IBADAN NAIROBI HARARE GABORONE
PORTSMOUTH NH (USA)

ISBN 0 435 10193 5

Copyright © 1987 Sue Davies

First published 1987
95 14 13 12 11

For Gareth – with thanks for all his help and encouragement

Printed in Great Britain by The Bath Press, Avon

Contents

Part Three: Communication

Part Four: Coursework

Introduction

This book is intended to provide a course of work for fourth and fifth year pupils who are working towards a final assessment in GCSE English. The author has taken full account of the National Criteria as they apply to English, as well as the differing needs of examining groups throughout the country. The author's own school was involved in pilot scheme work for GCSE and this book formed the basis of the course followed.

The book is divided into five parts dealing with: **Writing; Reading and Responding; Communication; Oral Skills** and **Coursework**. Each part is structured so that it can be used flexibly according to the needs of the pupils. This flexibility means that each part may be worked through from beginning to end or dipped into and used alongside other materials. It should be noted, however, that in the writing and the reading and responding sections exercises get progressively more difficult.

Writing deals with the three different types of writing that pupils need, namely imaginative, factual and argumentative. Each type of writing is dealt with in turn. Imaginative writing, for instance, is broken down into its component parts, setting, character and plot. Each aspect of the writing is then discussed and its importance emphasised through the use of examples. There are assignments for the pupils to tackle and practical and helpful hints in HELP sections throughout the book to assist any pupil who experiences difficulties.

The author's experience in running a pilot scheme for GCSE highlighted the teacher's need for ample ready-made resource material. Material of this kind is to be found in the chapters on factual and argumentative writing. This material, it is hoped, will provide not just written work but oral work as well. The argumentative essay section deals with popular topics for classroom discussion and poems provide some integrated literature work. This has been prompted by the requirement that English be seen as a 'single unified course'. It is felt that this section will prove invaluable, providing information and structured assignments for discussion and written work and addresses to write to for further information.

Reading and Responding also takes full account of the National Criteria. It provides material from many different genres including factual and fictional prose, poetry and drama. The aim has been to produce resource material that fulfils a multiplicity of functions. Not only can passages be used for conventional testing of a pupil's understanding, they can also stimulate writing that can be included in coursework folders through the 'write on' sections that follow many of the passages.

The **Communications** section on advertising, newspapers and letter-writing follows. Here it is hoped that pupils will gain an understanding of how language is used by the media as a persuasive force in our society.

Coursework, now an integral part of any examining group's syllabus, is discussed in some detail. On the written side, practical hints about how pupils can present their folders and log their work are given. On the **oral** side, particular attention is paid to the type of activities that pupils might find difficult and practical help and advice suitable for all abilities is given. Much of the material found in this section has been included as a direct result of the author's experiences whilst teaching the GCSE course.

GOLDEN RULES introduce each section of the book. If pupils' attention is drawn to these at the outset they may then be used as a constant reference as to how a specific piece of work can best be tackled.

Finally, this material can be used to best advantage if it is seen as a flexible teaching resource. Not only is each part adaptable to the individual needs of the pupils, but the resource materials provided can be interchanged and integrated with other coursework. Opportunities for oral and coursework occur throughout the book, for instance, information in the argumentative sections can provide work for factual writing; poetry and drama extracts could provide a stimulus for imaginative writing and discussion. The book provides a rich source of lesson material suited directly to the needs of the GCSE course.

Part One

Writing

General Introduction

Part One of this book contains chapters on three main kinds of writing descriptive and narrative; factual and informative; argumentative. Each chapter has its own Introduction and Golden Rules to tell you more about each form of writing and to help you with the assignments.

Descriptive and narrative writing makes the most use of your imaginative skills, whereas factual and informative writing should be based on fact or information that is known to be true, rather than imagined. Factual writing requires you to look at the information carefully so that you can answer questions about it using the most appropriate material. The third kind of writing, argumentative, asks you to argue your point of view on a subject using logical reasons. It also involves recognising that there is more than one side to the question and it requires you to look at your opinion on the subject very critically.

Your GCSE English work will involve all these different writing forms in your coursework and perhaps in a final exam. Your teachers will ask you to do assignments that will develop these different skills. Sometimes you will be asked to write a plan or notes for your assignment. At other times a continuous piece of writing, a paragraph or longer essay, a poem or dialogue may be required. Other assignments will focus on writing reports, leaflets, articles or advertisements. The skills you learn here will help you with your other GCSE subjects.

Golden Rules

1 If you are given a choice of topic to write about always choose carefully – poor writing is often the result of poor subject choice.

2 Make sure that you can write well and at length on the topic you have chosen. At some time you may have found yourself half-way through a piece of writing and not known how to finish it. You must try to avoid this happening.

3 All written work needs a structure and will require careful planning. (A plan is a brief outline of what you are going to write and the order in which you will write it.) It must have a good beginning to involve the reader, a middle full of the main information or detail of the writing and a satisfactory ending. A weak, unsatisfactory ending may indicate that you have run out of ideas and the reader will feel cheated. If you are writing an argumentative essay always provide a conclusion. This is a paragraph that sums up all the points you've made.

4 The first line or sentence of your writing is important, it should read fluently and should be free of errors. Remember, first impressions are important.

5 Remember to paragraph your writing – nothing looks worse than a piece of writing without a paragraph in sight.

6 Never begin successive paragraphs with the same word or phrase. For example, 'Then he did...' and 'Then he did...' or, 'Another point against ... is ...' You can avoid this by checking that you have used the same word or phrase at the beginning of a paragraph no more than twice in one piece of writing.

7 Punctuate carefully – if you include direct speech, remember to include all speech marks and begin a new line or paragraph for each new speaker.

8 Try to include interesting and mature vocabulary in your essays. Examiners and teachers expect to see this. They soon get bored with words like 'lovely', 'beautiful' and 'nice' in imaginative writing and words like 'terrible' in argumentative and factual writing.

9 Finally, *always* read through your work carefully before submitting it for marking. Check the grammar, punctuation and spelling. For instance, if you know that you always spell a certain word wrongly, check that it's not mistakenly spelt. Make sure that you have used a wide vocabulary and that you haven't used the same words many times over.

Descriptive and Narrative Writing

Introduction

Descriptive and narrative writing is probably the type of writing you are most familiar with because you began to do it as long ago as your primary school days.

Descriptive writing

This is where you describe a person, place or thing. For instance, you might be asked to write about a park in which case you would possibly describe the park itself, the things in the park and the people in the park (we call them characters). In descriptive writing the things you write about may be unrelated one to another and you may write about them in differing order but together they will build up an overall picture. They are like a series of snapshots which together give an impression of the place.

Narrative writing

Writing of this kind also contains descriptions of characters, places and things but, in addition, it has a plot – it tells a story. In order for the story to be understood there must be a plan of action, a sequence of events. A piece of narrative writing is rather like a family photo album, where the pictures are in a particular sequence and the characters and events are related. Many of the books that you read in class are narratives, they tell a story which may be true or false and which will often involve a group of characters.

Golden Rules

1   Look at the essay titles and choose carefully. If there is an essay about camping and you have never been camping it might not be the best choice of essay for you to write. However, if you know a lot about this type of holiday and feel confident you could tackle this question it could be a good choice, even if you've never camped.

2   Once you have chosen a title decide what you are going to write. Make a plan of the contents of the essay, paragraph by paragraph. Remember, a plan is not the same as a plot. All essays require planning, not all essays require a plot. If you have difficulty in *planning* a particular essay you may have difficulty in writing it. If this happens you could either rework your plan or change your choice of title without losing too much time. Of course, you will need to begin another plan if you choose a different title.

3   Whether your essay is descriptive or narrative, it will need a well described setting and probably some well described characters and things. This helps to involve the reader in the essay and make it more interesting. After all, isn't this what happens when you read a book? Don't you form a picture in your mind of the setting for the book and the characters in it?

4   Good vocabulary will help make your descriptions interesting. Try to make a list, before you begin your essay of words that you could use in it. After a while you will get into the habit of using more mature vocabulary. A wide vocabulary will help your other English work as well as your work in other subjects. Effective descriptions often include similes and metaphors. Look out for these when you are reading and try to include some in your writing.

5   Punctuation is important at all times but poor punctuation will stand out in an essay. Remember to use capital letters at the beginning of all new sentences and that 'i' is written as 'I' when it stands alone to mean 'I' or 'me'. Remember also to use paragraphs. If you are using direct speech, don't forget to use speech marks and to begin a new paragraph for each new speaker.

6   Always use a good pen; one that leaks will tend to make your work look untidy. Try to space your work out and leave a line between paragraphs since this makes your work easier to read. If you have poor handwriting try to spend a little time improving on it. You will certainly benefit from this in the long run.

Section 1 Writers and Writing

Introduction

All pupils are expected to be able to write an essay, especially by the time they reach the fourth and fifth years. However, many pupils find this difficult – maybe you are one of them. It is important to realise that no writing 'comes easy'. Authors spend a lot of time thinking about an idea before committing it to paper and most write a plan and work on it in some detail before they begin their book or piece of writing.

Writing an essay is obviously different from writing a book. With a book everything is on a much larger scale. After all, an essay is possibly only 500-600 words long whereas a novel is probably about 70,000 words. However, it is worth remembering that the main ingredients are often the same for both. They are often very similar in format; both may contain a setting and characters and, in the case of a narrative essay, a plot as well.

Here are two authors telling us something about the way they write a story. Obviously they are talking about the writing of a novel – you will not be expected to write a novel in a lesson or in an examination but what they have to say is also relevant to essay writing.

Read the passages carefully and then do the assignments.

Robert Westall

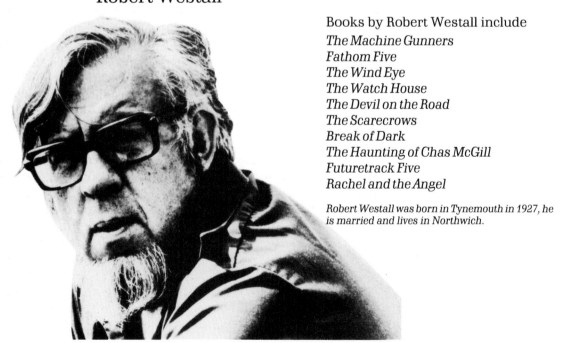

Books by Robert Westall include
The Machine Gunners
Fathom Five
The Wind Eye
The Watch House
The Devil on the Road
The Scarecrows
Break of Dark
The Haunting of Chas McGill
Futuretrack Five
Rachel and the Angel

Robert Westall was born in Tynemouth in 1927, he is married and lives in Northwich.

I began writing novels when I was twelve; the first was a novel of about 12,000 words called *The Mystery of Dead Man's Bay* and it was total rubbish .... I continued to write pure rubbish for many years because I used clichés borrowed from other books I'd read. But, the main thing was, I couldn't stop writing. Thousands and thousands of words.

I first began to write decently when I began to write about things I actually knew about; things I had done. This is the only way. The first piece I had published was after I had taken part, as a student, in an assault on the Russian Embassy in London, as a protest against the invasion of Hungary in 1956. I went home thinking, 'Tomorrow morning the papers will be full of the story of the riot from the police point of view. I want to tell people how it is from our point of view.' I got home from the riot at midnight and wrote till 4 a.m and posted it off to the editor of the *Newcastle Journal* before going to bed. It was published two days later and I got three guineas for it ....

Nor do I believe in a good deal of planning, I'm afraid. I do, of course, do very thorough research. If my hero is going to use plastic explosive (as in *The Devil on the Road*), I make sure I know how it is used before I start the book. I do gather all the facts I need, locations, etc, and digest them long before I start.

The book or the story is always carried by a hero or heroine, whether it is in the first person or the third, and the hero or heroine is always me or part of me, in some odd way. (Luckily I have a fairly well-developed *anima,* or female streak in me, for the heroines – though I am told that my heroines are not as strong as my heroes.) The other characters are all observed externally – and are usually comprised of bits and pieces culled from my long-suffering friends and aquaintances. It is best not to make characters up, unless they come into your unconscious and insist on being included.

The Machine Gunners is largely autobiographical. I wrote it because I wanted my son to know what it was like for me during the war. All the people in it are taken from my own childhood ....

Stories tend to grow with me; I will give you an example. I have recently written a short story called 'Rachel and the Angel' [published in a collection of that name]. This story started with a visit to a particularly fine Gothic church Upwell in the Fens – in 1979. It is interesting that I carried this story asleep in my head until I finally wrote it in 1985 – stories with me can take an awfully long time to be born.

What started me off, as I said, was this visit to Upwell on a very hot day in August, when the whole village was asleep and deserted. The church is not only very fine, but full of historic carving – an angel-roof, reclining knightly tomb, effigies, etc. Outside were exceptional tombstones. As I walked round, the feeling that I had this whole gorgeous treasure-house of history to myself excited me – I became a child again. But, the odd thing was, I became, or the heroine became, a girl of ten or eleven, a highly intelligent child, but bored with the summer holiday, who knew the church well, loved it, and in her loneliness and boredom had made it her toy (very respectfully, of course). The place of her imagination. But who was the antagonist? I knew he was there amongst the carved figures – I could sense him, but he would not come into focus. And there the matter rested for six years ...!

Joan Lingard

Books by Joan Lingard include
The Twelfth Day of July
Across the Barricades
Into Exile
A Proper Place
Hostages to Fortune
The Clearance
Strangers in the House
The Resettling
The Pilgrimage
The Reunion
Snake Among the Sunflowers
The Gooseberry
The Winter Visitor
Liam's Daughter
The File on Fraulein Berg

Joan Lingard was born in Edinburgh and brought up in Belfast for much of her younger life. She now lives in Edinburgh and is a full-time writer.

I started to write when I was eleven years old and living in Belfast and I began because I was absolutely crazy about books and couldn't get enough to read. The first book I wrote was about a girl called Gail and it was set in Cornwall where she went to stay with a granny. She stumbled on a secret passage which led to a secret cave and found that she was on the track of smugglers, whom, needless to say, she brought to justice! Shades of Enid Blyton!

I went on to write, during my adolescent years, books set in the Yorkshire moors, Wester Ross and even Brazil. I'd never been to any of these places. I didn't write a word about Belfast. I didn't think that dull, dreary, old Belfast could be the stuff of fiction! I thought that novels were only set in exotic places and that the characters had to go to boarding schools and have relatives who were in the Secret Service and such. It was only when I came into my twenties, that I realised I would write convincingly if I wrote about people and places that I knew and understood. So I wrote an adult novel called *Liam's Daughter,* set in Ireland and France, and it was accepted for publication.

I get ideas for books in all sorts of ways, sometimes from incidents, sometimes from overheard snatches of conversation. *The File on Fraulein Berg* is the most directly autobiographical book I have written. In the story there is a German teacher, who comes to a girls' school in Belfast during the war, and there are three girls who pursue her thinking she is a spy. I am one of those girls. Which is not to say that I appear in the book as myself. I created the characters but I used the situation from my childhood....

I think a lot about the structure beforehand and I decide on the point of view. Who will be at the centre of the book? Will it be in the first person or the third? The first person has the advantage of immediacy but the disadvantage of only being able to see the development from one viewpoint. But I quite like that. And, when I came to write the Maggie quartet, I knew at once that I would use the first person as the story was very much hers and I only wanted to show the world through her eyes. First person narrative has the advantage of giving a feeling of unity to the novel.

When ideas for a new novel start to form in my head I open a notebook on it. I make notes on possible characters, giving them names and physical characteristics, and on locations I might use. I often use streets and even houses that I know or have lived in. For instance, *The Gooseberry* is set around the corner from where I live in Edinburgh, *Strangers in the House* in a street I lived in as a student.

I write down snatches of dialogue in my notebook too. I might even write the opening paragraph. And gradually I think my way into the characters and their lives and their environment. I make a rough plan of how the novel will develop though often, when I come to write, it changes course. I enjoy that. I wouldn't want to know every step of the way beforehand. It's got to be a voyage of discovery for me as well as for the reader. And then the day comes when I really must begin....

When I finish the first draft I put it aside for a month and then go back to take a more objective look. During the first draft I am totally involved, in that I feel I am leading the characters' lives, but after that stage one must withdraw a little, otherwise one cannot even see what one has actually conveyed to the reader. And one must remember that there is going to be a reader. I think that the day one ceases to be critical of one's work is the day to lay down one's pen....

When I began to write I used to write at great speed, now I take my time. I feel I'm much more thoughtful about my writing. I stop to question myself so that I feel sure, as I write, that I know where I'm going.

Assignment 1   These two authors give hints which might help you in your writing. Make a list of the main hints that you find in each extract.

Assignment 2   Make a list of the books you have read that are written in the first person. Why do you think authors sometimes choose to write from this viewpoint? What might be the advantages or disadvantages?

The first person means using 'I'.

The third person means you write as 'he' or 'she' or 'they'.

Assignment 3   In about a page, describe a street accident or the inside of a disco, using the first person. Then try to describe the same scene writing in the third person. You might like to discuss in a small group which pieces are most effective and why.

Section 2   Descriptive Writing

Setting the scene – where

Where the action is to take place is important and needs to be described accurately. This is called 'setting the scene'. In descriptive writing the whole piece can deal with this description alone. If you want to see how important setting the scene is to a story, try this simple test. Take any three books from the fiction section of a library and open them at the first page. As you read, you should find that this page, more often than not, includes some description of the setting for the story.

When you set the scene you build up a picture using words. This makes it easier for the reader to understand your story and certainly makes the story more interesting. If books had no description in them, if there were no setting, they would be dull.

Does your writing have a recognisable setting or is it dull because it lacks one? The easiest way to describe a setting is to imagine you are there – maybe you are a fly on the wall – slowly move around the room, or wherever you're supposed to be, and write down what you see.

Read the following short extract. It builds up in the reader's mind a very clear picture of a setting in a short space of time, which is exactly what is required of you when you write an essay.

In a hole in the ground there lived a hobbit. Not a nasty, dirty, wet hole, filled with the ends of worms and an oozy smell, nor yet a dry, bare, sandy hole with nothing in it to sit down on or to eat: it was a hobbit-hole, and that means comfort.

It had a perfectly round door like a porthole, painted green, with a shiny yellow brass knob in the exact middle. The door opened on to a tube-shaped hall like a tunnel: a very comfortable tunnel without smoke, with panelled walls, and floors tiled and carpeted, provided with polished chairs, and lots and lots of pegs for hats and coats – the hobbit was fond of visitors. The tunnel wound on and on, going fairly but not quite straight into the side of the hill – The Hill, as all the people for many miles round called it – and many little round doors opened out of it, first on one side and then on another. No going upstairs for the hobbit: bedrooms, bathrooms, cellars, pantries (lots of these), wardrobes (he had whole rooms devoted to clothes), kitchens, dining-rooms, all were on the same floor, and indeed on the same passage. The best rooms were all on the lefthand side (going in), for these were the only ones to have windows, deep-set round windows looking over his garden, and meadows beyond, sloping down to the river.

From The Hobbit by J.R.R. Tolkien.

10

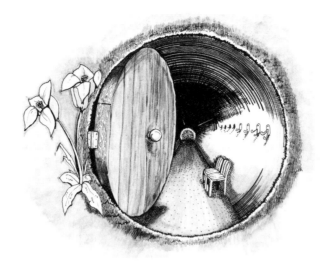

Assignment 1 Imagine you are invited to this hobbit's home for tea. Briefly describe, in one or two paragraphs, the room in which you sit and the refreshments that are laid on for you.

How big is the room?

Is it square or round?

Are there cupboards?

Is it a comfortable room?

Is there something mysterious about it?

What sort of things do you think hobbits have for tea?

Assignment 2 Write a short piece describing the setting of another party, perhaps one you have been to. Do not describe the party itself but build up a picture of the place where the party was held.

Assignment 3 Write a short piece describing a room in a house you have visited. It could be a house you know well or one you have only visited once, perhaps while on holiday. Try to build up a picture of the atmosphere of the room and the sort of person whose room it was.

Time and action – when

The setting is not just *where* the action takes place, there is more to it than that. It is also *when* the action takes place. When means the year it is, the season it is, or even the time of day it is.

You don't have to tell readers the exact time that your essay is set in, sometimes it is obvious. If you're writing an essay about the Vikings it is self evident that it's not set in the twentieth century unless you are writing about time travel. Similarly, if the sun is rising at the beginning of your essay, you do not need to tell the reader the exact time of day. They should have a rough idea at least!

In the following extract we are told that it is morning and we are told a little bit about the climate of the region. It is a rather different type of description from that found in *The Hobbit* and depicts a setting which is factual rather than imaginary. Information about the climate and the time of day adds to our impression of the place. We don't need first-hand experience of this type of climate. We are all made aware of how the scene described would look. Through our general knowledge gained from study in other subjects, from our watching of TV or from our reading of books we recognise the picture painted for us by the author.

READ

Far away, the desert dawn-wind blew through a British Military Cemetery. Neglected; unlike most. Surrounded by barbed-wire so rusty that the Arab children could reach up and grind it to red dust between finger and thumb. Then spit on the sand inside.

The peeling white gates had been wired up, by order of the Flossies. Nobody dared go in, even if they wanted to. Only balls of rolling desert weed ran through, caught on the arms of the leaning white crosses, then blew away back to the desert. Rags of Arabic newspaper caught and fluttered like dying birds on the wire. And in the morning the windswept sand was scribbled with the tracks of sandsnakes, passing in the night.

Major Wood's cross leaned less than most. The newest and last. Beneath, Major Wood slept on with honour. He had not heard; was not disturbed.

From *The Scarecrows* by Robert Westall.

Assignment 1   Add another paragraph describing the scene in the cemetery. Begin where the description ends.

HELP!

Is it a different time of day?

Has the sun risen fully?

What effect would this have on the scene?

Is there any movement in the cemetery?

What does the rest of the cemetery look like?

Concentrate your mind on one corner. What do you see?

Assignment 2 Write a paragraph describing a shopping centre when it is busy and another describing it when it is empty.

When is it likely to be most busy?

When might it be deserted?

Do buildings and places look better at certain times?

Using knowledge from other subjects

You will gain a lot of information about different times and places from your other studies, interests and so on. Do you ever use it? Very often pupils tend to compartmentalise subjects and keep them separate. This means that even if you've learnt about the Vikings and Romans in history, you may not think of using this valuable information in your English writing. The same is true of geography. Pupils tend to write about their own area or country and this means that there is no variety; similar settings are used time and time again. Do not be frightened to set your essays in a different time or in a foreign country, if you know enough to do this – it will make your writing more interesting and set your essay apart from others.

For instance, if you are given an essay title 'The Market' it is often tempting to write an essay about a local market. There is nothing wrong with doing this as long as the essay is interesting, well planned and obeys all the 'Golden Rules'. However, sometimes it is better to make your essay a little different, so that it stands out from those that are produced by the rest of the class. This can make writing more interesting for you as the writer as well!

You should use *all* your senses to enable you to describe scenes, not just your eyes. Your essay describing a market would be much more vivid if you were to include details of the mingled smells of hotdogs, fresh bread, fish, etc. The sounds of people chattering, of vendors selling their wares, of children playing and so on. Of course, sounds and smells would differ depending on the time and place you're in. They didn't have hotdogs in medieval England!

Assignment Imagine that you have been asked to write the essay entitled 'The Market'. Make a plan and list some of the words and phrases you might like to use. You must try and set your essay either in a different country or in a different time. If you are feeling very adventurous you might like to try both!

Atmosphere and mood

The following extract was written by an American staying in London on holiday. The writer has tried to build up a picture of two parks that are very different.

Setting a scene in a story means that we must be careful to note not only *where* we set our story, or *when* we set the story but also *how* something is set. Stories have different moods. There was a different mood evident in these two parks. The London park was quiet and serene whilst the other, New York's Central Park, was teeming with life, activity and noise. *How* you describe a setting influences the reader's reaction to it.

13

I'm lying under a tree in St James's Park. There are three downtown parks adjoining each other – St James's and Green, both small, and the big one, Hyde Park.

All the parks here are very serene, very gentle. Young couples go by arm in arm, quietly, no transistor radios or guitars in hand. Families picnic on the lawn sedately. Dogs go by on leashes, equally sedate, looking neither to the right nor to the left. There was one exception: a woman came by with a small grey poodle on a leash, I said hello to the poodle and he veered toward me, always-glad-to-meet-a-friend, but the woman yanked him back.

'Please don't do that!' she said to me sharply. 'I'm trying to teach him good manners.'

I thought, 'A pity he can't do the same for you,' and had a sudden vision of Dog Hill on a Sunday afternoon and wondered how everybody was....

Dog Hill is a broad, sloping hill in Central Park, and the largest canine Social Hall in the world. On a weekend afternoon you'll see forty or fifty dogs up there, charging around off leash meeting friends. (You don't take a dog to Dog Hill unless he's a friend to the world but I never met a New York dog who wasn't.) On a good day you'll see everthing from Afghans and Norwegian elkhounds to Shih-tzus and Lhasa Apsos, not to mention all the standard brands. The dog owners sit on the grass or stand around like parents at a children's party, keeping an eye out for sudden spats over whose stick it is or whose ball it is.

'George, if you can't play nicely we're going home!'

'Mabel, get off him! I don't wanna hear about it, just get off him!'

You do not stretch out on the grass to sunbathe because if a couple of great Danes and a collie are having a race and you're lying in their path they're not going to detour for you ....

I walked back down through the park to the Seventy-second Street entrance, past a baseball game and an impromptu marimba band fighting a rock concert that penetrated clear up from Fifty-ninth Street.

Lying in peaceful St James's, I realise how much a city's parks reflect the character of its people. The parks here are tranquil, quiet, a bit reserved, and I love them. But on a long-term basis I would sorely miss the noisy exuberance of Central Park.

From *84 Charing Cross Road* by Helene Hanff.

Assignment 1   Write a poem describing a park that you know about. Write about it when it is bustling and full of people and when it is empty.

What time of the year is it?

What is the weather like?

What are the people doing?

Is there something of interest that you can focus attention on? A particularly pleasant part of the park perhaps?

Assignment 2 Write a page describing 'Bonfire Night'. Think carefully about the mood you wish to convey.

Are there many people there?

Who is in charge of the fireworks?

Is the event well organised?

Are there adults as well as children?

Is the weather good for the time of year?

Reader's response

How you describe a setting — the mood you convey — is important and affects the reader's response. The setting can be peaceful or it can be grim and foreboding. The choices are endless and depend on the effect you wish to create. Sometimes, you may even wish to mislead the reader. To do this, you could build up a picture of a peaceful scene and then shock the reader by describing something sinister that they had not expected. Remember that the vocabulary you choose will play an important role in conveying an atmosphere to the reader.

Read carefully the following descriptions of a castle. As you read, watch for words that build up the mood in each extract.

It was a warm day and the birds had suddenly decided it was spring. They chirped away merrily as they set about nest building. The trees they were in lay at the foot of a steep embankment and their singing could be heard a long way away. Towering over the trees, like some giant, was a large stone castle, its two front-facing turrets guarded the valley that stretched out beneath it. From inside the castle could be heard the sounds of merry-making; laughter mingled with the sounds of the spring birds to produce a musical interlude. Soldiers could be seen on the ramparts but they were merely a precaution, there had been peace for a long time now.

The draw-bridge remained permanently down, almost as a welcoming gesture to strangers who sought shelter or food. Below the draw-bridge the moat didn't look dark and forbidding but warmly inviting; splashing in the distance indicated someone else thought so too. Along the banks wild spring flowers bloomed and their scent hung on the air like some potent perfume.

READ

There were buds on the trees and the day felt like a spring day but it was altogether too silent. Where were the birds? The beginning of the nests in the budding trees suggested they should be there. Fear hung among the branches and the birds hid too. Over the trees the castle shed its ominous shadow. It too was silent. The flags hung limply, as near to their poles as possible, their colours, once bright, had faded until they were hardly distinguishable.

Soldiers patrolled the ramparts; they too were silent, as if some heavy weight were pressing down on their spirits. The sun peeped from behind a cloud, it shone directly onto the draw-bridge; it was firmly shut. The moat below looked dark and forbidding, the black, murky waters lapping against the grassy banks, made a nasty sucking sound. Along the banks spring flowers began slowly to unfurl – they were black in colour. The scent they gave off was somehow cloying, almost like that of a sick room where someone had met their death.

Assignment 1   Make a list of the words and phrases in the first passage that help build up a peaceful, happy mood. Then make a list of words from the second passage that create a frightening picture. See how many words of your own you can add to each list.

Assignment 2   Write approximately one page describing the castle *either* as the setting for a school outing *or* as the setting for a spooky horror story.

What century are you in? Could you be in the future?

What is the weather like?

Is it day or night?

Section 3 Introducing Your Characters

Ways to describe characters

Descriptive writing often contains characters as well as a setting. These characters may be described in some detail and the way in which they are described may affect how the reader reacts to them. We learn about characters from:

---

1 Their appearance.

2 Their interests.

3 Their personality.

4 Their actions – what they do in the story.
    The deeds they perform. How they perform them.

5 What they say.

6 What other characters say about them.
    (Essays are often too short for this method to be incorporated.)

General impressions

In this extract the author builds up a picture of her grandfather so that at the end we have a very good idea of him.

Without a doubt my mother's father is an eccentric. My mum says he always has been, and I can believe that. You can only be that eccentric through years of practice.

He has ten adult children, and lives in a tumbledown country house where the family has lived for thirty years or so. It is rented, but the owner wants to demolish the house and sell the land. My grandad won't move out because he refuses to leave behind all the sheds, workshops and garages he has built around it over the years. He says they'll carry him out feet first.

His philosophy is that everything has a use, so in front of his house there is, what resembles, a scrapyard. Usually there is a used mound of turf too, as every year he goes up to 'The Hill' to cut peats. He never sells any, but gives it away to anyone who asks. It's the same with his vegetable garden. He grows everything, and gives it all away to his family in huge bagfuls.

In his day, before he supposedly retired, he was a blacksmith. He still occasionally, when asked nicely, will make beautiful wrought iron gates, which are his specialities. He once made a headboard for my bed which was too heavy to be carried upstairs.

He is religious, although he doesn't look it. He was born Protestant, but became a Jehovah's Witness when an adult. He left school when he was

twelve to start his apprenticeship. He started to smoke then, but gave up when he was sixty-five because he thought it was against his principles.

In his younger days he fancied himself as an inventor. He once connected all the lights to a wind generator. Unfortunately he did nothing to regulate the current, so on a fine day, with a light breeze, there would be little or no light. On the other hand during a gale, the lights would get very bright. My mother tells a story of how, one night when she was doing her homework, a gale was blowing outside. The lights got brighter and brighter, until, suddenly, every light in the house blew. That was the end of that invention.

He also deals in second-hand cars. He will fix them too, given half a chance. At any one time there will be half a dozen wrecks of cars lying around outside the house, because bits of them will come in useful, and, 'the engine is perfect, but it needs a new body'.

As my granny says, he can't understand that he's getting old. Last year he was seventy, and even though he says that he's living on borrowed time he can't understand why he gets tired quickly.

He is, at first sight, a strange character. As he is always working at something, he wears tatty old clothes. Now, that is acceptable, but he wears better clothes beneath. He wears his oldest clothes on top, and his Sunday best will be the bottom layer, so, at any one time, he could be wearing four pairs of trousers (and probably is). You wouldn't know it to look at him. I didn't realise until someone told me.

Not many people get on with my grandad. Even his sons and daughters frown at his stubbornness. He fights incessantly with his older grandchildren (my generation) and teases the younger ones. Strangely, my grandad and I don't argue. In his eyes I am the clever one, and he's always singing my praises to my cousins, Anne and Ruth, who are the same age as I am. This really annoys my aunt who replies that I may be at a grammar school, but Anne is a brilliant games player, and Ruth is good with her hands. All the same, I am the only one to get, 'free run of the milk bottle'. This is the device used to gauge your popularity with my grandad. In his house, they drink tea continually, and my grandfather is in charge of the milk. You can also help yourself to buns, butter, bread and sugar, but he pours the milk. He's mean with it too. Most people have to drink scalding tea, because he won't give them more milk. But I am one of the privileged few, and I get as much milk as I like! This, at times, causes much embarassment when my cousins are drinking black tea, and my cup is milky. I'm teased a lot about it.

He doesn't read much, as he seldom sits down for long enough. He reads the paper, and his religious magazines, but seldom books. He used to read to his children, and his favourite book is *Robinson Crusoe*. He absolutely refuses to believe that this is fiction, saying that nobody could make up a story like that. He must have read the book more than twenty years ago, and he still talks about it.

To sum up, I would say that he is a very generous (except with milk), argumentative, hard working, spoiled old man, who always gets his own way. As my mum once said, 'He's a loveable eccentric, who needs a good kick!'

'My Grandfather' by Tracy Starrett from *Young Writers 26th Year*.

Assignment 1   With a partner or as a class discuss whether the author has described her grandfather in the six ways suggested on page 18?

Assignment 2   Robert Westall says that in his books he often describes people he knows (see p.6). Choose two or three people you know well – they can be relatives, friends or people you just know – and describe them. Try to write a page about each of them.

Remember to think about the following:

Their appearance.

Their personality.

The way you feel about them. Do they have irritating habits?

Are they very helpful people?

Would you confide in them?

Describing how people look – appearance

Have you ever read a book that was made into a TV series or a film? Sometimes the actor or actress who plays the part of the main character may not look as you imagined they would. This is because *you* had built up a picture in your mind that was different from that built up in the mind of the casting director. (The casting director is in charge of finding the actors and actresses for the parts in the film, etc.)

Authors build up a picture of what their characters look like through their use of descriptive language. Most essays can be made a lot more interesting if there is some character description, no matter how limited. Since the first thing you notice about a person is usually their outward appearance this is often the best place to start a description. Think also about the type of clothes your characters are wearing. Clothes tell us a lot about people. Look around the classroom you are in; you will find that even if the pupils are in uniform they will have adapted it in some way to highlight their personality. If there is no uniform in your school, then look closely at the way people have chosen to dress. What does their appearance tell you about them?

When you write, try to picture in your mind what your characters look like. Think about them carefully – their looks, their physical characteristics, their clothes, etc., and do your best to convey this information to your reader. You may decide to describe a character briefly at first and build upon the initial information gradually throughout your essay or book.

Read the Gerald Durrell extracts which follow. They are a good example of this style.

Considered as a group my family was not a very prepossessing sight that afternoon, for the weather had brought with it the usual selection of ills to which we were prone. For me, lying on the floor, labelling my collection of shells, it had brought catarrh, pouring it into my skull like cement, so that I was forced to breathe stertorously through open mouth. For my brother Leslie, hunched dark and glowering by the fire, it had inflamed the convolutions of his ears so that they bled delicately but persistently. To my sister Margo it had delivered a fresh dappling of acne spots to a face that was already blotched like a red veil. For my mother there was a rich, bubbling cold, and a twinge of rheumatism to season it. Only my eldest brother, Larry, was untouched, but it was sufficient that he was irritated by our failings.

It was Larry, of course, who started it. The rest of us felt too apathetic to think of anything except our own ills, but Larry was designed by Providence to go through life like a small, blond firework, exploding ideas in other people's minds, and then curling up with cat-like unctuousness and refusing to take any blame for the consequences. He had become increasingly irritable as the afternoon wore on. At length, glancing moodily round the room, he decided to attack Mother, as being the obvious cause of the trouble.

From *My Family and Other Animals* by Gerald Durrell

Assignment Choose one of the characters named in the above extract. Continue the description concentrating on the outward appearance of the character. Aim to write about a paragraph.

What is the character wearing?

How old is the character?

What is s/he doing?

What colour hair has s/he?

How heavy is s/he?

Describing people's interests

Later in his book, Gerald Durrell tells us more about these characters by introducing us to their individual interests.

Read the extract to see how he is building upon the initial information.

We all travelled light, taking with us only what we considered to be the bare essentials of life. When we opened our luggage for Customs inspection, the contents of our bags were a fair indication of character and interests. Thus Margo's luggage contained a multitude of diaphanous garments, three books on slimming and a regiment of small bottles each containing some elixir guaranteed to cure acne. Leslie's case held a couple of roll-top pullovers and a pair of trousers which were wrapped round two revolvers, an air-pistol, a book called *Be Your Own Gunsmith* and a large bottle of oil that leaked. Larry was accompanied by two trunks of books and a brief-case containing his clothes. Mother's luggage was sensibly divided between clothes and various volumes on cooking and gardening. I travelled with only those items that I thought necessary to relieve the tedium of a long journey: four books on natural history, a butterfly net, a dog and a jam-jar full of caterpillars all in imminent danger of turning into chrysalids. Thus, by our standards fully equipped, we left the clammy shores of England.

From *My Family and Other Animals* by Gerald Durrell.

Assignment 1 Choosing two of the characters mentioned above (Margo, Mother, Larry, Gerald), write a diary entry for both of them, focusing on their individual interests.

Assignment 2 Choose a relative or friend of yours and write about them. Emphasise their interest in a particular hobby or activity.

Defining a personality

At the beginning of a story you, as the reader, know very little about a character. It is as if someone has put a matchstick man or woman in front of you. Gradually, as the story develops, you learn about the character and the matchstick person acquires an appearance that makes him/her different from other matchstick figures. As the story develops you even get to know how the figure walks and talks and even how they would react in certain situations. It is as if the matchstick figure has gained padding from somewhere – this padding is the description that the writer has given to the figure. It is this information which makes the figure not just *anyone* but *someone*.

Earlier, whilst talking about settng, I pointed out that it is often easy for readers to recognise a setting. Even if a reader has never been to a desert, s/he will have some knowledge of what one looks like. Recognising characters is very much the same. We don't need to know an evil person to recognise a description of one. Readers are able to relate to a character through the writer's description and through their own knowledge of different types of people.

Read the following passage about a soldier. This episode occurs when the author, Laurie Lee, meets the soldier for the first time. He is a deserter who has been living rough in the woods near Laurie Lee's home. Note how Laurie Lee gives only the important information about the soldier in a short space of time. This type of character introduction is particularly suited to essay writing.

We went down and found him sitting by the fireside, smiling, wet and cold. I climbed up to the breakfast table and stared at him, the stranger. To me he did not so much appear to be a man as a conglomeration of woody things. His face was red and crinkled, brilliant like fungus. There were leaves in his mud-matted hair, and leaves and twigs on his crumbling clothes, and all over him. His boots were like the black pulp you find when you dig under a tree. Mother gave him porridge and bread, and he smiled palely at us all.

'It must have been cruel in the wood,' said our mother.

'I've got some sacks, mam,' he said, spooning his porridge. 'They keep out the wet.'

They wouldn't; they'd suck it up like a wick and wrap him in it.

'You oughtn't to live like that,' said mother. 'You ought to get back to your home.'

'No,' smiled the man. 'That wouldn't do. They'd jump on me before you could say knife.'

Mother shook her head sadly, and sighed, and gave him more porridge. We boys adored the look of the man; the girls, fastidious, were more uncertain of him. But he was no tramp or he wouldn't be in the kitchen. He had four bright medals in his pocket, which he would produce and polish and lay on the table like money. He spoke like nobody else we knew, in fact, we couldn't understand many of his words. But Mother seemed to understand him, and would ask him questions, and look at the photographs he carried in

his shirt and sigh and shake her head. He talked something of battles and of flying in the air, and it was all wonderful to us.

He was no man from these parts. He had appeared on the doorstep one early morning, asking for a cup of tea. Our mother had brought him in and given him a whole breakfast. There had been blood on his face and he had seemed very weak. Now he was in a kitchen with a woman and a lot of children, and his eyes shone brightly, and his whiskers smiled. He told us he was sleeping in the wood, which seemed to me a good idea. And he was a soldier, because Mother had said so.

I knew about war; all my uncles were in it; my ears from birth had been full of the talk of it. Sometimes I used to climb into the basket chair by the fire and close my eyes and see brown men moving over a field in battle. I was three, but I saw them grope and die and felt myself older than they.

This man did not look like a soldier. He was not brassoed, leather-belted and wax-whiskered like my uncles. He had a beard and his khaki was torn. But the girls insisted he was a soldier, and said it in whispers, like a secret.

And when he came down to our house for breakfast, and sat hunched by the fire, steaming with damp and coated with leaves and dirt, I thought of him sleeping up there in the wood. I imagined him sleeping, then having a go at the battle, then coming down to us for a cup of tea. He was the war, and the war was up there; I wanted to ask, 'How's the war in that wood?'

But he never told us. He sat drinking his tea, gulping and gasping, the fire drawing the damp out of his clothes as if ghosts were rising from him. When he caught our eyes he smiled from his beard. And when brother Jack shot at him with a spoon, saying, 'I'm a sodger,' he replied softly, 'Aye, and you'd make a better one than me, son, any day.'

When he said that, I wondered what had happened to the war. Was he in those rags because he was such a bad soldier? Had he lost the war in the wood?

When he didn't come any more, I knew he had. The girls said some policemen had taken him away in a cart. And Mother sighed and was sad over the poor man.

From *Cider With Rosie* by Laurie Lee.

Assignment 1   In this extract the appearance of the soldier is important. Most of us have a picture in our minds of what a soldier looks like – does the soldier described in the passage differ in some way from your idea of a soldier? Why is this? What does it tell us about the soldier?

Write an essay describing two soldiers. One should be a portrayal of a conventional soldier. The other should be of a soldier who is not typical – perhaps from another country or century.

Assignment 2   Did you notice that although the author has given us only small pieces of information we have a fairly complete picture of the soldier? Is it because all the pieces of information are important?

Discuss as a class why this should be the case.

Assignment 3   Read the passage about the soldier again. Imagine you met this soldier one day whilst out for a walk and write the conversation that you might have with him. Remember to expand the details given about the character so far.

How did you meet the soldier?

Where did you meet him?

Did you first observe the soldier before actually speaking?

What was your impression of him?

How did you feel, talking with the soldier?

How did he sound?

What type of voice did he have?

Remember to begin a new paragraph every time you change speakers.

Assignment 4   Write a poem about two people meeting after a long time apart. Think about the mood you wish to convey as well as how you wish to describe the characters.

Are they meeting on friendly terms?
Are they old friends?
Were they apart because they wanted to be?
Would you describe their looks, personalities and interests?
Would you use a lot of dialogue?

Assignment 5   Sometimes when you read a book or a play you will find that a character is so well described that you find it difficult to forget them. Choose a character that has affected you in this way. Describe the character and explain the methods that the writer used to introduce you to the character.

Why did they remain in your mind?

Did you like them or hate them?

Did you find them humorous?

Do you wish to be like them?

Did you feel sorry for them?

Section 4 Inventing the Story

The plot

QUESTION What has a narrative essay got that a descriptive essay hasn't?
ANSWER   A plot.

Narrative writing differs from descriptive writing in one important way – it contains a plot. The plot tells a story which may be true or false. It is a sequence of actions, the main events of the story, and the order they occur in. With a plot the actions are in some way related one to another, even if at first this doesn't seem to be the case. It is when the characters and their actions are all, or nearly all, related and when there is a definite sequence to the actions, that a plot can be seen to be in evidence.

Do not confuse the plot in a narrative essay with the planning you will need to do for *all* your writing. Descriptive essays need a structure or plan but they do not have a plot.

Narrative essays, or stories that contain a plot, also contain a climax. The climax is the term given to the culmination of the action. The point when the tension of the story reaches a peak, when all the characters and events are in some way drawn together. The climax may not be at the very end of a story and there may be more than one climax in a single story. Sagas on TV are a good example of writing which contains more than one climax. Descriptive essays don't contain climaxes and this is the essential difference between a narrative essay and a descriptive essay.

READ

When I found her, the dawn was just mature, mist gently lifting from hazy fields. A water droplet surprised a hawthorn leaf, springing itself up, up and then down again. Its glassy surface shimmering in the weak rays was but an acorn to the oak of my new problem.

Down in the dyke, she lay, barely twitching, gasping for breath, a female badger. The thin steel of a self-lock snare, encircling her neck. She was once such a beautiful creature, clean well-groomed hair, white distinct from black on muzzle. Now, leaves stuck to the mud on her thighs and head, a wreck of her beauty, the wire was pegged, three feet into the undergrowth. The more she tugged, the tighter became the noose, and it never slackened because it was a self-lock.

I cursed the ass who had laid this victim's grave for her; already she was bleeding from her neck.

I traced the wire back to the peg, only to find that it was a double spike, virtually impossible for an animal to break out. Kicking made the sow whimper as the wire tugged at her, but then out it came. She made no attempt to escape, even now the peg was free. That made my heart cry out with anger. That man was so cruel and inflicted pain to such a degree, that an animal would no longer even attempt to rid itself of human company.

Now, what to do?

A full-grown sow is far too heavy to carry and dragging her was definitely 'out'. I had to get help from somewhere. There was a scare of bovine T.B. This meant no help from a farmer or labourer; my parents or family would not help either. But my friend would!

I ran hell-for-leather through the branches, my legs and shins, shining with wet as the undgergrowth embraced them.

'Teth, Teth! Cum quick!'

I turned to see a question on his face.

'N'er mind, git your cart, oi' got a badger ain't I.'

We both hurdled the fence adjoining the fields and dragged his rough-slapped cart under it. We fair flew across those grassy squares to the copse. The sun was blazing itself yellow as it tried to climb up out of the mist into the day.

The poor creature was hardly alive, just a corpse with a whisper of life.

'Quick Teth! Steady 'er head and shoulders.'

It was like a dream, a bad one. All the way back, twice I stopped, brimming with tears, believing that I had just to push her off into the mud, but as if she knew my thoughts, she blinked and uttered a strangled cry. We did not speak much, except to say that we wished to exchange positions, from pushing to pulling.

It was only when we came to the fence that I fully understood the predicament: What should I do? Lie to my family and say nothing about it; lie to the authorities, or dispose of her?

I ran to get the pliers and buried my hand into the cold, wet, grey coat of hair. Warm blood kissed my hand as I sought in the rolls of muscle for the wire. Pushing the pliers into the skin a gasp of breath escaped as did a cry. But it was done and I carefully raised the head to take away the wire.

'Teth warm milk, quick as snakes!'

Most of it ran into the wood frame, but a little was taken in, but not enough to benefit a movement or response.

'More!' I rasped.

Teth looked surprised at my tone of voice, but he understood as tears rolled down my face and splashed on the ground like a gannet to the sea.

The area surrounding my home had been gassed several times by the 'men'. The setts were all vacated but more badgers poured back in, sure as water finds its own level. Whole populations of badgers had been destroyed because it was thought that badgers carried the disease which affected cows, bovine tuberculosis. Vast herds had had to be slaughtered and disposed of. But now, after some more detailed research it seems that the badger is not responsible for the disease as it was first thought. But all this was to come.

Orders had been posted up to kill any badger that was seen around. I couldn't do it. My family were as bad as the 'men'. 'Kill it, and don't be so irresponsible.' Only Teth and I loved her. She was in pain, the scar on her neck having become septic and her eyes were glazed. She could stand up though and I fed her on dor beetles and slugs with milk and treacle. But she was a pity to look at.

The chill was nearly frosty as the mist clamped down again. There was now no distinction between dawn, day or dusk. Just a faint murmur of light in between. I was in a worried stupor all that week. What if the authorities, the 'men', found out? Would it be as bad as harbouring a spy? 'Kill her! Don't be so irresponsible. Kill her.'

'Kill her. Don't be so irresponsible. Kill her!'

'No. Not for something which isn't her fault. Never. Not for nobody!' I found I was screaming, crying, for nothing anyone had said just then.

She ceased eating and grew visibly smaller. The hair around her shoulders was matted with pus and blood and she could barely stand. But still I could not kill her. If I went to the local veterinary, he would only tell the 'men' and I would be in trouble.

She was now in great pain, unable to rest, starving, almost rotting alive. 'KILL HER.'

'No, not for nowt.'

'Irresponsible.'

'No.'

But still Teth and I loved her.

She was in extreme agony.

I did it.

It was the most unheroic deed I could do. Not for the 'men', not for the farmers, but for her. It was for her good and relief; never would I do it for the 'men'.

Never.

Again the sun rose and sank but it was a different day. Teth and I stayed away from home for the whole day. We never spoke, but aimlessly wandered the fields, woods and hedges, and copses, seeking her dead lost soul.

We never found it and nobody ever will either, thank God.

'Dilemma' by Gavin Bridge from *Young Writers 26th Year.*

Assignment 1   Read the essay again carefully and write down a plan of the action as it occurs.

Assignment 2   TV sagas always end with a climax so encouraging you to 'tune in' for the next episode. Choose a particular series that you watch and, bearing in mind how the last episode ended, write the next programme. Remember that you will need to finish 'your' episode with some kind of climax.

Assignment 3   Choose a favourite book or short story with a good plot. Make notes to outline the plot, concentrating on the main storyline. Highlight where the main climaxes of the book come.

Order or disorder?

Look at this cartoon.

In this cartoon strip there is no sequence. This could be a cartoon of a descriptive essay. It contains in pictures, a description of various people and actions but it follows no set sequence.

Now look at this cartoon.

This cartoon strip is different. Here, there is a logical sequence of events and the characters could be related to one another by the events. Narrative essays, by their nature, must contain and follow a set sequence of events which we call a plot.

Assignment 1 With a partner discuss and write out a plan for an essay based on the above cartoon. Decide whether you would like to make the essay comic or dramatic

Assignment 2 Write the essay that you have planned. Remember to give it a suitable title. When you have finished compare your essay with your partner's. You will be surprised at how one plan can still produce very different end results.

Simple anecdotes

An anecdote is a narrative which relates an amusing or interesting incident. The plot is usually quite simple. Most of us have anecdotes that we could relate about our family, friends or pets. When you write about a real life experience and you recount it in a logical manner, you have included a simple plot just as Jasper Carrott has done in this example of an anecdote.

Read the following extract from Jasper Carrott's autobiography. An autobiography is a story written by a person about his or her own life. It differs from a biography which is a story about someone's life written or told by someone other than the person.

I bought Biffer as a guard dog. He's a labrador who will do anything for a fuss. He will growl, bark and look ferocious. But you've only got to pat him on his head and he will roll over on his back and show you where the money is.

The only time I've seen him really roused was one night when all his hackles were raised and he was tense and snarling. I thought there must be at least a troupe of rapists in the garden, so I dashed out with a piece of iron piping in my hand. He paced twenty yards, dribbling and snarling across the back lawn – and came to a halt in front of the watering can. He leapt on top of it and ravaged it before I had time to stop him. To this day it's the only thing he will attack along with other male dogs.

If a pack of male dogs armed with watering cans tried to rob this house he would respond. But humans – no. He's not too keen on people who make essential deliveries, either. The postman, milkman or paper boy. But if someone wanted to steal the family silver – great!

He has this terrible habit of running away. After a time I found out where he was going: he lopes off down the towpath of the canal at the back of our house, runs along for three bridges and then walks in to the village of Knowle. There's a fish and chip shop where he sits outside and allows people to feed him.

I was always having to go out at all hours to pick him up in the car, so I decided to put a stop to it. If he went missing I would scramble into my car, drive for a mile and a half up the Warwick Road and stop at the canal bridge. There's a restaurant near this bridge and I would park my car there, dash out, down the towpath and hide behind the bushes to wait for Biffer.

When he came into sight I would leap out, usually with my right shoe in my hand.

All the diners in the restaurant have grown used to this. They see Carrott arrive in his car, park it and hide. This apparently innocent dog comes loping along the path by the canal only to be attacked by me with a shoe. I always shout: 'In your box – now.'

His 'box' is back at the house. He never twigs the fact that I'm not hard on his heels chasing him down the canal, so he turns tail and runs back. I get my shoe back on, I'm across the bridge, into the car and arrive in the house before he does. So when Biffer comes through the door I can see him thinking: 'How the hell has he got back here before me?'

This ritual has been going on for five years now. Supposedly laugh-a-minute Carrott turning up with a face like thunder to beat an apparently lovable, friendly dog. It's a wonder I haven't been arrested.

From *A Little Zit On the Side* by Jasper Carrott.

Assignment   In about a page and a half write a short anecdote about a pet of yours. If you have no pets write about a friend instead.

Choose carefully the incident you are going to write about and spend a while planning the information you wish to include. You may make up the incident.

Have you had a pet that has caused some damage?

Have you had a pet against your parent's wishes?

Has a pet of yours ever bitten you or someone else?

Have you ever had a pet for some reason, for example a cat for mousing, and found they were hopeless at the job?

Writing in the first and third person

The extract from Jasper Carrott's autobiography on page 32 is written in the first person. The first person is 'I', in this instance, Jasper Carrott. When you write in the first person you tell the story as if you are there and personally involved.

Essays may also be written in the third person. The third person means that the story is written, not using 'I' as in the first person, but using 'he', 'she', or 'it'.

Read the following extract which is written in the third person. Again, it is an example of an anecdote. In this extract Spike Milligan has written about something that happened while he was there. Many authors write at least one autobiographical book in their writing life. Note that although the writer uses 'I' and 'we' the extract uses mainly the third person 'he'.

Southern Command Sports were coming up. One of our competitors was Gunner Alexander Naze who had entered for the high jump. This puzzled us. He was the most unathletic person I'd ever met. Such was his confidence, he never trained. Came the day and Bexhill Sports Ground was crammed with shouting soldiers and things. The weather was perfect, sunny, warm, with a delightful cool, salt-scented breeze from the Channel. The grass was a fresh cut green. How can people have wars! Among the contestants were professional athletes from pre-service days; some Canadian high jumpers were clearing the bar at five-foot-eight just as a warm up! To date, no sign of Gunner Naze. Then we saw it. Issuing from under the stands was a figure. It was wearing a red hooped football jersey, elastic-waisted blue military P.T. shorts that reach just below the knee, grey army socks dangling round his ankles and white, slightly over-large plimsolls. He ran in a series of peculiar little bounds and leaps, flicking his feet behind him, which I thought was some sort of expertise muscle-loosening exercise. He was blissfully unaware of the comparison his comic garb made with his sleek-muscled professionally-clad opponents. By then he had arrived at the jump-off; the warming up had been terminated. The official had taken down the bar and temporarily rested it at the three foot level…Naze eyed it…He walked some hundred yards from the bar, then turned and started to run. It wasn't until he was half-way there we realised he intended to jump. He gathered a sort of lumbering momentum but never got faster…finally reaching his goal, he launched himself into a schoolboy 'double-your-legs-under-you' style jump and *just* managed to clear it. He seemed well pleased, unconscious of the puzzled look that followed his effort. Came time for the jump off. An official signalled Naze and asked him if he was competing. Naze nodded. Naze walked twenty yards away, turned, and now saw that the officials had set the bar at five foot. For the first time he looked worried. He walked back a further fifty yards. He started his approach. The stadium fell quiet as the great athlete bounded across the grass. We all felt that something unusual

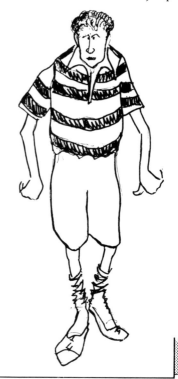

Gunner Naze about to commence his famous jump.

was about to happen. On and on he came, making little clenching gestures with his hands… he reached the bar and with a triumphant shout of 'Hoi Hup la!' and an almighty effort he hurled himself upwards. The bar broke across his forehead. Cheering broke out from the stands. Gunner Naze kept running, he left the field, he left the stadium, he left athletics.

From *Adolf Hitler: My Part in His Downfall* by Spike Milligan.

Assignment 1   Choose one incident from your childhood that you remember well but where you were not the main character involved. Writing in the third person, that is using 'he', 'she' or 'it', relate briefly what happened. Now write about the same incident in the first person as if you were the main character.

Can you think of an incident where you or your friend were in some sort of danger?

Has a friend of yours ever done anything that has got them into trouble?

Have you ever been involved in the wedding of someone close to you?

Is there a sad occasion you feel you can write about?

Have you ever been on a trip with a friend or to a party with them?

Assignment 2   Write an anecdote about your school sports day, jumble sale or a class outing. Decide whether you wish to write it in the first or third person.

Which way to go?

When you plan a narrative essay you have a lot of decisions to make. Many of these are to do with the way the plot will work. For instance, in an essay entitled 'The Escape' the plot is implicit in the title – by that I mean that obviously some form of escape has to take place at some time.

However, you must decide the following.

When the escape takes place.
Who is escaping.
From where they are escaping.

If you think of all the books you have read about escapes, or films you have seen, you will realise that there are thousands of ways of writing this essay. However, here we will limit ourselves to just a few possibilities. Remember, we are concerned with how the plot will work and nothing more at the moment.

1 You could begin at the beginning and describe who the prisoner is. Then you could relate the planning of the escape and finish the essay with the escape itself.

2 You could begin in the middle of the action with the escape already in progress and continue the story from that point.

3 You could begin at the end of the story and relate the whole escape as if it were a memory. In this way the reader would know the outcome of the story, that is, that the person did escape, or didn't, beforehand. In this type of story the writer works to keep the reader involved and in suspense. Sometimes this is called writing in flashback and this technique is discussed on p.43.

Beginning at the beginning

Look at this extract. Here the story begins at the beginning and works up to the point where Ray is tempted to steal the bike. Probably many of the essays you write are structured like this one. Certainly many novels are written in this way.

The bike was a dare – not by anyone else, because he was alone, but a dare to himself. The day had been draggy at school. He had drifted from lesson to lesson, half paying attention at first but gradually losing interest and spending most of the time doodling or signing his name. Eventually four o'clock had arrived, and he'd gone back home. He'd enjoyed the walk because the weather was bright and sunny although there was a real winter snap about it.

At home he'd eaten tea, then gone to his room and tried to do some work, but somehow he just couldn't concentrate. He'd played some music, but after one side of some heavy Rock, he'd looked at his other records and just couldn't choose what to play. He seemed to know them all so well – and he wished he could buy something new.

His father came home from work and called out, 'Hello', then went to eat in the kitchen. It was then that Ray suddenly decided to go out. He went about getting ready – putting on a thick sweater and his fur-fringed parka almost without thinking, almost as if he didn't want himself to know what he was doing.

He walked silently down the stairs, opened the front door, and closed it behind him gently.

It was dark and still, and high above the houses the glow from the yellow lights of the main road caught and reflected in a fine mist. He began walking towards the end of his road and turned left. Almost immediately he began to feel better, and he stamped his feet on the pavement to listen to the click echo against the houses. Although it was only just past seven, the back streets were deserted. He turned right, and about fifty yards down the road was the gash of bright sodium light of the main road; he hurried towards it, seeing if he could hold his breath all the way. He reached the end, turned right on to the main road, and gasped in air to his tightening lungs. Out in this yellow glare he felt that there ought to be bustle and excitement, but there wasn't. An occasional car roared by, taking late workers home, but the pavement was empty. He shivered and bundled his hands tight into his pockets and hunched up his shoulders as he headed towards the parade of shops.

He stopped outside a sweet shop and felt in his pocket for a coin to put in the chocolate machine – but he'd forgotten to bring any money and, he discovered, as he felt a drop swell at the end of his nose, he'd also forgotten his handkerchief.

None of the shops was open, and they all seemed dingy and cheap with just one light burning at the back. He looked idly at the advertisements behind the glass-covered notice-board – mostly for second-hand equipment for babies: cots, prams, and toys. Ray looked for one that he'd seen last week offering part-time work as a gardener, but it had gone.

Three shops farther on was the one brightly lit and open place in the whole parade, the launderette. There were three people inside sitting watching their clothes going round in the machines. The bright lights made their faces pale, and they looked bored and tired. He wandered on down the road and came to the pub. There was a low, hooped-iron fence bordering a patch of grass in front of the building, and he jumped it and walked up to the window. Through the net curtains he saw into the main bar and watched two old men playing bar billiards. It looked warm, friendly, and lively inside, and he wished he could go in, but he was young-looking for fifteen, and he knew he couldn't fool anyone that he was old enough to drink. He'd even been turned out of the Astoria once when he and two others had tried to get in to see an 'X' film. The other two had got in OK and had enjoyed telling him what he'd missed when he saw them next day at school.

Ray was turning away, thinking that all he could do was wander home again, when a motor-bike drew into the small car-park at the side of the pub. The rider got off the bike, pulled it back on to its stand, leaving the engine running, and walked towards the off-licence bar, undoing the strap of his crash-helmet. He opened the door and went inside.

Ray walked slowly over to the bike. It was a Honda 125 with a yellow tank. The engine sounded good, he noted, and he suddenly felt a temptation to sit on it. He glanced quickly at the bar. He could see the bike's owner standing waiting to be served. Ray ran his hands along the handle-bars of the bike and then swung his leg over the seat and sat astride the machine. He was sitting facing the bar door, and he could see that the man still hadn't been served. Suddenly, he felt the urge to go – to take the bike and ride.

From *Collision Course* by Nigel Hinton.

Did Ray steal the bike? That's another story isn't it? One thing has led to another. You have all heard people say 'But if So-and-So' had done this it wouldn't have happened. Look at the 'ifs' involved here. If Ray had bought a new record he wouldn't have been bored and gone out at all. If Ray had had money for chocolate, he might not have been at the off-licence at the same time as the bike was left outside. If the person had turned off the bike's motor Ray wouldn't have been tempted to steal it.

However, these things didn't happen. That is because the author had decided to follow a certain course of action. He had constructed a plot.

Assignment 1 Make a plan of the plot as it is seen to emerge in this extract.

Assignment 2 Imagine that you are going to write about a theft of some kind. It could be planned or, as in this case, it could be a 'spur of the moment event'. In a page describe the events that lead up to the theft.

Is the theft planned?

What type of people might plan a robbery?

What can you steal apart from the obvious things like cars?

Why might two people be tempted to steal? Read the passage from *Twopence to Cross the Mersey*, page 41. It might give you some ideas.

Assignment 3 Plan and then write two episodes of a story. The first episode must end in a cliff-hanger situation which will be resolved in the second part.

Assignment 4 Choose one narrative essay that you have written. Either write another essay featuring the same characters in some form of adventure, or write a sequel to the first essay to take the reader further on in the story.

While writing the second essay you should assume that the characters and their previous actions are known by the reader. Occasionally, however, you could remind them of what has gone before.

An essay of this kind needs a good deal of planning and you will need to think very carefully about the characters and the setting of your essay.

Have you written about a family? Could you introduce another member of the family?

Could you involve a character you've used before in another adventure?

Previously you were asked to write about your friends at school. Could you write another episode involving them? Did the incident concerning your friends have a natural sequel?

Have you ever written a science fiction story? Could you get the characters to visit another planet or another time?

Beginning in the middle

We may meet characters in the *middle* of an action. This means that we have not met them at the beginning. The information that we might have missed is often given to us later in the passage or book.

Read the following extract. (It is taken from the second book in a series of five.) Sadie and Kevin have not seen each other for some time when they suddenly bump into one another.

'Sadie! Sadie Jackson!'

She looked round. For a moment she could not see who was calling her. The pavement was thick with people heading homewards. Then she saw him coming through the midst of the throng. Tall, dark, broader than she had remembered, but with the same bright spark in his eyes. She waited for him to reach her.

'Kevin,' she said. 'Kevin McCoy.'

'It's me all right.' He was grinning.

'Haven't seen you for ages. It must be nearly three years.'

'Suppose it is. It's funny seeing you again after so long.'

They only lived a few streets away from one another but it might as well have been a thousand miles. They stood and looked at one another and let the hurrying people push round them.

'Fancy a cup of coffee?' asked Kevin. 'Have you time?'

'Don't see why not,' said Sadie. There were many good reasons why not, her mother would say, but Sadie was not one to be put off by reasons, especially her mother's.

They walked side by side to a coffee bar without talking. They felt a little awkward walking together but once inside the café, seated across a table from one another, their tongues broke free again.

'How's Brede?' she asked.

'How's Tommy?' he asked at the same time, and they laughed.

'Brede's fine,' he said. 'She's working as a nursery nurse.'

'She always was soft on kids, wasn't she? Tommy's in the yard apprenticed as a welder.'

They were silent for a moment, Sadie thinking of Kevin's sister Brede and Kevin of Sadie's brother Tommy as each had been three years ago. They had all been at school then, different schools. They had started as enemies, had even fought with stones and fists; then for a while they had been friends but eventually had drifted apart because of the difficulties of meeting.

'And you, Sadie, what are you doing?'

'Me?' She shook her long fair hair back over her shoulder in a gesture that he remembered. 'Well, first I went into an office' – she wrinkled her nose – 'and then I got a job in a linen mill…'

He laughed. 'You always were a restless one!'

'Look who's talking!' They were used to sparring with one another; it came back to them easily. It was as if the three years had never been.

From *Across the Barricades* by Joan Lingard.

Assignment Write an extended story that begins in the middle of a situation and then goes back to what caused the situation to arise and what happened afterwards.

Some ideas could be as follows.

An accident, going back to what caused it and forward to what happened afterwards.

A robber in the middle of stealing something, going back to why s/he did it and forward to what happened afterwards.

The bride not turning up for her wedding, going back to why she did not appear and forward to what happened afterwards.

Beginning at the end

To begin a story at the end is an unusual way to go about things. However, it can often work well and it is yet another approach to writing that is open to you.

You may have come across this technique in your reading already. Have you ever read a thriller or suspense novel where you are given some crucial information at the beginning of the story? It might have been the identity of a murderer perhaps. This doesn't happen often because the writer usually creates suspense by withholding the vital clue. Obviously, when the writer gives this information away first suspense must be created in other ways.

Now read the extract. Here, on the first page of the book, we start at the end of the story. We already know that the person telling the story of her childhood is grown up, married and has a son.

Liverpool is a city through which visitors pass on their way to other places. It is to them a dull world of shipping and commerce which sprawls untidily along the north bank of the River Mersey. Many of them will not know that it has a sister port, Birkenhead, on the opposite bank, which is linked to it by ferry-boats, a railway tunnel and a road tunnel. Beyond Birkenhead lie the small seaside towns of the Wirral peninsula and beind them is pleasant countryside. My widowed grandmother lived in the Wirral, and here, while visiting her, I spent the happiest days of my childhood, on sandy beaches or in wind-swept gardens. I remember with love the rain-soaked hills looking out on to stormy seas and the turbulent estuary of the Mersey.

It used to cost twopence to cross the river on the ferry-boat from Liverpool to Birkenhead. Twopence is not a very large sum, but if one has no money, the river is a real barrier, and, during the Depression years, was an impassable one to many of the poverty-stricken people of Liverpool.

Not so many years ago, I took my little Canadian-born son to see Liverpool and the places of my childhood.

'Did you live here when you were small, Ma?' he asked incredulously, his strong North American accent sounding strange amid the thick, nasal speech around him.

'Yes, I was in Liverpool for part of my life.'

'My, it's dirty! Do you mind it being dirty?'

I smiled, seeing it all through his stranger's eyes, eyes accustomed to new buildings, miles of neon signs, miles of prairie golden with wheat or diamond-white with snow.

I laughed down at him a little ruefully.

'Yes, at first I did mind. Not now, though. I soon learned that people and cities which do the hard unpleasant work of the world can't help getting dirty. Liverpool's a wonderful place when you get to know it.'

He looked at me derisively and said, with all the cold logic of a five-year-old, 'They should use more soap and – wash the streets.'

My smile faded, as cold shadows of winters past crept over me. That was how I had felt, when first I had really looked at the city and not passed through it as a traveller. God, how I had minded the dirt! How terrified I had been! How menacingly grotesque the people had looked; children of the industrial revolution, nurtured for generations on poor food in smoke-laden air, grim and twisted, foul-mouthed and coarse, shaped in this strange gloomy world to serve the trade to the Americas. And I, a middle-class girl of the gentler south-west of England who had been shielded from the rougher side of life by a private school system and obedient servants, had nearly gone mad with panic when, with little warning, I had been thrown amongst them. Gone was the protection of money and privilege; I had to make what I could of this grimy city and its bitterly humorous inhabitants and share with them their suffering during the Depression years.

I clutched my son's confiding little hand in mine, as, for a second, I felt again the fear which had enveloped me that January day in 1931, when, at the age of twelve and a half, I arrived in Liverpool, not to pass through it as I had done before, but to live in it.

It seemed to me that it was not my son's hand which I held so tightly but the hand of my youngest sister, Avril, and that I could hear her snivelling, as we looked out from the entrance of Lime Street Station and saw, through icy, driving rain, a city which seemed to be slowly dying, unloved and unsung, in the Depression of the nineteen-thirties.

From *Twopence to Cross the Mersey* by Helen Forrester.

Assignment 1 Imagine that you have grown up and now have a family and that you are writing your life story. Write an essay, beginning with details about your life now and then moving gradually towards giving details about your younger days.

How do you see yourself in a few years' time?

Would you be happy to re-visit your old home town or area?

How do you think it would seem to an outsider?

Are you interested in your parents' childhood?

Do you think your children would be interested in yours?

Assignment 2 From your reading choose a book which begins at the end of the story. Discuss in groups how the author manages to keep the reader interested having given away the end. Plan and write a suspense story using this structure.

Assignment 3 Select three books or stories that you have read. One should begin at the beginning of the story, one in the middle and one at the end. Discuss why the author might have chosen to construct the story in this way.

Flashback

Flashback is often used in films or books. It is where a character thinks back to an incident that has occurred in the past. Flashback is seen when a writer refers every now and then to an incident from the past and in between the story continues taking us closer and closer to its climax. It is a way of revealing to a reader or to an audience an important or haunting memory.

READ

Read the following extract carefully. In it Ponyboy (that is the name of the person speaking) is recounting to Cherry an incident that occurred a few months earlier. It is a good example of a flashback as it helps to explain the behaviour of one of the characters.

As you read think about why flashback is used. What added information is it giving you? Could the information have been written into the story in a more straightforward way?

'Your friend — the one with the sideburns — he's okay?'

'He ain't dangerous like Dallas if that's what you mean. He's okay.'

She smiled and her eyes showed that her mind was on something else. 'Johnny ... he's been hurt bad sometime, hasn't he?' It was more of a statement than a question. 'Hurt and scared.'

'It was the Socs,' I said nervously, because there were plenty of Socs milling around and some of them were giving me funny looks, as if I shouldn't be with Cherry or something. And I don't like to talk about it either — Johnny getting beat up, I mean. But I started in, talking a little faster than I usually do because I don't like to think about it either.

It was almost four months ago. I had walked down to the DX station to get a bottle of pop and to see Steve and Soda, because they'll always buy me a couple of bottles and let me help work on the cars. I don't like to go on weekends because then there is usually a bunch of girls down there flirting with Soda — all kinds of girls, Socs too. I don't care too much for girls yet. Soda says I'll grow out of it. He did.

It was a warmish spring day with the sun shining bright, but it was getting chilly and dark by the time we started for home. We were walking because we had left Steve's car at the station. At the corner of our block there's a wide, open field where we play football and hang out, and it's often a site for rumbles and fist fights. We were passing it kicking rocks down the street and finishing our last bottles of Pepsi, when Steve noticed something lying on the ground. He picked it up. It was Johnny's blue-jeans jacket — the only jacket he had.

'Looks like Johnny forgot his jacket,' Steve said, slinging it over his shoulder to take it by Johnny's house. Suddenly he stopped and examined it more carefully. There was a stain the colour of rust across the collar. He looked at the ground. There were some more stains on the grass. He looked up and across the field with a stricken expression on his face. I think we all heard the low moan and saw the dark motionless hump on the other side of the lot at the same time. Soda reached him first. Johnny was lying face down on the ground. Soda turned him over gently, and I nearly got sick. Someone had beaten him badly.

We were used to seeing Johnny banged up — his father clobbered him around a lot, and although it made us madder than heck, we couldn't do anything about it. But those beatings had been nothing like this. Johnny's face was cut up and bruised and swollen, and there was a wide gash from his temple to his cheekbone. He would carry that scar all his life. His white T-shirt was splattered with blood. I just stood there, trembling with sudden cold. I thought he might be dead; surely nobody could be beaten like that and live. Steve closed his eyes for a second and muffled a groan as he dropped on his knees beside Soda.

Somehow the gang sensed what had happened. Two-Bit was suddenly there beside me, and for once his comical grin was gone and his dancing grey eyes were stormy. Darry had seen us from our porch and ran towards us, suddenly skidding to a halt. Dally was there, too, swearing under his breath, and turning away with a sick expression on his face. I wondered about it vaguely. Dally had seen people killed on the streets of New York's West Side. Why did he look sick now?

'Johnny?' Soda lifted him up and held him against his shoulder. He gave the limp body a slight shake. 'Hey, Johnnycake.'

Johnny didn't open his eyes, but there came a soft question. 'Soda?'

'Yeah, it's me,' Sodapop said. 'Don't talk. You're gonna be okay.'

'There was a whole bunch of them,' Johnny went on, swallowing, ignoring Soda's command. 'A blue Mustang full ... I got so scared ...' He tried to swear, but suddenly started crying, fighting to control himself, then sobbing all the more because he couldn't. I had seen Johnny take a whipping with a two-by-four from his old man and never let out a whimper. That made it worse to see him break now. Soda just held him and pushed Johnny's hair back out of his eyes. 'It's okay, Johnnycake, they're gone now. It's okay.'

Finally, between sobs, Johnny managed to gasp out his story. He had been hunting our football to practise a few kicks when a blue Mustang had pulled up beside the lot. There were four Socs in it. They had caught him and one of them had a lot of rings on his hand – that's what had cut Johnny up so badly. It wasn't just that they had beaten him half to death – he could take that. They had scared him. They had threatened him with everything under the sun. Johnny was high-strung anyway, a nervous wreck from getting belted every time he turned around and from hearing his parents fight all the time. Living in those conditions might have turned someone else rebellious and bitter; it was killing Johnny. He had never been a coward. He was a good man in a rumble. He stuck up for the gang and kept his mouth shut good around cops. But after the night of the beating, Johnny was jumpier than ever. I didn't think he'd ever get over it. Johnny never walked by himself after that. And Johnny, who was the most law-abiding of us, now carried in his back pocket a six-inch switchblade. He'd use it, too, if he ever got jumped again. They had scared him that much. He would kill the next person who jumped him. Nobody was ever going to beat him like that again. Not over his dead body ....

From *The Outsiders* by S.E. Hinton.

Assignment 1   Can you think of any films or novels which used flashback?

     Write a brief outline of one of these and explain why you think flashback was used.

Assignment 2   As a class, discuss how and why you might use flashback in your writing.

Section 5 Extra Assignments

Writing to a given title

1 'A Day I Will Remember for the Rest of my Life'

2 'Sport in Winter'
The joys or sorrows of sport on a Monday afternoon in the winter on the school field.

3 'The Outsider'
You could use this title to write a poem rather than an essay.

4 'The Visitor'

5 'Childhood Memories'

6 'Lost Friends'
Many of us make friends through life but sometimes we lose touch with someone we were very fond of. Can you think of people that you once knew and whom you don't see now? Describe them and the type of fun you used to have.

7 'The Antique Shop'

8 'A Part-Time Job'

9 'Modern-Day Vampires'

10 'A Parable from the Bible'
'The Good Samaritan', for instance, or 'The Prodigal Son'. Re-write one such story and set it in modern times.

11 'Grandad'/'Grandma'
Write about one of your grandparents. Describe your grandparent and explain why you wish to write about him/her. You may like to describe your relationship with them.

12 'A Long Journey'
You meet a most unpleasant person. Describe the remainder of the journey.

13 'Training Pets is Never Easy'

14 'A Busy Town Street'
Describe the street in the summer and in the winter.

15 'The Race'
You could use this title to write a poem instead of an essay.

16 'View From the Top'
You have climbed a very steep cliff or hill and are overlooking a beach or a small industrial town. Describe carefully the climb and what you can see from the top.

17 'Disaster'
Describe an area after a disaster of some kind.

18 'Castles in the Air'

19 'The Unlikely Hero'

20 'Three Wishes'

Imagine that you are granted three wishes and that you are allowed to use them to alter events that have occurred in the world's past or in your own time. (You could write about a combination of the two.) What would you alter and why?

21 'Is Life Better or Worse?'

Many teenagers complain that they are not as happy at 16 as they were at 11. They also complain that school, which they once enjoyed, is now a bore. How do you think your life and attitudes have changed in the last few years? Is life better or worse?

Writing on ...

Sometimes you may be asked to continue an extract or an idea in any way which seems appropriate to you. If you attempt an essay of this kind in an exam do not waste time copying out all the extract given. Ensure that you number your essay well and include the last sentence of the extract at the beginning of your essay.

1 This year the Sunday School Outing was different. We were going to ...

2 I looked at the floor and watched in horror as water came bubbling through cracks between the boards. In panic I ran to the window and threw back the curtains. The clouds had lifted and there was a full moon. There was no land any longer. The sea was black and silver in the moonlight, it stretched from the kitchen window to the horizon. It was swirling past at speed, rising every minute, not in great waves and torrents but in an almost orderly fashion, like a bath filling. Then there was a tremendous crash as the door burst open and the water surged towards me. I rushed for the stairs as the lights flickered and went out ...

3 At three o'clock in the morning it was dark and the hotel slept. The only sound was the creaking of the window frames in the rising wind off the sea, and the slap-slap of the rope against the flag-pole that stood outside the hotel. The residents were few in number. Twelve were asleep, but the thirteenth was not ...

4 A fine April morning, even though it was Monday. Somewhere or other the sun was shining and the birds were singing their heads off; but not in this particular street. It was dark and narrow; it was old, shabby and broken-down and even the air seemed tired of being breathed. A clock banged out seven and, with a grisly rattle of chains, the shop doors opened, like so many dirty mouths, and drab boys came out, exchanged insults, took down the shutters and went back inside. At all except one shop ...

Source: WJEC Examination paper

Writing using poems and pictures

You might be asked to write an essay having read a poem or having seen a picture first.

1 *Read the poem and then write an essay describing the resort at both times of the year.*

The Isle of Wight

When the trippers found this island
They publicised its charm
And camped on it and tramped on it
And picnicked on its farms,
The paddle-boats brought the strangers
To the half mile pier at Ryde,
In linen slacks and aertex shirts
Their women by their side,
The folk of the little dolls' houses
Out of speaking range,
To the little fields came holiday camps,
Speed boats to the river,
The little boats were dinned and thronged
By bus and boat and flivver
To the garden isle came the tourist trade;
The Needles an afternoon trip
'Five bob all round the island'
In a snorting little ship
But the first hard frost of winter
Sends the hiker to his den,
The islanders come through unbolted doors,
Into their own again,
The foreigners' cars are ferried away
The little roads are clear,
The island men in island pubs
Slowly quaff their beer,
In the quiet night they saunter home,
They linger to talk at street corners
In voices unhurried and deep.

Leslie Thomas

2 *Read the poem and then write an essay describing London, or any town or village you know well, early in the morning.*

Composed upon Westminster Bridge
September 3, 1802

Earth has not anything to show more fair:
Dull would he be of soul who could pass by
A sight so touching in its majesty:
This City now doth like a garment wear
The beauty of the morning; silent, bare,
Ships, towers, domes, theatres, and temples lie
Open unto the fields, and to the sky;
All bright and glittering in the smokeless air.
Never did sun more beautifully steep
In his first splendour valley, rock, or hill;
Ne'er saw I, never felt, a calm so deep!
The river glideth at his own sweet will:
Dear God! the very houses seem asleep;
And all that mighty heart is lying still!

William Wordsworth

3 *Read the poem and then write a narrative essay about the drowning incident.*

Not Waving But Drowning

Nobody heard him, the dead man,
But still he lay moaning:
He was much farther out than you thought
And not waving but drowning.

Poor chap, he always loved larking
And now he's dead
It must have been too cold for him his heart gave way,
They said.

Oh no, no, no, it was too cold always
(Still the dead one lay moaning)
I was much too far out all my life
And not waving but drowning.

Stevie Smith

4 *Look at the two pictures below and write either a narrative essay or a descriptive essay based on each picture.*

Factual and Informative Writing

Introduction

Factual and informative writing is made up of facts. Facts are things which are known to have occurred or which are true. Have you ever written up the details of an experiment in science or the directions from your home to your school for a geography teacher? Both of these tasks involve the use of facts and you need to think carefully about the order the facts should be put in. What would happen if you put the directions in the wrong order, for instance?

Think about all the factual writing you do in a week in school. The amount is quite surprising. In English you are often asked to write a summary of a book you have read. In this case your whole summary would contain facts. The facts about the book. You can probably think of many other tasks that you have undertaken that have involved you in using information and facts.

How did you decide what facts or information to use and what to leave out? How have you planned your writing? How have you used these facts? All these questions you have, no doubt, tackled without even realising you were doing do. From now on think about them before you begin your essays.

In English you will be presented with material in various forms and you will be asked to use the information and the facts it contains in various ways. Obviously, you won't want to use it all. You will manage best if you go through the information carefully twice. The first time just to understand it, the second to decide what information you need for the task you have to do. Once you have decided this you will need to plan your writing by making notes on the information and putting it into some sensible order. Finally, you will need to decide how best to set the facts out. You may be asked to write a pamphlet, design a poster, write a newspaper article and so on. In each case you would set out the facts slightly differently.

Whenever you are given factual information to read, look carefully at who is presenting the facts for your scrutiny. 'Statistics can be made to prove anything you want them to prove' is a well-known saying. Organisations may present facts in a biased manner – choosing facts that suit their own point of view and ignoring or distorting others. Politicians often give a biased view of the facts.

Golden Rules

1 Work on factual material, like any other, needs thorough planning. Great care must be taken to ensure that work is ordered logically. Often, facts follow one another naturally. If you are not careful and this does not happen, your writing can become confusing and sometimes nonsensical to the reader.

2 Factual writing often asks you to write in a different format from that normally used in an essay. For instance, you might be asked to write an article for a magazine. Make sure you do exactly what is asked. Teachers are not amused when you make up an answer to your own question!

3 If you are given information make sure you read it carefully. Some people try to read only what seem to be the main points. Never do this as often vital information is missed. It saves time but wastes marks.

4 Once you have read the information, write down the heading then jot down briefly the important points. Always number your points, it makes it much easier later to separate the information. If you don't do this you could end up including unnecessary information which is time wasted.

5 Arrange these points in a logical order (one thing naturally following another) before you begin to write and not as you write. Your essay will then read easily and sensibly.

6 If you are asked to design a poster remember the main emphasis will be on the written form, not the artistic output.

7 Very often pupils panic when they see a question which involves factual writing. Always remain calm and attempt to plan your answer by taking it one step at a time. Remember, if you are in an exam and you leave out a question you will score zero; if you attempt it, you will gain some marks at least. When you are in a classroom and you find something difficult always ask for help from your teacher.

8 There is a difference between a fact and an opinion. Look up both words in a dictionary.

Section 1 Sample Assignments

What type of assignments might be required?

The following examples will give you some idea of the type of question that may be set.

Assignment 1 New pupils at your school are provided with a brief description of the various clubs and societies available. Write a description of the activities of one club or society, giving all the relevant information, for someone who may be thinking of joining.

Assignment 2 Using the information given below, write an article giving general advice on the cost of heating systems available (indicating the cost of purchase and installation and annual running cost) and end by making your personal recommendations.

BUYING A NEW HEATING SYSTEM: WHICH WILL BE MOST ECONOMICAL?

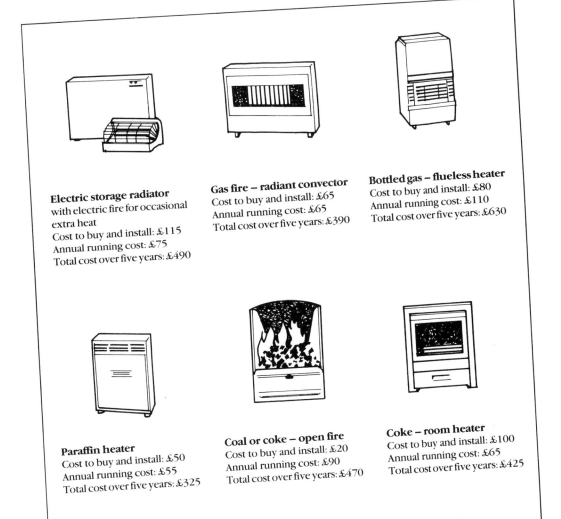

Electric storage radiator
with electric fire for occasional extra heat
Cost to buy and install: £115
Annual running cost: £75
Total cost over five years: £490

Gas fire – radiant convector
Cost to buy and install: £65
Annual running cost: £65
Total cost over five years: £390

Bottled gas – flueless heater
Cost to buy and install: £80
Annual running cost: £110
Total cost over five years: £630

Paraffin heater
Cost to buy and install: £50
Annual running cost: £55
Total cost over five years: £325

Coal or coke – open fire
Cost to buy and install: £20
Annual running cost: £90
Total cost over five years: £470

Coke – room heater
Cost to buy and install: £100
Annual running cost: £65
Total cost over five years: £425

Source: WJEC Pilot Scheme Paper 1986.

Discussion of sample assignments

As you can see from these examples there is no set pattern to the questions. They can vary dramatically in what they require from you. In both these instances you are asked to write something for someone in particular. It is important that you are aware of your audience. Who you are writing for will affect the way you write.

In these cases who would your audience be? Do you write in different ways depending on the audience? Why is this?

As a class look at and discuss the points put forward concerning the two assignments then attempt each one.

Assignment 1 Although you are left to choose exactly what to write about, you are still expected to structure your writing logically. Does the assignment tell you this? No, it does not. However, information is required in the form of facts and wherever there are facts there should be order of some kind. Obviously, you are entitled to fabricate some of these facts, only your teacher will know whether or not the facts are true.

Where would you find a description of this kind? Would it be on a leaflet to be handed out to pupils? What would a leaflet of this kind look like? Might the information be found in a school magazine, perhaps? What does a school magazine look like? Has your school got one?

How would this type of factual writing differ from narrative or descriptive writing? Would the heading be different? In what way?

Does the style of writing differ? Look at a short story then look at a magazine article or even a newspaper article. The difference you find between these forms of writing should help you.

What sort of information about the club should be included? Think about which day it meets, who can join, whether or not there is a subscription and the sort of things the club does.

Assignment 2 This question gives you some information. You are expected to write a factual article on different heating systems. To do this you will need to present your information in a logical way. Your article must only contain facts taken from the information given.

Does the question ask you to do anything extra at the end?

As a class discuss logically which you think would be the most practicable form of heating to install. Remember to weigh up all the advantages and disadvantages – some of these may not be given. Here the examiner is expecting you to use logic in order to decide which heating system is the best and why.

Extra assignments

Assignment 1 Devise a leaflet about your school aimed at providing new pupils with all they need to know to enable them to survive! You may provide diagrams and details about staff, etc.

Assignment 2 Describe the rules of a well-known sport to a visitor from another planet. Set your work out in the form of a conversation.

Assignment 3 Describe for a specialist magazine how you would do or make something. Use diagrams where appropriate.

Assignment 4 Write an article for your school magazine on the subject of buying and keeping a pet.

Assignment 5 Write a review for a local newspaper of a book you have read or a film you have seen.

Section 2 A Stay at Stackpole

Stackpole Basecamp

The basecamp at Stackpole provides full board for up to 30 children in two dormitories on the first floor of newly renovated farm buildings, with separate rooms for two accompanying teachers. On the ground floor there is a large common room and refectory with adjacent kitchen, showers, storage and drying rooms, all centrally heated. Full board includes full cooked breakfast, packed lunch, cooked evening meal and supper. There is also a tuck shop.

There are three resident instructors and the Basecamp is open for nine months a year from March to November.

The activities offered include ornithology, orienteering, canoeing, swimming, pond studies, sea-shore studies, woodland studies, trapping, tracking, beach combing, beach games and historical and geographical trails. Trips to castles and museums can be arranged on request.

The estate was given to the National Trust in 1976 in lieu of death duties and still contains a working farm. The beautiful lakes, woods, beaches and cliffs give pleasure to locals and to thousands of visiting tourists every year. Children are also encouraged to visit places of historical interest.

Orienteering

Cliff walks

Church Rock

Canoeing

Lily ponds at Bosherston

Visit the following:
Pembroke Castle
Carew Castle 3m E of Pembroke
Manorbier Castle 5m SW Tenby
The Tank Range
Dolaucothi Gold Mines (64 miles)
Aberdulais Falls (73 miles)

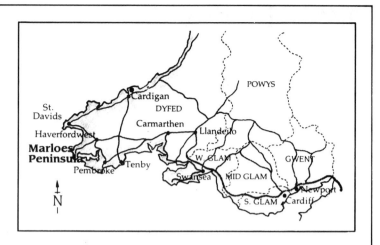

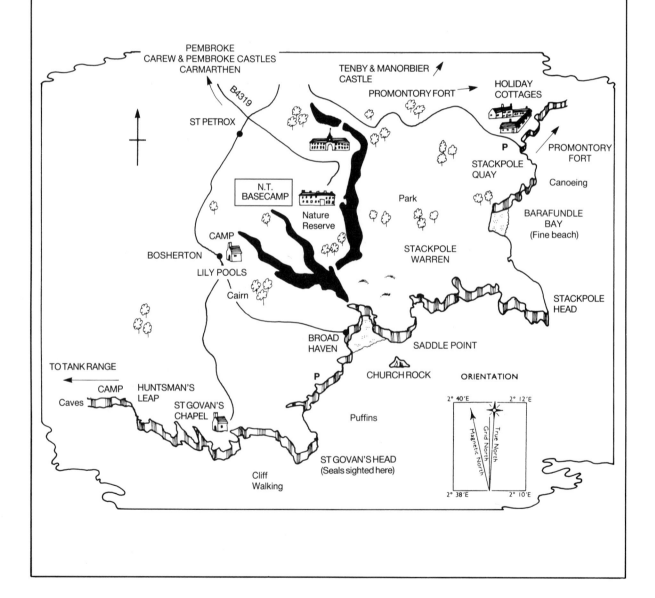

Places to visit

PEMBROKE

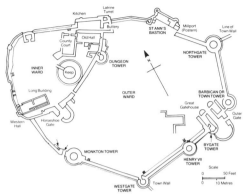

PEMBROKE CASTLE GROUNDPLAN

First founded during the original Norman scramble for South West Wales, Pembroke Castle was completely rebuilt in stone by William Marshall, the greatest English knight of the Middle Ages. His magnificent castle, never captured by the Welsh, remains unaltered to this day. Birthplace of Harri Tudur, the Welshman who became the first Tudor monarch, it had otherwise an unexciting history until the Civil Wars, when it withstood a seven-week siege led by Oliver Cromwell himself, finally surrendering through lack of water.

DOLAUCOTHI ROMAN GOLD MINES ·

Pumpsaint, Llanwrda SA19 8US. Between Lampeter and Llanwrda on A482 (140(146) : SN6640) - The only place in the country where the Romans mined gold; a close examination of the workings has shown archaeologists that they belong to the most technically advanced industrial site of the Roman period yet discovered in Britain; some gold was mined here before the coming of the Romans by the natives who had discovered deposits of the mineral which had been washed down into the gravel of the bed of the River Cothi; last mined in 1939; now used by University College, Cardiff, and Saint David's University College, Lampeter, for field study courses; underground and surface tours during summer months.

Carew Castle

Gerald of Windsor's private castle, Carew, has been altered several times. It contains unique medieval 'maisonettes' for the constable and chaplain of the garrison; also two successive Tudor wings of palatial grandeur, all standing two or three storeys high.

Aberdulais Falls

WEST GLAMORGAN ·

ABERDULAIS FALLS ·

Aberdulais, nr Neath, tel. Neath (0639) 56674. On A465 3m NE of Neath 153 (170) : SS772995.

Aberdulais Falls is a combination of natural beauty and a fascinating industrial history. For almost a hundred years this important historic site had remained largely forgotten and hidden from view; recently it has been opened to visitors and gradually its secrets are being uncovered.

A short walk alongside the river through the wooded gorge reveals one of the most famous waterfalls in the Vale of Neath. Its waters have been harnessed since 1584 to provide the power for a variety of industries; copper smelting, iron working, a corn mill and a tinplate works.

Aberdulais Falls is a dynamic site and its history is constantly unfolding. To the visitor, the site offers a unique and fascinating insight into the early metals industry of South Wales. There is an excellent display housed in the recently re-furbished visitor Information Centre. Open every day (except Christmas Day), Aberdulais lies adjacent to other sites of interest, all within walking distance.

Source: National Trust Offices, Kings Head, Llandeilo, Dyfed

Assignment 1   Imagine that you are organising a stay at Stackpole and that you would like to encourage other pupils to join your group. With this in mind, design a poster to display on a school noticeboard.

Remember that posters contain written information as well as pictures.

What type of person would enjoy this type of holiday?

How can you make the poster attractive to them?

People who produce tourist information make a place sound attractive by choosing their words carefully. Can you do this?

Assignment 2   At the end of your stay at Stackpole the National Trust have asked you to write an article for their newsletter. You are asked to include details of your week's activities and explain why you enjoyed your week there, as well as how it benefited you – if indeed you thought it did. You may like to make a few recommendations as to what aspects of the holiday could be improved upon. For instance, you may have some ideas about activities that could be added to those already offered.

Use the maps carefully and base your facts on the locality.

Sometimes the points you need to make are to be found in the diagrams or pictures, not just in the written information.

It is easy to get carried away and write only from imagination, not using any factual information at all. Writing of this kind should be a mixture of the two.

Make a list, in point form, of all the activities you could have been involved in.

Remember that this is an article, try to make it eye-catching.

I'm sure you are aware that no organisation would include an article in a newsletter that did not do it justice. Your article should be praiseworthy, at least for the most part!

Assignment 3   Research the amenities and tourist attractions in your area. Design and write a tourist brochure for your locality. You will need to include information about places to visit, plus a map.

Make a list of local attractions like cinemas, theatres, swimming pools and so on.

Provide details of the necessary amenities such as doctors, shops, post offices, and anything else that the visiting public might find useful.

Useful organisations to contact would include your local Tourist Information Office, or, in some areas, your local National Trust Office.

Section 3 The Police Force

The Beginning of the Police Force
An explanation of the words in italics appears at the end of this extract on p.61.

It is difficult for us to imagine how rough, lawless and brutal life was in English towns in the eighteenth century. During the Industrial Revolution England changed from being a farming country into an industrial country. Thousands of people left the countryside and poured into the towns to look for work and to seek their fortunes.

Country communities were very cut off. There were no cars, railways or buses, no radio, television or telephones. The roads were mostly mud, very bad and unsafe, and the only transport was by horse. The local landowners had their property protected by armed game-keepers and villagers still relied on the old method of *hue and cry*. But crime prevention was easier in the country where the population was small and everyone knew what everyone else was doing.

Towns like Manchester and Birmingham grew at a staggering rate. There was not enough housing, sanitation, or work for the huge increase in population. There was no social welfare and enormous numbers of people lived in slums with little work, little to eat or wear and no education; it is not surprising that many became desperate and took to crime.

By far the largest town in the country was London. The small square of the City of London had organised its *constables* and watchmen reasonably well.

The artist Hogarth pictures here the terrible disorder that was brought to eighteenth-century London by poverty, drunkenness and neglect.

Source: The Mansell Collection

In 1663 the City of London began to employ watchmen to guard the streets at night. In later years these watchmen were nicknamed 'Charlies'. They were paid very little and only men who were too old or too decrepit to do any other kind of work were employed. They all carried a bell, a lantern and a rattle and were armed with a staff though there was not much a feeble old man could do to stop active gangs of thieves and robbers. However, in spite of the fact that they were so inefficient, the Charlies of London were probably the most effective night police force anywhere in the country until the end of the eighteenth century.

Life on the streets was far from safe even with the constables and night watchmen. In 1743 the poet Shenstone wrote that London was 'really dangerous…pickpockets…made no scruple to knock people down with bludgeons in Fleet Street and the Strand'. In 1752 Horace Walpole said, 'One is forced to travel, even at noon, as if one were going into battle.'

In 1750 Henry Fielding began the first small detective force. He realised that to be successful he was going to have to get the public to help. He published the descriptions of criminals and crime and asked the public to help with information. Very soon this little force had improved the state of London's streets. They became known as Mr Fielding's People and they were successful in breaking up a number of criminal gangs. Later they were known as the Bow Street Runners.

When Henry Fielding died in 1754 his blind half-brother took over from him. John Fielding improved on his brother's work and was later knighted for his efforts. Despite their hard work, however, the two Fielding brothers had little immediate effect on crime in London. Their efforts began a 75-year campaign to police London adequately and they left the Bow Street Runners who remained a useful band of 'thief takers', able to work in any part of the country.

The new towns went on growing at an amazing rate in the nineteenth century and were becoming ungovernable. Even so, when William Pitt, the Prime Minister, tried to get Parliament to set up a new police force for London, he met with such opposition that he had to drop the idea.

Little by little the policing of London improved in the early years of the nineteenth century. But they were troubled times and there were far too few constables to deal with any serious outbreak of social unrest or crime.

In 1815 Napoleon was defeated and the long war with France ended. Thousands of soldiers added to the growing numbers of unemployed, caused by the use of labour saving machinery in the factories. Social unrest grew and there were a number of riots.

One famous episode occurred in the summer of 1819 when a crowd of 60,000 people gathered in St Peter's Field in Manchester to listen to Henry Hunt, a famous speaker. Mounted *yeomanry* were ordered to arrest Hunt but instead they turned on the crowd. Eleven were killed and 400 were injured. The government became unpopular but still failed to do anything about law and order. Order was kept by the local *militia*. They couldn't patrol regularly but when called into action they often used more violence than was necessary.

Many people throughout the country still opposed the idea of a police force. However, some progress had been made in London and by 1828 the Home Secretary, Sir Robert Peel, controlled about 450 men in London. It was a tiny force, about one policeman to every 3,000 people. They were nicknamed 'Peelers' or 'Bobbies' after their founder.

Source: *The Story of the Police*, published by the Home Office

In 1829 the Metropolitan Police Act was passed by Sir Robert Peel. This provided for a single police force for the whole of London – that is for an area roughly within a circle of seven miles from the centre of London. The new Metropolitan Police force worked only in London, the rest of the country remained unchanged. The example, however, showed other cities and towns what could be done to clear the streets of crime. Finally, in 1835, the government passed an Act that ordered all areas to set up a police force and the government met a quarter of the cost of this but only if the new forces were found to be efficient.

Source: 'The Story of the Police'
Home Office Publication

The new police wore a dark blue uniform with a top hat. They were nicknamed 'Peelers' or 'Bobbies' after their founder, Sir Robert Peel.

Source: Barnaby's Picture Library

Vocabulary

Hue and cry People say that the word 'hue' comes from the sound of the hunting horn and 'cry' from the shouts that encouraged others to join a chase. The only way to raise the alarm in olden times was to shout and if someone saw a burglar in the act of stealing he or she would raise a 'hue and cry' to encourage others to help catch the villain.

Constables were appointed by the parish to help keep the peace. They were unpaid, had no uniform and were expected to carry out their duties as a constable as well as their everyday job. Needless to say they were highly unpopular as part of their job included reporting their neighbours' behaviour to the courts. Arresting criminals and guarding them until their trial and calling out a hue and cry when necessary was also part of their job.

Militia A military force raised from the civilian population and used in times of trouble to back up the regular army.

Yeomanry A yeoman was a person who cultivated a small piece of land. The yeomanry were a volunteer mounted cavalry force raised chiefly from the yeoman class.

Assignment 1   Design a poster which aims to attract people to join the police force at the time it was started in 1829.

Why did they need a police force?

How did the police force benefit the people?

What image would you present of the police in your poster? Would they be seen as heroes?

What type of character would the force want?

Assignment 2   Imagine that you are the chairperson of the History Society and you have been asked to give a talk explaining why the police force came into being.
   Make notes for your talk which should last for five to ten minutes. You may include facts not given in the extract but the main body of information should come from what has been supplied.

Do not be put off by the length of the talk.

What information from the extract would an audience find most interesting?

Look at each paragraph of the material provided and jot down, in point form, any information you feel you should include. This provides you with the skeleton on which to base your talk.

Think about your audience. Since you are giving a talk you will need to capture the attention of your audience immediately.

Sometimes speakers illustrate their talks with pictures. These are called visual aids. Could you make some for this talk? Remember that the main marks will be for the written details.

Assignment 3   Imagine you are a policeman who joined the force in 1829. Write three extracts from your diary that emphasize the lawlessness of the time. Explain the difficulties that you, as a member of the police force, have encountered in trying to uphold the law and in catching criminals.

Assignment 4   Look at the reasons given for the growth of crime in the nineteenth century. Are these problems responsible for crime today and are there any new causes now which are not mentioned in the extract? Discuss this as a class then write an essay entitled 'Crime in the Nineteenth Century and Today'.

Useful organisations to contact

Information on the police force can be obtained from your local police station or library.

Section 4   The Bin Sin

Half a ton of rubbish! That's how much garbage every person in our country chucks out each year! Disposable calculators, throwaway torches, non-returnable bottles – these are the symbols of our society.

In many developing countries one person's rubbish is another person's lifeline. Recycling and re-using materials – sacks, tyres, metal boxes – is an important means of survival for many of the world's poorest. In India last November I met families sorting rags and sacks from the Madras rubbish tip to be made into paper. Jayanti Singh, a metal worker, sat by the side of the road in Hyderabad city beating scrap iron into kerosene stoves. In northern Ethiopia, they've fulfilled Isaiah's vision of swords being hammered into ploughshares, as discarded ammunition boxes are crafted into musical instruments.

While our neighbours in the developing world scavenge on the rubbish heap, we Christians of the West gorge ourselves on the world's resources. In your lifetime you will consume twenty times as much energy, raw materials and food as the average Indian.

Source: Christian Aid.

Source: Christian Aid.

If the many millions of tonnes of material already reclaimed and recycled annually were not recovered, they would be added to the enormous quantities of household, industrial and commercial refuse collected and disposed of mainly by the local authorities. Collecting and disposing of rubbish costs money. If it wasn't collected, then it would be left to pollute the environment. Before long we would be buried in our own waste.

It is cheaper for industrial producers to use reclaimed materials. Not only are they cheaper but they save the world's resources.

Many charities organise collections of certain kinds of waste. Bottles, cans, tin-foil and paper are the most well known. They sell the items to industry for recycling and thus make money. However, Britain still lags behind other countries when it comes to recycling waste and saving resources.

Source: British Reclamation Industries Confederation.

Assignment 1 Discuss as a class the charities that raise money by collecting waste.

What types of things do they collect?

What other things, not mentioned in the chart, are recycled?

Do they advertise? Where would they advertise?

Assignment 2 a) Try to find out how much money a local charity makes from collecting waste material.

b) Find out from your local authority the amount they spend on the collection of rubbish, household and otherwise, each year.

c) Find out about facilities for recycling waste in your own area from your local authority. Find out the cost of recycling this type of waste.

You will need to do your own research for this assignment. This might involve phoning or writing to various bodies. If you are going to write a letter make sure that you have read the chapter on letter writing first. Telephone numbers and addresses can be found in local directories.

Your local authority and charities such as Oxfam, Dr Barnardos and charities for the blind should be able to help you.

If there is a bottle or tin bank in your town you local council may help.

Waste not, want not!

NOTE: All products can be recycled profitably as long as
  1. they are not contaminated
  2. the distance from the collection point to the recycling plant is not too great.

Product		Amount recycled	Money available to collectors	Savings on energy and resources
Paper		2,000,000 tonnes (still import 1.5m tonnes of wood pulp	Variable but profitable	1 tonne saves 15 medium size trees*
Tin Aluminium		⅓ recycled	12 cans = 1p 1 tonne = 14,000 cans	Takes 20 tonnes more energy to make tins from ore than to recycle
Glass		100,000 tonnes 10% of all waste	Variable but profitable	9 million gallons of oil saved (less fuel used in recycling
Rubber		140,000 tonnes (20% total)	Variable but profitable	100,000 tonnes crude oil saved by recycling
Foil			10p = 500 tops	
Copper Lead		⅓ recycled	Variable 30p kg	Will re-cycle (3.2% of total energy used to convert copper from ore)
Steel/Iron (cars, fridges, etc)		7m tonnes (50% total)	Variable but profitable	Recycling uses ⅓ of the energy to make new steel
Sump Oil Chemicals		Not available	Variable but profitable	30,000 tonnes of used sump oil can be recycled, therefore saving on oil resources

* The Government is helping to create a stronger demand for waste paper by allocating £23 million towards new plant to process waste paper and to develop improved ways of recycling paper.

Source: Information based on National Anti-Waste Programme.

Assignment 3   Using all the information you have now acquired, as well as that provided, write an article for a school magazine or community newspaper on how we, as a nation, could recycle refuse and save resources.

Be careful not to get carried away. Read the title carefully, it is not asking you to recycle tins, bottles and so on yourself.

Think carefully of all the things that could be recycled.

How could you make your article eye-catching?

Don't forget that when you are writing an article it must be of the appropriate length. A paragraph is not enough!

Assignment 4   Write a letter to your local newspaper suggesting ways of cleaning up your area. Don't just consider the problem of litter; think of all the other things which can spoil an area, abandoned cars, tips, coal tips and so on.

Useful organisations to contact

The Christian Aid Education Department, P.O. Box No 1, London SW9 8BH.

National Anti-Waste Programme, Ashdown House, 123 Victoria Street, London SW1E 6RB.

Industry Committee for Packaging and the Environment (INCPEN), 161-6 Fleet Street, London EC4 2DP.

Friends of the Earth Ltd, Environmentalists, 377 City Road, London EC1

Section 5   Poverty at Home

Child Poverty Action Group (CPAG)

Source: Child Poverty Action Group

The Child Poverty Action Group was set up in 1965 by a group of Quakers to draw attention to the millions of people living on or below the poverty line. The poverty line is an imaginary line. Various organisations have assessed that every family needs a certain income on which to survive. This income will allow them to buy the essentials needed for the family in the way of food, accommodation and heating. If families do not have this minimum income they are said to be living below the poverty line.

When CPAG was set up many people thought that Britain's post-war boom had put an end to poverty. CPAG argued that despite improvements in living standards poverty continued to be a fact of life for many children and their families. Since then, things have got worse and now there is a growing poverty crisis. The rising tide of poverty already affects the lives of millions of people and threatens to engulf more. Over two million children are now being brought up on or below the poverty line!

Source: Child Poverty Action Group.

CPAG Survey

CPAG conducted a survey of families living on Supplementary Benefit (SB). This is a cash amount paid to families who have no other source of income. It is seen as the state 'safety net' for those not in full time work. It is frequently treated as the conventional poverty line. 7.2 million people were dependent on SB in 1983 – enough people to fill London – yet the government estimates that three out of ten of those entitled do not claim!

This is what some families told CPAG about living on Supplementary Benefit.

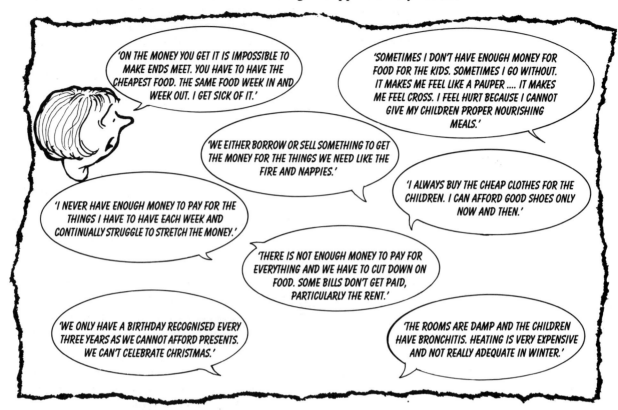

'ON THE MONEY YOU GET IT IS IMPOSSIBLE TO MAKE ENDS MEET. YOU HAVE TO HAVE THE CHEAPEST FOOD. THE SAME FOOD WEEK IN AND WEEK OUT. I GET SICK OF IT.'

'SOMETIMES I DON'T HAVE ENOUGH MONEY FOR FOOD FOR THE KIDS. SOMETIMES I GO WITHOUT. IT MAKES ME FEEL LIKE A PAUPER .... IT MAKES ME FEEL CROSS. I FEEL HURT BECAUSE I CANNOT GIVE MY CHILDREN PROPER NOURISHING MEALS.'

'WE EITHER BORROW OR SELL SOMETHING TO GET THE MONEY FOR THE THINGS WE NEED LIKE THE FIRE AND NAPPIES.'

'I ALWAYS BUY THE CHEAP CLOTHES FOR THE CHILDREN. I CAN AFFORD GOOD SHOES ONLY NOW AND THEN.'

'I NEVER HAVE ENOUGH MONEY TO PAY FOR THE THINGS I HAVE TO HAVE EACH WEEK AND CONTINUALLY STRUGGLE TO STRETCH THE MONEY.'

'THERE IS NOT ENOUGH MONEY TO PAY FOR EVERYTHING AND WE HAVE TO CUT DOWN ON FOOD. SOME BILLS DON'T GET PAID, PARTICULARLY THE RENT.'

'WE ONLY HAVE A BIRTHDAY RECOGNISED EVERY THREE YEARS AS WE CANNOT AFFORD PRESENTS. WE CAN'T CELEBRATE CHRISTMAS.'

'THE ROOMS ARE DAMP AND THE CHILDREN HAVE BRONCHITIS. HEATING IS VERY EXPENSIVE AND NOT REALLY ADEQUATE IN WINTER.'

Benefits

The Supplementary Benefit rates as at April 1987 are given below. These are basic weekly rates which are supposed to cover all items of normal day-to-day living, excluding housing.

Weekly Benefits		*LTB
Single person Age 16-17	£18.75	£23.70
Single person Age 18-25 Non-householder	£24.35	£30.95
Non-householders over 25 qualify for additional £4.05		
Single person Age 18+ Householder	£30.40	£38.65
Married couple Non-householder/householder + each child under 11 over 11	£49.35 £10.40 (Less child benefit of £7.25) £15.60 (Less child benefit of £7.25)	£61.85
* Long Term Benefit. This is not paid to unemployed people but to those unable to work due to ill health/one parent families etc. Not everyone on Supplementary Benefit qualifies for this.		

NB. Figures frequently change. These give an indication of the problems faced by some members of our community.

In some circumstances a couple can get extra benefits to meet additional requirements. However, in 1982 the average weekly expenditure of couples with two children was more than twice as much at £134.05. (Expenditure means the money spent per week on the family for food and day-to-day living and does not include housing.)

The Supplementary Benefit rate and Child Benefit for a child under 11 amount to a mere £1.49 a day. How did you spend your last £1.49? Every parent of a child in Britain is paid Child Benefit, it is paid till the child is sixteen.

What is poverty?

Some people argue that we have no 'real' or 'grinding' poverty in Britain today. Instead, they talk about starving children overseas – as seen on TV or on Oxfam posters – or compare the situation today with the horrors of Dickens's day or George Orwell's 1930s. Neither comparison makes sense. As a social security minister has put it.

'… it is not sufficient to assess poverty by absolute standards; nowadays it must be judged on relative criteria by comparison with the standards of living of other groups in the community…beneficiaries must have an income which enables them to participate in the life of the community.'

This ministerial view is widely held by the general public, as a survey recently carried out by a London Weekend TV channel for a programme called 'Breadline' and MORI polls have shown. Of those interviewed more than two out of three felt that the following were necessities.

---

1 Self-contained, damp-free accommodation with an indoor toilet and bath.

2 Adequate bedrooms and beds.
  Heating and carpeting in living rooms.

3 A weekly roast meat joint (or its equivalent) for the family and three meals daily for the child.

4 Two pairs of all-weather shoes and a warm, waterproof coat.

5 Sufficient public transport.

6 Enough money for special occasions like Christmas.

7 Toys for children.

The survey found that not only do many people suffer hardship because they have to do without these necessities, but that millions of people regularly go without a meal because they can't afford it.

Assignment 1 Summarise in your own words the types of problems faced by the families interviewed by CPAG. Make notes, then write an essay.

Make notes under three headings: food, housing, clothes.

Include all the detail you can find.

Before you begin your essay make sure your notes are in a logical order.

Assignment 2 You are a member of a family contacted by CPAG and you have been asked to speak on the radio, highlighting the plight of people like yourself. Write a radio talk of 300-400 words explaining your problems.

How would writing a radio talk differ from writing an article for a magazine? Think about how the audience is receiving the information.

Would you want to burden your audience with lots of facts and figures?

How would you best get sympathy from the audience?

How do appeals for charities sound on TV or the radio? What tone do they adopt?

Assignment 3  You are an interviewer for a radio documentary asking questions about the type of life poor people have. Write down the dialogue between yourself as the interviewer and the person being interviewed.

Look at the information on interviews on page 211. Note how an interviewer draws out information from the person being interviewed.

What questions would you ask? Plan these before you begin. Also think about the answers you might get.

Assignment 4 Discuss how society could help families who are unable to manage on a low income.

Who would be in a position to help them – nationally, locally?

Are there other organisations like CPAG that could help? In what way?

Do people always find it easy to accept help? Consider feelings of independence, pride, and of not wishing outsiders to know details of their lives.

Useful organisations to contact

Child Poverty Action Group, 1 Macklin Steet, London WC2B 5NH.

SHELTER (Look up their address in your area.)

Section 6 Smoking

SMOKING KILLS SMOKERS!

THERE ARE KINGS AND THERE ARE STUPIDKINGS

CIGARETTES: THEY'RE LESS PAINFUL THAN LICKING YOUR FINGERS AND STICKING THEM IN ELECTRIC LIGHT SOCKETS BUT JUST AS EFFECTIVE!

Source: North West Regional Health Authority.

HOW MUCH SMOKING COSTS THE NHS

On average each day **4,009** beds are occupied in hospital by patients with these diseases, an annual total of **1,463,400** bed days used unnecessarily. This costs the National Health Service **£111,325,000** a year for England and Wales.

Population **MEN:** 18,213,600 **WOMEN:** 19,217,700
TOTAL: 37,431,300

Lung Cancer

Lung cancer kills more people than any other type of cancer and 90% of deaths from this disease are caused by cigarette smoking.

Source: Health Education Council.

Passive Smoking Kills

Non-Smokers' Health WARNING:

OTHER PEOPLE'S SMOKE CAN DAMAGE YOUR HEALTH

A cigarette produces two kinds of cigarette smoke:

Roughly 75% of the smoke from a lit cigarette goes straight out into the air as **sidestream smoke**. The smoker inhales the remaining 25% as **mainstream smoke**, and breathes half of this out again. In total, 85-90% cigarette smoke gets into the air which others breathe.

The smoker

The smoker inhales mainstream smoke which contains a treacly tar (which irritates the lungs and can cause cancer), carbon monoxide (which starves the body of oxygen and may lead to heart attacks), and nicotine (a very addictive poison) plus a variety of other gases and poisons.

The passive smoker

The passive smoker breathes in sidestream smoke, diluted in the air. This is unfiltered smoke, and contains higher concentrations of the poisonous chemicals and gases than mainstream smoke. It contains twice as much nicotine, 3 times as much tar, 5 times as much carbon monoxide 50 times as much cancer causing chemicals

Effects on babies

Passive smoking begins in the womb. Pregnant women who smoke are more likely to have small babies, and small babies are more likely to die at birth or shortly afterwards. Pregnant women shouldn't smoke, but neither should fathers-to-be, because the sidestream smoke from their cigarettes may be breathed in by the mother and affect the baby.

Would-be-fathers are also warned that smoking can affect fertility. Results of work done on a group of men in an Edinburgh infertility clinic showed that smokers produced higher numbers of abnormal sperm than non-smokers.

Effects on children

Babies run twice the risk of developing a serious chest illness if both parents smoke. The children of parents who smoke are twice as likely to suffer from colds, coughs, phlegm, and, more seriously, pneumonia, bronchitis and tonsillitis, than children of non-smokers. Smokers' children also grow up with less healthy lungs, and have more days off sick from school. Parents who smoke set a bad example, and their children are more likely to start smoking than are children of non-smokers.

Source: Health Education Council.

Adults
* Many non-smokers find that tobacco smoke causes:

  sore or runny eyes   sneezing

  a runny nose   a blocked up nose

  a 'stuffed up' feeling   headaches

  coughing   wheezing

  hoarseness
* People with asthma may find that breathing other people's tobacco smoke brings on an attack.
* People with allergies often find that tobacco smoke makes their allergies worse.
* Many contact lens users find that tobacco smoke affects their vision. And lens users who have a lot of trouble with tobacco smoke may become more prone to eye infections.
* Non-smokers run only a small risk of getting lung cancer. But that risk is increased if they have lived or worked with smokers over many years. For example, researchers have found that the non-smoking wives of *smokers* are more at risk of developing lung cancer than the non-smoking wives of *non-smokers*.

Children
* The children of smokers are more likely to get bronchitis, pnuemonia and other chest infections than the children of non-smokers.

Many non-smokers feel angry or frustrated by tobacco smoke and the lingering smell of stale smoke at work, at home, on buses, in cinemas, cafés and restaurants. Tobacco smoke can cause a lot of friction between smokers and non-smokers.

Source: Health Education Council

Mel Calman

I hope my eating isn't spoiling your cigar

No smoking

Source: ASH

Assignment 1   Devise a leaflet, suitable for distributing at school, aimed at deterring pupils from smoking. It should be based on information you have read.

Who is the audience?

What information should the leaflet contain?

Since it is a leaflet would you need to present the information in a special way?

Could you use illustrations to make it more effective?

Assignment 2 Discuss as a class why you think young people start smoking. What pressures are there on them to start? Why do you think that for the first time ever more females than males are taking up smoking?

Assignment 3 In your own words write a summary describing the ways that smoking affects smokers and non-smokers alike. Think about the financial side as well as the health side.

Divide your answer up into how it affects adults, children and babies.

What diseases are caused by smoking?

Are there any other side-effects you can think of? Bad breath, for instance.

How much does hospital treatment for smokers cost?

Are only smokers affected by cigarette smoking?

Why is it unpleasant for non-smokers?

Assignment 4
a) Find out how much revenue the government gets from smokers. Where **and from whom does this money come?**

b) Discuss what measures governments have taken to make people aware of the dangers of smoking.

c) Should governments do more to stop people smoking? Are there reasons that might prevent them from going too far?

You will need to use your local library and possibly the Health Education Authority, or the Health Education Unit in your area, to research this assignment.

Useful organisations to contact
Note: All these are anti-smoking organisations.

Tacade 3rd floor, Furness House, Trafford Road, Salford M5 2XJ.

GASP (Group Against Smoking in Public), Box 20, 37 Stokes Croft, Bristol, BS1 3PY.

ASH (Action on Smoking and Health), 5-11 Mortimer Street, London W1N 7RH.

Health Education Authority , 78 New Oxford Street, London WC1A 1AH.

3 Argumentative Writing

Introduction

Argumentative writing is possibly one of the most difficult tasks you will be set and very often it is hard to find just the right information, on just the right topic, when you need it. The aim of this chapter is to provide the facts upon which you can base an opinion. Where the subject is of a debatable nature the chapter aims to present impartially some information taken from both sides.

More and more examining boards are expecting you to argue a point of view in an essay. Questions may be set on examination papers, or pupils who are preparing coursework for the GCSE may be set essays of this kind by their teacher. The topics chosen are often controversial and therefore there are two opposing viewpoints. You are encouraged to make a decision and to reveal how and why you have reached such a decision. It is good practice for life outside school, where often you may come into conflict with others over certain matters. This chapter will help you gain the skill to argue your case successfully.

It is hoped that after reading this chapter you will be able to make up your own mind about a number of important issues, some of which might affect you in the future. You will have a chance to air your views on paper and verbally in a debate.

Golden Rules

1 Writing of this kind needs careful planning; think very carefully about the subject matter of the question. Argumentative writing requires you to use your imagination to a lesser extent because knowledge of the subject matter is far more important. Always choose to write on a subject you know something about and one for which you could come up with some ideas.

2 Your opinion on a subject will be required. For instance, the question might ask if you are in favour of field sports or not and you must have formed an opinion before you can begin to write convincingly. A poor answer is one where the writer finds his or her opinion changing halfway through.

3 Writing of this kind is much easier if you have jotted down the points in favour of something and the points against. Make a careful plan before you begin to write. Argue your case logically, dealing with each point completely before moving on to the next.

4 In your writing you will need to put forward reasons to support or oppose some topic *and* you must also develop these reasons into an argument. It is possible that your views may not fall neatly into being either for or against a subject. If this is the case, state exactly how you feel, what reservations you have about adopting one viewpoint or the other, and why you have these reservations.

5 Your answer must contain more than an opinion, it must be backed up by reasons and these reasons need to have a basis in fact. Make sure you know the difference between a fact and an opinion.

FACT 3,000,000,000 canned drinks are consumed each year.
OPINION I think we drink far too many canned drinks.

FACT Capital punishment has been abolished in this country.
OPINION I do not think capital punishment should be restored.

Look at some newspaper articles with your teacher and see if you can distinguish between a fact and an opinion.

6 The structure of your writing is important and so too is being logical. Avoid jumping backwards to a previous point because you have forgotten to include something. This suggests that a) you can't organise your thoughts and b) you didn't complete your plan thoroughly enough. It also confuses the reader who is trying to make sense of your ideas.

7 Whether you are arguing in favour of something or against *always* be aware of the opposition's points of view and try to anticipate their criticism in your answer. Do not use over-emotional arguments or allow your feelings to take over.

8 Be bold when you are beginning your writing: make some reference to the title, perhaps by answering immediately a suggestion made in it. Adhere firmly to answering the question only, don't get side-tracked.

9 Argumentative writing needs a conclusion. A conclusion is a suitable end and it is normally brief – a review, in about a paragraph, of all the points you've made. It brings your writing to a natural end and ties the whole structure together neatly.

Section 1 Sample Assignments

The following topics show the type of essay you may be expected to write.

Assignment 1 'There would be no violence if there were no TV programmes, films or newspaper articles highlighting violent acts. The media have a lot to answer for.'
Do you think there is any truth in this view, or is it just an excuse for people to ban violence on TV and in films?
Write an essay giving your views on this subject.

Assignment 2 'In view of the rise in organised dog-fighting and the profusion of organisations to protect animals we cannot surely believe ourselves to be a nation of animal lovers.'
Would you agree with the view held by this writer?
Write a 300-400 word essay illustrating, with reasons, your point of view.

Assignment 3 'The only way to get rid of soccer hooliganism is to get rid of soccer! I'm sick of hearing the excuses put forward for violence on the terraces: boredom, lack of jobs, lack of money. In my day there was a shortage of jobs and certainly a lack of money, it didn't make me a soccer thug.'
How do you feel about this person's point of view? What do you think are the causes of soccer hooliganism and how can it be stopped?

Assignment 4 In about 400 words discuss whether you think that teenagers have a bad image as far as the general public are concerned. What things could you say in defence of youth today against any harsh criticism?

Assignment 5 How do you feel about the threat of nuclear war? If there were a referendum tomorrow would you vote to keep the bomb or not. Give reasons for your views.

Assignment 6 If you had a choice of which century you could live in which would you choose and why?

Section 2 Capital Punishment

Introduction

Capital punishment refers to the taking of the life of someone who has been found guilty of committing a crime. It is used when someone has committed a capital offence; that is a crime punishable by death. Although in the past a person could be hanged for various offences, capital punishment has been used mainly when a person has been found guilty of murder or treason.

There is a difference between murder and manslaughter. Manslaughter is the term used when someone has been killed but the act is considered to be unintentional. In cases such as this the death penalty would not be used. Murder implies intent to kill. Anyone who is convicted of murder but is found to be insane or of 'diminished responsibility' would also avoid the hangman's noose.

The death penalty for murder was abolished in this country in November 1965 by the Murder (Abolition of Death Penalty) Act 1965. Prior to that the law was governed by the Homicide Act 1957, which created two categories of murder, capital and non-capital, with only the first carrying the death penalty. The types of murder designated capital included murder in the course of furtherance of theft, murder by shooting and the murder of a police officer or prison officer.

Many people still believe that only the death penalty can control or diminish the growth of terrorism, hijacking, kidnapping and taking of hostages. There are many, too, who hold that even if it had no effect on those crimes, the death penalty would be appropriate on the 'just deserts' principle – the offender deserves to be hanged even if his death may worsen the general problem. Others believe that the death penalty should be brought back for other categories of murder as well, the murder of children, for instance.

Murder

For weeks we've had them, all the photographs:
Johnny from Johnny's passport – 'The police
Believe this man could help them.' Easy laughs
From quotes by Johnny's fourteen-year-old niece –
The picture shows a fluffy dance-hall chick.
Today's the day the state wrings Johnny's neck.

Then here's Johnny, raincoat over face;
He's stumbling from a squad car, on each side
A small crowd of the ghoulish gives him place.
Here's Johnny's mother – see her trying to hide
Behind her handbag as she hears the click.
Today's the day the state wrings Johnny's neck.

Here's Johnny's father at the law-court gate –
Grey rubber mask – 'We hope for a reprieve.'
But still the little men with cameras wait –
Visiting-hour is up and soon she'll leave.
'Get us his wife, in tears outside the nick!'
Today's the day the state wrings Johnny's neck.

'The taking of a life I have raised from a boy to a man is very hard to accept'

from RICHARD SHEARS in Melbourne

DOOMED Briton Kevin Barlow met his mother yesterday and patched up a family row it was feared he would take to the grave.

Barlow, who is facing the gallows later this week for a drugs offence, chatted with her for four hours in Kuala Lumpur's Pudu Jail.

A day earlier he had refused to see her after mistakenly believing his family had spent £5,000 in legal aid money.

As she emerged from the prison's huge brown-painted steel doors, Mrs Barbara Barlow, 47, said: 'The taking of a life of a boy I have reared from a baby and brought up to be a man is so difficult to come to terms with.'

She sat in a reception room just across the courtyard from the main gates with her son and 17-year-old daughter Michelle who had also flown out from the family home in Australia.

'We sat chatting about everything and anything,' said Mrs Barlow.

'We were doing flashbacks of when we were on holiday together, when all the family was together.

'We went back to the times when we were all younger – ...talking about the sort of things you discuss when you haven't seen somebody for a long time.

'We didn't discuss the future. It's something I've been deliberately avoiding for the time being.

'I can't see that it's too late for them to show compassion. While there is life there's hope.

Mercy

'I've always hoped. You don't stop hoping. I know they've got a drug problem here, but this is not the way to beat it. They are not punishing him. They will be for the moment, but then he will be free.

'They are punishing all of us, and we haven't done anything. We have realised the death penalty doesn't do anything except kill the one person each time.'

Mrs Barlow, who emigrated to Australia with her family from Stoke-on-Trent in 1971, spoke as the Malaysian official who helped turn down her son's final plea for mercy was now considering a stay of execution.

Australian prime minister Bob Hawke had earlier ruled out any further government action to save Mr Barlow and 28-year-old Brian Chambers who is awaiting the same fate.

Today, Tuesday 24 June 1986.

Capital Punishment for Terrorists?

The National Campaign for the Abolition of Capital Punishment sees the problem in the following terms.

* Great Britain has decided, like most countries, that judicial killing has no place in a civilised state, and that this applies to the execution of terrorists as much as to that of any murderer.

* In any case, the practical arguments against executing terrorists are peculiarly strong. Judicial killing is unavoidably slow. There is a preliminary hearing, a trial, usually one or more appeals against conviction; and it can all take many months — in some countries, years. During that time other coercive crimes are likely to happen, including the taking of hostages whose lives will depend on the fate of the prisoner.

* 'Terrorism' today is often the work of minors, female as well as male, whom it would be virtually unthinkable to execute. And the death penalty for terrorists of 'executionable age' might have the ghastly effect of increasing the use of minors for the purpose of homicide.

* Moreover, it makes no sense to kill terrorists whose aims, whatever we think of them, may to them be idealistic, and not to kill those who murder for personal gain.

* Recent years have seen a tragic sequence of convictions against innocent people. With terrorism as with other forms of homicide, there is a constant risk of convictions against innocent people.

* The death penalty, like any other penalty, will deter some killers, but there is no evidence that it does so more than any other. It is in the nature of political 'terrorism' that it is the work of fanatics who accept (indeed sometimes relish) the risk of death 'for the cause'. The judicial killing of terrorists, more often than not, has the opposite effect to that which is intended.

* Reprisals will often follow executions, leading to the loss of still more innocent lives.

Source: NACRO.

Former Home Secretary on terrorists

They are fanatics who, however perverted they may be in their thinking and feeling, see themselves as fighting for a cause higher than themselves and who are living in a state of mind of dangerous exultation, in which they hold their own lives at a relatively low price.

Robert Carr, now Lord Carr, 20th April 1982.

Should the Death Penalty be Restored?

Police Federation view

We have always maintained that capital punishment should be available for the crime of murder. Last year more than 250,000 ordinary members of the public took the trouble to write to us to express their support for the restoration of capital punishment, and we know that many citizens have written to their Members of Parliament asking them to support the restoration of the death penalty.

In the 20 years since abolition, 36 police officers have been killed by criminals in England, Scotland and Wales compared with 12 such deaths in the 20 years before abolition. Each year about 15,000 police officers are assaulted on duty, and about 4,000 sustain injuries which warrant compensation from the Criminal Injuries Compensation Board. In his Annual Report for 1981, the Chief Constable of Strathclyde said that there were 21 attempts to murder police officers in his force. Whilst we recognise that police officers are more likely to find themselves in conflict with criminals, if this is happening to a group which represents no more than one in five hundred of the population, what is happening to the rest? We are particularly concerned about attacks on elderly citizens and lone women.

Terrorism has added an awesome dimension to the question of capital punishment. When the House of Commons voted to abolish capital punishment for a 5-year period in 1965, acts of terrorism in Britain were virtually unknown. The vote to make abolition permanent took place in 1969, just before the present troubles in Northern Ireland degenerated into terrorism. Over the past ten years, the United Kingdom has witnessed terrorism on a scale without precedent in our history. Well over 2,000 people have been killed in Northern Ireland alone, including more than 150 officers serving in the Royal Ulster Constabulary, and more than 400 members of the security forces. Attempts to spread the campaign of bombing and murder to the rest of the United Kingdom have seen the outrages of the Hyde Park and Regents Park bomb explosions last year, and the Guildford and Birmingham bomb explosions and the attacks on the Tower of London and elsewhere. There have also been deliberate attempts, in some cases successful, to murder prominent persons who were outspoken in their condemnation of terrorism. Members of Parliament will not need to be reminded that two of their colleagues have been assassinated in recent years.

►

81

Britain has also witnessed examples of terrorism perpetrated by murder gangs whose targets have been their opponents in the politics of the Middle East. There have also been hi-jacking incidents at London Airport, and the siege of the Iranian Embassy.

We have carefully considered the strong arguments advanced by people in responsible positions who maintain that the application of the death penalty to terrorists would not deter others, and could lead to further outrages. It is also said that an executed terrorist immediately becomes a political martyr. We do not accept these arguments.

One of the most disturbing features of criminal activity since the abolition of the death penalty has been the increased use of firearms in the commission of crime. To some extent this has been mitigated by the stringent requirements of the law in respect of the possession of firearms, and the legislation which has empowered the courts to impose salutary penalties. Notwithstanding this, the evidence is clear that ruthless criminals are prepared to band together and to use firearms in the commission of crime, usually with the objective of stealing huge sums of cash or other valuables. We believe that this is the direct result of the abolition of capital punishment.

The overwhelming view of the police service is that capital punishment should be restored for the crime of murder. We accept, of course, that there are degrees of murder and we are not saying that all persons who are convicted of homicide should suffer the death penalty.

Source: The Police Federation, 1986.

RESTORE CAPITAL PUNISHMENT

More than 40,000 readers of the <u>Daily Star</u> took part in an opinion poll. A massive majority of 83.6 per cent want the return of capital punishment for murder. In the absence of the death penalty, an even larger majority believe that 'life imprisonment' should really mean 'imprisonment for life'.

An overwhelming 92 per cent want to see a mandatory minimum sentence of 25 years for rape.

The biggest vote, 95.6 per cent, was in demand of the prosecution's right of appeal against lenient sentences. The House of Lords showed itself to be grossly out of touch with public opinion when it threw out that motion.

Source: Tebbit Campaign for Law and Order.

Group work   Work in groups for Assignments 1, 2 and 3. Elect a group leader who will report back to the class and a secretary who should make notes.

Assignment 1   Make a list of arguments that people make for and against the reintroduction of capital punishment.

Assignment 2   Make a list of the crimes you feel particularly strongly about. Try and explain why you feel this way.

Some people find crimes against women, children and the elderly particularly disturbing. Do you? Why is this?

Have any recent crimes upset or shocked you?

Assignment 3   Some children are killed by their parents or step-parents. Most of the time parents are not actually charged with murder but with manslaughter. How do you feel about these crimes? Are penalties strict enough?

Assignment 4   All groups should now be in a position to report back to the class. Listen carefully to what other groups have to say and jot down any extra points they make.

Assignment 5   Work in small groups of about six. (Alternatively this can be done by just one group putting on a performance for the rest of the class.) You will need a group leader and a secretary who will take notes.
Choose three members of your group to play the parts of Johnny's mother, father and wife. Let them relate their experiences with the press and the public during the trial and the time leading up to the hanging. Imagine that the other members of your group are relatives of the victim. After the performance discuss as a class who is the victim in such a case. Is it only the person who is killed?

You may have knowledge of another case that has had a lot of publicity. You could use this case instead of the poem as the basis for your role-play.

Explain how you feel as the parents or wife/husband of the victim.

Assignment 6   *Write an essay on one of the following.*
   a) '"An eye for an eye and a tooth for a tooth" is a line often quoted from the Bible by people who wish to reintroduce capital punishment. However, the Bible also says, "thou shalt not kill". Hanging is barbaric and medieval, we can't possibly live in the twentieth century and suggest hanging people.'
   How do you feel about this view?

   b) 'Last year I was against the reintroduction of hanging. This January my son was forcibly taken from a park near our home where he was playing with some of his friends. His unclothed body was found three days later.

He was six. Now I would be happy to hang the murderer myself. No-one can understand the grief the victim's family has to bear. No-one really cares. Everyone wants to protect the killer, my son was six, who protected him?'

What is your reaction to this statement? Do you think that hanging should be brought back for crimes of this kind? Write explaining your views.

c) 'All over the world terrorists kill and maim hundreds of people. Four hundred in one plane, twenty at an airport and the list goes on. Some mass murderers have deprived at least a dozen people of their lives. What happens to these terrorists and murderers? They spend their life in jail. Big deal! They're still breathing, eating, sleeping. Some of them escape, some are let out after twenty years. As far as I'm concerned, they have given up their right to live in a civilised society, we're better off without them.'

What do you think about this person's view? Can we justify hanging in these cases?

Useful organisations to contact

Police Federation of England and Wales, 15-17 Langley Road, Surbiton, Surrey KT6 6LP.

Organisations against capital punishment

The National Prisoners' Movement, 50 Westbourne Avenue, Hull.

Radical Alternatives to Prison, BCM Box 4842, London WC1N 3XX.

Women in Prison, Unit 3, Cockpit Yard, Northington Street, London WC1 2NP.

The Howard League, 322 Kennington Park Road, London SE11 4PP.

The National Campaign for the Abolition of Capital Punishment, 2 Amen Court Road, London EC4.

CHILD, Farthings, Pawlett, Nr Bridgewater, Somerset.

Organisations in favour of capital punishment
Campaign for Law and Order, The Tower, Rainhill, Prescott L35 6NE.

Section 3 Field Sports

Introduction

The term 'field sports' refers to sports that take place normally in the countryside and involve the hunting and subsequent killing of animals or fish. The term 'blood sports' is sometimes used to describe the same sports by those opposed to such pursuits.

The Stag

While the rain fell on the November woodland shoulder of Exmoor
While the traffic jam along the road honked and shouted
Because the farmers were parking wherever they could
And scrambling to the bank-top to stare through the tree fringe
Which was leafless,
The stag ran through his private forest.

While the rain drummed on the roofs of the parked cars
And the kids inside cried and daubed their chocolate and fought
And mothers and aunts and grandmothers
Were a tangle of undoing sandwiches and screwed-round gossiping heads
Steaming up the windows,
The stag loped through his favourite valley.

While the blue horsemen down in the boggy meadow
Sodden nearly black, on sodden horses,
Spaced as at a military parade,
Moved a few paces to the right and a few to the left and felt rather foolish
Looking at the brown impassable river,
The stag came over the last hill of Exmoor.

While everybody high-kneed it to the bank-top all along the road
Where steady men in oilskins were stationed at binoculars,
And the horsemen by the river galloped anxiously this way and that
And the cry of hounds came tumbling invisibly with their echoes down
through the draggle of trees,
Swinging across the wall of dark woodland,
The stag dropped into a strange country.
And turned at the river.

Hearing the hound pack smash the undergrowth, hearing the bell-note
Of the voice that carried all the others,
Then while his limbs all cried different directions to his lungs, which only
wanted to rest,
The blue horsemen on the bank opposite
Pulling aside the camouflage of their terrible planet.

And the stag doubled back weeping and looking for home up a valley and
down a valley
While the strange trees struck at him and the brambles lashed him,
And the strange earth came galloping after him carrying the loll-tongued
hounds to fling all over him
And his heart became just a club beating his ribs and his own hooves shouted
with hounds' voices,
And the crowd on the road got back into their cars
Wet through and disappointed.

Ted Hughes

Information in Favour of Field Sports

A small but vociferous body is intensifying a long-running campaign to persuade major parties to include in their policies the abolition of country sports.

In a nation with a reputation for its affection for animals, this is understandably an extremely emotive subject – but one where issues can easily become obscured.

We ask you to ensure that you are well informed on the issues and make a decision on the basis of the facts, which are often hidden behind the shouting.

VITAL STATISTICS

Country sports, far from being the privilege of a few, involve up to six million people from all walks of life who take part, or are actively concerned in them.

The largest sport, fishing, is supported by 3.6 million anglers, and the smallest, falconry, by up to 2,000 enthusiasts. Between these extremes are sizeable numbers supporting hunting, shooting, and hare coursing. Over one million, for instance, are licensed to own a gun or rifle.

* There are:
  293,000 people who hunt regularly, either mounted or on foot
  2,500 people who take part in coursing
  4,000 people involved with Highland stalking
  3,600,000 people who fish (either game, coarse or sea)
  2,000 falconers
* In Great Britain in 1981 there were 867,000 holders of shotgun certificates worth £2¼ million to the Exchequer. A recent survey undertaken by NOP Limited on behalf of the British Association for Shooting and Conservation shows that the majority of users of shotguns are skilled manual workers.
* The annual turnover in relation to hunting, coursing and ancillary trades is £160 million, attracting tax valued at £22 million.
* Gameshooting is worth £100 million annually in taxes, sporting rates, rearing, wages and goods sold – much of it in foreign currency. At least a further £100 million is spent in other forms of shooting such as wild fowling, rough shooting, stalking and clay pigeon shooting. £10.75 million of game meat were exported in 1980.
* £420 million a year is spent on angling and equipment.
* Some 62,500 jobs are dependent on country sports (not including the thousands who assist in driven game shooting as paid beaters and as pickers-up).

Source: British Field Sports Society

We Are Conservationists

The River Trent. From the beginning of industrialisation in the North Midlands, the story of the once magnificent River Trent was one of gross deterioration due to pollution. First the salmon, trout and grayling disappeared; then coarse fish and nearly all other wildlife vanished from extensive stretches of the river below where darker tributaries discharged their filth. Then came an historic High Court action brought by the Anglers Co-operative Association against three major polluters. From their victory stemmed a will to rescue the Trent, followed up admirably by the Severn-Trent Water Authority who have responded to the articulate demand of a million anglers in their area by instigating a massive programme of improvement in the main river and the tributaries.

The Trent today is one of the finest coarse fisheries in Britain and in 1982 the salmon began to return. Without angling interests would any of this have happened? And what in the way of kingfishers, grebes, coots, moorhens, ducks, and dragonflies does an open sewer support? To these questions there can be only one answer.

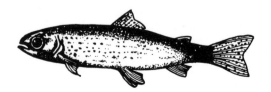

What others say

'Most of the species of mammals and birds which are killed by hunting and shooting none-theless exist in larger numbers than would obtain were these sports to be eliminated. In most cases additional cover on the landscape of intensive farms encourages other species of wildlife which would not survive in the bleak landscape.'

Professor Kenneth Mellanby CBE, 1981
(Director, Institute of Terrestrial Ecology 1961-1974)

A few miles south of Newbury, between Basingstoke and Hungerford, stretches a ridge of chalk hills embracing some of the loveliest scenery in England. Here, (on the Highclere Estate), as in many of the other corners of the countryside that retain a thick growth of deciduous trees, the woods have been maintained not for the timber they provide, but as cover for pheasants. Pheasants are reared at Highclere every year to provide sport for the owner and his guests. To guarantee the availability of this sport much of the uncultivated land throughout the estate has been left unreclaimed and, largely for the benefit of pheasants, the whole of the northern one-third of Highclere has been maintained as woodland.

Marion Shoard, Author on Conservation
('The Theft of the Countryside', 1980)

'The future for wildlife looks rather grim. With growing economic constraints it is likely that loss of habitat will continue at an accelerating rate due to forestry and agricultural requirements. Conservation interests are neglected or ignored in the interests of high productivity.

Many people do realise how important the responsible sportsman is to the well-being of our countryside...'

Professor F.G.T. Holliday CBE FRSE, 1981
(Chairman, Nature Conservancy Council 1977-1980)

Source: British Field Sports Society

Information Against Field Sports

Foxhunting

The picturesque scene of a fox hunt meeting on the village green is often used to window-dress a savage activity. The basic facts are concealed, even from Hunt members.

FOR EXAMPLE

Fox earths, badger setts and drains are blocked up the night before a hunt so that when a fox is found by the hounds, it is forced to run and run until it is totally exhausted. Then the hounds literally tear it apart.

The hounds used are slow-runners with plenty of stamina, the purpose being to prolong the chase to give the horse-riders a good gallop. If fast hounds were used the whole thing would be over in two minutes or less, which would spoil the recreation, even though the quarry would receive shorter torment.

These simple facts clearly prove that unnecessary suffering is inflicted on the fox, solely for the purpose of providing amusement.

If a fox does manage to find an unblocked underground refuge and cannot easily be 'bolted' for further hunting, the Hunt moves on and the 'spade and terrier brigade' takes over. These characters, who have no interest in horses and hounds, set their terriers onto the trapped victim and dig it out. Eventually they either kill the fox or place it in a sack, take it to the Hunt and release it, confused, battered and bleeding, in front of the hounds.

FOXES – NOT GUILTY!

Government Scientist Refutes Fox Damage Claims

Scientists working for the Department of Agriculture and Fisheries for Scotland (DAFS) have discovered that whilst up to 24% of lambs born in the Scottish hills are born dead, or later succumb to disease, hypothermia and malnutrition, only one per-cent fall victim to foxes.

The full report showed that only 1% of lambs are taken by foxes and that the massive mortality of sheep and lambs due to the harsh Scottish conditions leaves enough dead livestock lying around to feed every fox in Scotland – even if they had nothing else to eat, such as deer carr-ion, field voles and rabbits! The final paragraph of the report states, *"On the island of Mull, which has no foxes, lamb production was no better than in comparable areas of North Argyll, so that it is difficult to argue that fox predation makes sub-stantial inroads into the production of lambs."*

The DAFS Report proved that the fox is not the savage lamb killer of repute.

FOUL HUNTING

ONE OF the pathetic excuses trotted out these days by those who delight in chasing and killing wild animals is that they, above all others, can be relied on to ensure that the hunted species does not become extinct.

Their argument runs: *"We have a vested interest in ensuring the survival of foxes, deer and hares because, if they die out, we lose our sport."*

It is a simple matter to prove the bankruptcy of this argument, by pointing out that otters were hunted and killed for 'sport' right up until there were so few left that Parliament was forced to enact protective legislation in 1977. However, it is not so widely known that another British wild animal was hunted with hounds until the 'sport' died out simply because there were none left to be found.

Once Widespread

The victim was the polecat or, as it used to be known, the foulmart. These nocturnal animals are about two feet long and weigh two to three pounds. They were once widespread throughout England and Wales, but are now a rare sight.

The Foulmart was hunted by at least five packs of hounds in Cumbria alone — otter-hounds being considered ideal for the pur-pose, and the hounds were followed on foot from early morning meets.

Strong Scent

As the foulmart became scarce, hunters trapped them in cages and released them near the meet, where the hounds could easily

The Polecat - hunted nearly to extinction.

find the strong scent which gave the animal its name. Eventually the hunters and their pheasant-shooting friends virtually wiped out this British native species, which is now only found in odd pockets of Wales and the West Country.

The next animal to be driven into the en-dangered species list looks like being the harmless hare — unless a Government emerges which recognises bloodsport fanatics for the vandals they are and puts an end to their destruction of wildlife.

Source: League Against Cruel Sports

88

Hare Coursing

Some facts about coursing

Organised hare coursing is followed by approximately 1,000 people in Britain today.

The aim of this 'sport' is for two dogs, usually greyhounds, to compete against each other in pursuit of their quarry.

Hares are driven over a distance of ½ mile or more into the coursing field by some 30 or more people known as 'beaters'. The two dogs, straining at the leash, are released by the 'slipper' who gives the hare a recommended start of about 80 yards (although sometimes it is less). The already tired hare then has to run for its life. The mounted judge awards points to each dog according to its skill in turning the hare, which may or may not escape. The death is not a pretty sight. When both dogs catch the quarry, the hare can become a 'living rope' in a tug-of-war, being pulled and torn between the two powerful animals. Supporters of coursing say that the hare is always killed instantly.

Time and time again the League has proved this to be nothing more than a lie.

The hare's agony may last several minutes, depending on how quickly the handlers or 'pickers up' reach the dogs. The hare at this point is more often than not still alive and screaming. It is then taken from the dogs and killed, usually by having its neck broken.

Live hare coursing takes place between September and March every year.

The events are staged purely for entertainment. Betting has certainly helped to keep it alive for so long.

Coursing is NOT a form of pest control. The hare is becoming so rare that in more and more areas it is having to be introduced in order to provide 'sport'.

Between 600 and 1,000 hares are killed through organised coursing annually.

Quote:

'I think that practically all civilised people are against hare coursing ... I regard it as a barbarous anachronism.' *The Rt. Hon. Harold Wilson MP (speaking as Prime Minister).*

Source: League Against Cruel Sports

An article in *The People* says ...

'In the heart of the English countryside last week I watched hundreds of people indulge in what I regard as an orgy of sadism and savagery and sheer primeval blood lust. And they did it all in the name of sport.'

Reproduced by kind permission of the Editor of 'The People'

'... I became involved in a campaign against what is to my mind the filthiest stain on the sporting pages of Britain – hare coursing.'

'... A country which does not concern itself with deliberately inflicted cruelty on defenceless creatures – is a country that has lost its sensitiveness and its feeling of what is right and what is wrong ...'

Peter Wilson
World famous sports writer in the 'Daily Mirror'

Lord Kenyon
Hon. Sec. Waterloo Cup Coursing says ...

'We have a rule forbidding photographs of coursing. The ban was imposed to prevent these anti-bloodsport people from getting ammunition to use against us.'

Assignment 1 Look at the information provided by the British Field Sports Society on pages 86-7. It contains a lot of reasons in favour of field. Make a list of them.

Look at each item in turn.

Try and put the reasons under two main headings. Those connected with the sport and those connected with conservation.

Think of any other arguments in favour of field sports and add them to your list.

Assignment 2   Make a list of the different field sports you know of. Many are mentioned in the articles from the British Field Sports Society. What objections are put forward by the opponents of field sports? Find as many as you can and list them next to the sport.

Assignment 3   How do you feel about field sports? Are you in favour of some and not others? Why is this? Write down your views on the subject in note form.

Do you think there is a difference between hunting and shooting?

Is it all right to kill a fish but not to shoot a pheasant? If so, why?

Is there a difference between shooting something to eat and shooting wildlife only for sport.

Assignment 4   *Write an essay on one of the following.*

a) Imagine there was going to be a referendum on field sports. (A referendum is when the government allows the people to have a vote to decide whether or not something should be allowed.) How would you vote and why?

b) 'How hypocritical can society be? Yes, I go out and hunt, fish and shoot, but at least I'm catching my supper, not buying it cellophane wrapped in the supermarket. No one complains about all the lambs, calves or piglets butchered every day for Sunday lunch; but mention shot bunnies and that's it. My method of killing is just as humane as that used in a slaughter house! Maybe more so, I don't herd the animals out of a truck into a slaughter house where the smell of blood immediately frightens the life out of them.'
Do you sympathise with this person's point of view? Write giving your reasons.

c) Many people who are in favour of field sports maintain that they are conservationists. Would you agree with this belief or not? Write giving your reasons.

Useful organisations to contact
Organisations in favour of field sports

British Field Sports Society, 59 Kennington Road, London SE1 7PZ.

The British Association for Shooting and Conservation, Marford Mill, Rossett, Clwyd LL12 0HL.

Organisation against field sports

The League Against Cruel Sports, Sparling House, 83-7 Union Street, London SE1 1SG.

Section 4 Equal Opportunities

Introduction

This section of the book looks at the question of the position of women in Britain. Do they have the same chances as men? Are they treated equally? Do they have the same rights as men, equal pay for the same job? How have things changed? Is it now the turn of men to complain that they are not given equal opportunities?

READ

'Women,' said an 18th century gentleman, 'are only children of a larger growth: they have an entertaining tattle, and sometimes wit; but for solid, reasoning good sense, I never knew in my life one that had it.'

Did You Know...?

That women didn't get a vote till 1918 although they had been campaigning since 1867.

They were allowed a vote in 1918, chiefly because during the war they had carried out jobs previously done only by men.

They became bus drivers, van drivers, plumbers, electricians and porters. They even took up what are still regarded as men's jobs, work such as quarrying brick making, shipbuilding and foundry work.

In most jobs they founded trade unions and took another step towards equality.

Many men who fought for the country during the war didn't have a vote either as men had to own a house to be entitled to a vote.

An Act of 1918, called the Representation of the People Act, gave the vote to all men over 21 and to women over the age of 30, if they were householders, or the wives of householders, or possessed university degrees.

A later Act gave women the same rights to vote as men.

Sisters are Doin' it for Themselves

Now there was a time when they used to say,
That behind every 'Great Man',
There had to be a 'Great Woman',
But in these times of change you know
That it's no longer true.
So we're comin' out of the kitchen
'Cause there's somethin' we forgot to say to you.

Chorus
Sisters are doin' it for themselves.
Standin' on their own two feet
Ringin' on their own bells
Sisters are doin' it for themselves.

Now this is a song to celebrate
The conscious liberation of the female state!
Mothers – daughters and their daughters too.
Woman to woman
We're singin' with you
The 'Inferior Sex' has got a new exterior
We got doctors, lawyers, politicians too,
Everybody – take a look around
Can you see – Can you see – Can you see
There's a woman right next to you.

Chorus

Now we ain't making stories
And we ain't laying plans
Don't you know that a man still loves a woman
And a woman still loves a man
(Just the same though.)

Lennox and Stewart

Comments Made by Pupils in a Comprehensive School

'If all the women who worked stayed at home there would be no unemployment.'

'I think mothers should stay home and look after their children. My mum works and the house is empty when I get in, I hate it.'

'I wish my brothers had to do the washing up, or make the beds. They get away with mowing the lawn. It only needs cutting once a week in the summer. The dishes need washing every day.'

'My mother makes the whole family help with the housework. She says she works to pay for extras for us, therefore we should make an effort to help around the house. I feel a bit of a sissy washing dishes, especially if my friends come round and I'm up to my ears in "Fairy"!'

'I like doing some housework, when I leave home I don't want to live in a tip. I like being able to cook. All my mates starve when their mums go away for the day. I don't. They've started coming round here for lunch some Saturdays if their mums have gone to town. I charge them fifty pence for sausages and chips! Well, they eat a hell of a lot.'

'When I was young my father stayed home to look after us as my mum had a really good job. It was really weird when he used to come up the school to get us. I mean, there were all the mothers and my dad! I think he had a lot of guts.'

100-year-old Elizabeth Dean looks back on her life as a suffragette

In a rented room above a drapers shop in King Street, a group of women gathered. One of them, Elizabeth Dean, stands up to speak and out come the impassioned words of a woman who could never accept the injustices and the anomalies of being female in Britain during the 1900s. Today, Elizabeth Dean gazes out of the window of her pink-hued room at Oaklands Aged Persons Home on to the concrete jungle of Hulme. Last November this silver-haired, bespectacled lady celebrated her 100th birthday, making her Britain's oldest surviving suffragette. 'I used to speak a lot,' said Elizabeth Dean in a voice as loud and crystal clear as any you're likely to hear. 'I always had a ready reply to the stupid ones who used to say "Just fancy a woman doing that." I was a good speaker in those days.'

Those days were the bleak times at the turn of the century and into the bitter struggle of the war years. When women worked in ill-equipped, run-down factories earning half a crown for sewing a dozen shirts. Or in the sweat shops of the cotton industry, toiling seven days a week from 6 am until seven at night for 10 shillings a week....

Service

When she left school Elizabeth operated a drilling machine in a Manchester factory. 'I soon got out of that. I went to night school to learn pastry making and went into service as a pastry cook. I was very good at it and I liked the people.' Inevitably, Elizabeth, enraged by the refusal of the male university hierarchy to give Christabel Pankhurst her degree, joined the suffragette movement. It was 1912.

She showed her rebellious nature by refusing to marry in church. Twisting her plain gold wedding band, a ring worn thin with age, Elizabeth scoffed at the church and its ceremony. 'A load of poppycock. A load of old men spouting rubbish. Do you take this woman? To have and to hold? Pooh. I wasn't having any of that. I could see the impudence of it.'

Elizabeth was 65 when her husband died. He was 70. 'We were good companions. I was the leader of things. I've never been one of those women who took second place. So what could he do?'

But what was his reaction to his militant wife who was determined to break through the stranglehold men had on women. 'He didn't interfere. After I had joined the suffragettes my father told him he should stop me. But he didn't. He just said "She's your daughter, you try and stop her".'

Elizabeth refused to accept the notion that women were second-class citizens. Together with Manchester's other suffragettes – 'We were mainly working-class women. Not like the Pankhursts, they were middle-class,' – protest marches and meeting were held.

'People used to say that if people shouted at us we'd all run away,' said Elizabeth. 'That wasn't true at all. We did not run away. Emily Davidson, who died under the King's horse, showed courage.'

In London the radical suffragists embarked on a highly public campaign of militancy. Chaining themselves to railings, going on hunger strike, burning churches. In Manchester there were bombs, most notably in Alexandra Park. 'There was in Bolton, too,' confessed Elizabeth. 'They were planted by the suffragettes.'

Feminists

When the Great War came, Christabel and Mrs Pankhurst were traitors. They went to the House of Commons and offered their services in helping to get women doing all the jobs the men did. She shouldn't have done that. Nine years we had to wait after that before we got the vote.

Elizabeth remembers the Prime Minister Stanley Baldwin's speech at the time with horror. 'It has been decided,' Baldwin said, 'to allow women to use the vote when they reach the age of 30 years, and I hope the home and the family will not suffer.'

'Can you believe that?' added Elizabeth Dean, raising her voice. 'If I'd been there I would have smacked his face.' Resentment of the male dictum that a woman's place was in the home, continued to enrage Elizabeth Dean. 'At school I hardly learned to read and write. Girls were taught how to cook, bake, darn socks. The boys were given better educations. It was all wrong.' Elizabeth and her husband had children, two sons. 'I'm glad that I had children. But I couldn't have had a career as well.'

Although she is still a dedicated socialist, Elizabeth Dean openly expresses her admiration for Margaret Thatcher. 'Mrs Thatcher has been able to get where she is today because of the suffragettes. Don't forget that. I think she's very masterful. She's shown a lot of spirit of domination. But she's wrong. She's taken wrong decisions.'

Now being cared for by the staff at Oaklands, whom Elizabeth praises continually, this determined woman, whose mind is still as sharp as a razor, has years of memories to look back on. If she'd been a young girl of today's generation Elizabeth Dean says she wouldn't have got married, wouldn't have had children and would have had a career in politics or trade unions.

93

Source: *Manchester Evening News* 14.2.87

The population in 1984 was:
51·5% women
48·5% men

Further Education

Women comprised 41.5% of university students

There were more women on arts, education, health and welfare courses.

There were more men on science, engineering and technology courses.

Source: *University stats 83-84 Vol 1*

Employment

Few women earn as much as their male counterparts

In 1985 the average weekly wage of a woman over 18 in full time employment was £126.40. The average weekly wage of a man over 21 in full time employment was £192.40.

Source: *Employment Gazette, October 1985*

8% of top General Managers were women.

Source: *NGO Report for UN Decade 1985*

Politics

House of Commons	650 seats	28 are occupied by women
House of Lords	1174 seats	65 are occupied by women
		45 life peers, 20 hereditary peers

Awards

Few women have won a Nobel Prize.

WOMEN NOBEL PRIZEWINNERS		
1903	Pierre & Marie Curie	Physics
1911	Marie Curie	Chemistry
1935	Frederick & Irene Curie-Joliot	Chemistry
1963	Maria Goeppert-Mayer	Physics
1964	Dorothy Crowfoot Hodgkin	Chemistry

Source: *Emancipation of Women* by M.N. Duffy.

Following years of growth, the total number of university under-graduates fell by 9,000 between 1981-82 and 1983-84. Whilst the number of male students fell for the third year running, the number of female students fell for the first time. Despite this, women still increased as a proportion of the total – to 40.9%. At postgraduate level the numbers of both male and female students increased slightly, reversing the decline of the past few years. Again women increased as a proportion of the total – to 31.5%.

Boys' rights 'same as girls'

BOYS have just as much legal right to single-sex education as girls, a High court judge ruled yesterday.

Mr Justice Taylor said the proposed closure of a boys'-only comprehensive school in Bristol was in breach of the sex discrimination laws – because girls in the city would keep their single-sex schools.

'To deprive boys, but not girls, is to treat boys less favourably,' ruled the judge.

This was contrary to the 1975 Sex Discrimination Act.

The judge quashed a proposal by Avon County Council to close Merrywood Boys' County Comprehensive in South Bristol.

Jobs: Now men are complaining

WOMEN have always had a taxing time trying to made headway in 'a man's world', now it's men's turn as more of them try to get jobs in 'a woman's world'.

The Equal Opportunities Commission now find a third of their complaints about discrimination in some areas come from men – the jobs shortage has prompted them to take work in female-dominated offices, factories, social service departments, hospitals, health centres – and some have found the going tough.

Among their specific complaints are the following:

● Women in a particular warehouse are allowed to wear jeans but men are told they must wear trousers. (Could that possibly be someting to do with women's shape in the eyes of male managers, I wonder, because it does sound unfair?)

● A man was turned down for a job in an old folk's home 'because the residents feel more comfortable with women helpers,' he was told. Why?

Sexist prejudice can clearly be seen to work in two ways. But are the experiences reported to the EOC unusual, or merely the tip of the iceberg? I asked two men working in female-dominated worlds how they got on.

Both decided they could be more outspoken if their true identities were concealed. Both are in their mid-twenties.

TOM THE NURSE

'I HAVE worked for three years in various parts of the country and have seen and experienced discrimination of both a negative and positive kind.

'One incident which really annoyed me was when a ward sister described my work as "untidy and unsystematic – probably because he is a man". 'Maybe that report was fully justified, but what I resented was the assumption that my failing was "because I was a man".

'In another area where I have worked, the woman in charge used to regard the only male auxiliary nurse as incapable of doing anything wrong: she used to put all his faults down to his being "amusing" of it being a quirk of his personality ... even when he did things a girl nurse would have been severely rebuked for. He was just lazy.

'A lot of the problems in hospitals for people like me arise from women's perceptions of men still running on old traditonal lines. For instance, I don't think men are necessarily more dynamic than women, but there is an assumption male nurses will get on and be promoted and move from clinical nursing into management.

'Girls get to resent this – not surprisingly.

'From the patients' viewpoint men are often considered a good influence in a ward but I have had one woman patient refuse to let me carry out a pre-natal examination. And once I had a husband who refused to let me examine his wife.

'I think his was sheer sexual prejudice – he didn't like the thought of me seeing any of her private parts. But the point was, he would not have protested if I had been a doctor rather than a nurse.

'There is an assumption that people who nurse are automatically of a gentle, caring disposition. But that doesn't have to be so, for men or women. The idea of "We'll cope" whatever is still thought of as typifying the traditional nurse, but this is rapidly being worn away by political pressures, which are leading to us being overworked, underpaid and simply not able to reach the high standards we all aspire to. It is very frustrating. And it upsets both sexes equally.'

SEAN THE CLERK

'AFTER some months out of work (I had been a technician) I was ready to take anything offered and joined an office where I was the only man among 30 women.

'I realised I was in a sense resented and I found the gossip level amazing. There were times I felt so uncomfortable I wanted to leave. On many occasions I wanted to complain about the feminine aspect of females.

'There was a sense of envy, as if I as a man had more options facing me at work than they did. And if there was a barney between two girls, they expected me to take sides. I didn't.

'But once it was realised a member of the management (female) was giving me a lift into work, because we lived in the same village, people's tongues really wagged and I kept hearing laughter behind my back.

'Now I'm glad I stuck it out. If anything, there was discrimination against me because it was the females in this organisation who usually get promoted to a higher level. But I finally won promotion too, and I now know that when I decide to move on to something better my chances are 50 times better than they would have been.

'I have learned to work with people of both sexes and to stand up for myself in any environment.'

VALERIE GREEN

Source: *Daily Post*, Wednesday, 24th September 1985.

Girls join high-flyers

FEMALE STUDENTS at the University of Wales are being offered the chance to learn to fly with the RAF but only for fun.

The University Air Squadron is opening its cockpits to women for the first time – but if they want to join the Air Force after graduation they will have to do so at ground level.

Squadron-leader Tony Hooper said, "Most women recruits don't stay with the RAF long enough to justify the high cost of training them to fly. There are no female pilots in the RAF and previously this prevented women joining the University Air Squadron.

"This is a completely new scheme which we hope will encourage women to consider a career in the air force," he said.

Three female pilot cadets have been recruited by University Air Squadron based in St Athan, each studying for a degree at colleges of the University of Wales.

The women cadets will be fully integrated into the air squadron to learn about life in the RAF and attend certain camps throughout the year.

Squadron-leader Hooper said, "At this stage it is too early to say how the women will shape up, but we see no reason why they should not be as good as the chaps."

The cadets will learn to fly on a Scottish Aviation Bulldog T Mark 1. They will be taught up to the standard required for their private pilot's licence.

Many of the cadets apply to join the RAF on completion of their degree course.

The first three women cadets are Katherine James, aged 18 of St Athan, who is reading French and politics at Swansea; Karen Jones aged 18, from Guildford, reading oceanography and marine biology at Bangor, and Elvadia Tolputt, 19 from Pinner, Middlesex, reading physics at Cardiff.

Source: Western Mail

Assignment 1   Parents often expect children to help around the house. Write an essay of about a page in length explaining the types of things you're expected to do at home.

Assignments 2 and 3 are for class discussion.

Assignment 2   Do you think boys and girls are treated differently by adults? Give examples of ways in which this happens and why you think it happens. Would you treat your children differently?

Do boys and girls have different toys?

Have you ever heard someone say, 'Little boys/little girls don't do that'?

Are boys or girls encouraged to study certain subjects at school or to train for certain types of jobs?

Do you think boys get more freedom than girls? Why is this?

Are there some places that men may go to on their own, but not women?

Assignment 3   Would you expect to give up your job when you had children, or would you expect your wife or husband to do so? Explain why you feel this way.

Assignment 4   For many years women have complained about the lack of equal opportunities. Discuss as a group whether the situation has improved for women. Record your findings. Try to base your argument on facts rather than emotional feelings.

Assignment 5 Are women the only ones who feel as if they don't have an equal chance? List other groups that might feel they are unfairly treated. Discuss ways in which our society might try to remedy this discrimination.

What makes some people acceptable and some not?

How are handicapped people treated by society in general?

Are there adequate facilities for them?

Do shops make them feel welcome?

How are ethnic minorities treated? Consider racial discrimination.

Assignment 6 Conduct a survey of shops, banks, hospitals and factories in your area. Try to find out how many women are employed and the range of jobs they occupy. Then do the same for men.

How many men are employed as nurses in hospitals? How many women are employed?

How many women work on the check-outs in shops and how many men?

How many women bank managers are there in your area?

How many women are overall managers in big stores?

Assignment 7 *Write an essay on one of the following.*

   a) 'If all married women were expected to give up work when they had children there would be plenty of jobs for married men. Children would also be well cared for and not left to fend for themselves.'
   Write an essay of 300-400 words explaining your views on this writer's statement.

   b) 'They say that women and men are equal, don't believe it. Working women are still responsible for their families. It's no wonder that they don't get to the top of their professions, they're not given the chance.'
   Would you say this was true or false? Explain your views in 300-400 words.

   c) 'Women have never had it so good! They have the freedom to get jobs that were once just for men, the chance for equal pay and still they're treated like ladies. They're equal when it suits them but they still like men to pay when they go out – and to open doors for them.'
   Do you agree with this opinion? Explain your views in 300-400 words.

   d) 'It's about time all men joined together to ensure equal opportunities for men. It seems to be the case that it is now we men who have something to grumble about. Women seem to be doing OK.'
   Do you think this person has a valid point? Has equality for women meant inequality for men? Write giving your views.

Useful organisations to contact

Equal Opportunities Commission, 1 Bedford Street, London WC2.

Section 5 Euthanasia

Introduction

Euthanasia refers to instances where a person decides that they do not wish to go on living. It is not the same as suicide. In the case of a suicide the person takes his/her own life; with euthanasia the person wishing to die gets a willing party to help them bring about death in as gentle a way as possible.

Sometimes people who are seriously ill wish to take their own life. Often unable to carry this out, they ask loved ones to help them. This is an example of euthanasia.

Similarly, old people, who find the carrying out of routine tasks very difficult, or who can't get about due to illness, may feel that their useful life is at an end. They may wish to die and may ask someone to help them.

READ *One Reply to Euthanasia*

Poor dears, they'd be much better dead,
Chained fast by chains
invisible yet real,
By useless nerves robbed of
their erstwhile skill,
By muscles now so feeble,
once so strong....
It's better life is ended, 'ere
too long....

Well meaning souls, no
doubt, but we have still
The break of each new day,
sunrise, sunset;
Dawn chorus of the birds; the
grace of trees;

The smell of new mown
grass, the scent of flowers;
Music sweet solace for the
lonely hours...;
We have the joy of laughter,
blessed relief of tears,

The noise of children at play,
the bliss of silence,
For me the love of relatives
most dear,
Of friends, more precious
with each passing year.

All these great gifts and
many, many more
Come open-handed, an unending store....
And I would choose to live
my life's full span,
Perform the tasks set in the
Master's plan,
And when at last the
appointed day shall come
To hear, perhaps, my Lord's
Much prized, 'Well done'.

Doris E. Manning

98

Daily Mail MONEY MAIL TODAY

Son begged them to end his misery

PARENTS WHO KILLED OUT OF PITY SET FREE

NUM crisis over axed leader

Dr Barnard:'Headlines failed to stir any professional discussion'

SHAME ON OUR DOCTORS

Dr Christiaan Barnard on a crisis of conscience

TEN DAYS ago a British judge declared that Norman and Janet Houghton, accused of murdering their severely paralysed son, should walk free.

The crowded courtroom was told they required no further punishment. Their suffering would stay with them for ever.

It was a story that touched me deeply. I felt saddened that we live in a society where loving parents can find themselves forced to take the life of their own child. And I had an important message for Mr and Mrs Houghton.

While I was in Britain last week I spoke to them. It was the first time they have talked since the trial and, perhaps because I am a doctor, they opened up to me. Mr and Mrs Houghton, who have endured everything from the death of their son, police questioning and detention, a public courtcase and public suspicion and at times hatred, trusted me. But I felt only ashamed.

What I had to tell them was how sorry I am. I apologised, as a doctor, for the lack of compassion shown by the medical profession towards terminally ill people.

Shock

I point the finger of blame at my colleagues — their young son's doctors — who shelved their responsibility. Five years ago, after a terrible road accident, they should have allowed Robert to die.

I know that what I write may shock people. Where there is life there is hope, as they say. But I know this is not true.

When my mother suffered what can only be called a terminal stroke at the age of 80, it was not a difficult decision for me to allow her treatment to stop. I did not kill her. I gave her dignity in death. And I have done that for my patients in the past.

The goal is not to prolong life, but to improve the quality of it. At times a doctor may have to decide, however reluctantly, that death is the best option.

But doctors do not like 'letting people die'. The temptation, especially in the last decade since the invention of hundreds of life-supporting drugs and devices, has been to fight off death at all costs. There is an unspoken law to maintain life.

Against this tide, it has taken me my entire career to face up to writing a book in open support of euthanasia. Most of my colleagues prefer not even thinking about it.

But I was still surprised to find that the newspaper headlines about Robert's five-year ordeal failed to stir any professional discussion.

The silence was indicative of an attitude I discovered a long time ago: far safer to keep heads buried in the sand like ostriches, waiting for some great miracle cure.

'There have been stories of incredible spontaneous recoveries,' a distinguished colleague told me.

If there have, I do not know of them.

If you live in a house that no longer pleases you, you have the right to leave it. But if that house is your own body, the individual is by today's medical standards condemned to it almost interminably.

Dying is the only way to leave — and many doctors believe that their job is preventing death at all costs.

To me this attitude is a great shortcoming in our view of human life. And never has it been so clearly branded in my mind as when I talked to Janet Houghton.

Suffer

'Robert was a very proud person,' she told me. 'After the accident we tried to act as though things were normal and we'd take him out — to his favourite restaurant, for example. But he hated it.

'All those kind well-meant comments from friends and sympathisers. You could see him suffer as they congratulated him on how he was coping. He didn't want to live in their world any more.

'Of course I hated giving him those pills. But who else would have done it?'

Who else indeed? Especially facing conviction for murder.

I believe it is high time the medical profession demanded their right to help and insist that law makers act.

Is it such an awful thing to ask a person admitted to hospital to sign a form — like the consent to post mortem he already signs — saying he would like doctors to end his life if he became terminally ill?

This is not encouraging doctors to act as God. They are guilty of that in imposing a life sentence. What I am calling for is compassion, for doctors to act out of sound clinical judgment and take away from relatives the prospect of even contemplating the horror of Mr and Mrs Houghton.

I fail to see why my profession is not already living up to its responsibilities. Are we afraid we will be labelled as doctors who kill off our patients? Or is the reluctance a fear of administering the fatal injection?

I am not for one second encouraging a blasé attitude of life and death. I would never say to a patient: 'Right, tomorrow at midday we'll do the injection.' I believe the decision can be arrived at together.

Courage

I expect by speaking out I open myself to controversy and criticism again — not least from my colleagues. But I know from my mother, my patients and from Janet Houghton that I am right.

It is up to doctors to search their consciences about Robert Houghton.

We should not be impotent technicians in an ever more technological world of medicine. There were no medical miracles that could have saved Robert. It takes courage to admit it.

The miracle in his case was that he had parents who loved him enough to respect his wishes.

As a parent myself I cannot conceive of a worse decision. As a doctor I am ashamed they had to take it.

Reproduced by permission, from *The Mail on Sunday*, 26 May 1985.

'I was right to save mongol baby'

SOCIAL SERVICES boss Mr David Plank yesterday defended his decision to go to court to save the life of a mongol baby girl.

Doctors and parents were not always the best people to judge, said Mr Plank.

Mongol babies were often very affectionate and loving, he pointed out. 'I would adopt this one myself if I was able to.'

Mr Plank, 36, director of social services for Hammersmith and Fulham, West London, intervened last week after the baby's parents refused to give permission for life-saving bowel surgery. The Appeal Court allowed the operation to go ahead.

Yesterday it was revealed that the baby, 13 days old, will go to foster parents when she leaves Hammersmith Hospital. She was "progressing satisfactorily".

The parents had wanted nature to take its course, which probably would have meant death within days. Now the girl has a life expectancy of about 30 years.

Mr Plank had "no regrets". He said, 'Doctors aren't necessarily the best people to decide whether the child could grow up to have a good life or not. They might not have the specialised knowledge of the prospects and opportunities the child may have.'

He is married to a part-time research assistant with the Campaign for the Mentally Handicapped. He and his wife, Morag, have two children, a boy of 11 and a girl of eight who are not handicapped. Mr Plank is a member of the Independent Development Council for Mentally Handicapped People.

Last night, Mrs Plank said: 'Of course I support my husband in his action. We did not have any discussion about the case at all. I did not know about it till afterwards.'

Mr Plank explained: 'My wife had nothing to do with my decision. I never discuss professional matters with my wife.

'The only people I did discuss this with are the social workers on the spot and my immediate management colleagues.'

Last night the baby's parents were agonising over a decision whether to bring up the child or to allow her to be adopted.

In a statement through their solicitors, the couple, who live in Chester, said they still felt strongly that their daughter should have been allowed to die. Later they would seek a suitable opportunity to publicly explain their views.

The parents, a 49-year-old engineer and a dentist in her late thirties, already have a young child who is normal.

Mr Plank said a meeting was being arranged with them to discuss the mongol baby's future. He was waiting for the 'dust to settle' before contacting them.

by CLARE DOVER

Source: *Daily Express,*
Tuesday 11th August 1981.

Hospices

Many people who are against euthanasia state that people who are chronically sick and have no hope of recovery would not resort to such drastic action as euthanasia if there were more hospices. A hospice aims to alleviate pain and give a person dignity in death. People who opt for euthanasia are often frightened by the prospect of a painful death where all dignity is lost due to the suffering they have to endure.

Hospices are places where the terminally ill are cared for. (A terminal illness is one for which there is no cure.) Hospices try to provide a happy and relaxed atmosphere for the patient, as well as for the family. The aim being to help all concerned to come to terms with the death of a loved one. If required, they will provide spiritual help for the family, as well as legal advice, so that a person may put their affairs in order before they die.

Some hospices treat all their patients within the hospice itself, others, like St Joseph's, also run a Home Care Service which provides expertise and facilities so that a person may die in the comfort of their own home.

St Joseph's argues against the introduction of legalised euthanasia. It gives as one of its reasons the fact that fourteen people were admitted to the Hospice last year, supposedly with terminal cancer. Some were found to have no cancer at all or cancers that were still in the early stages and therefore treatable. What if euthanasia had been legal?

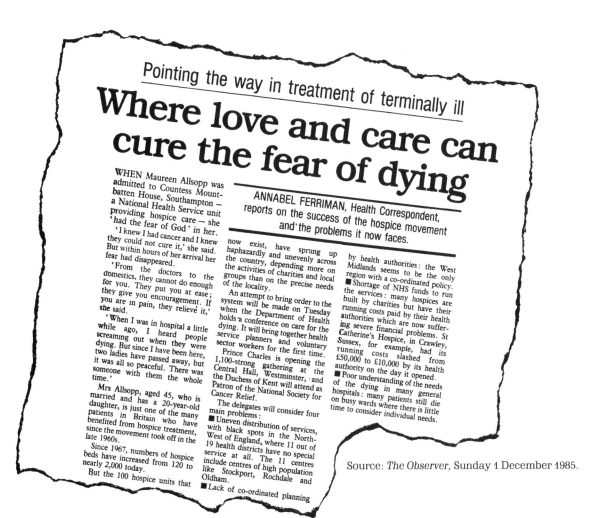

Pointing the way in treatment of terminally ill

Where love and care can cure the fear of dying

ANNABEL FERRIMAN, Health Correspondent, reports on the success of the hospice movement and the problems it now faces.

WHEN Maureen Allsopp was admitted to Countess Mountbatten House, Southampton — a National Health Service unit providing hospice care — she 'had the fear of God' in her.

'I knew I had cancer and I knew they could not cure it,' she said. But within hours of her arrival her fear had disappeared.

'From the doctors to the domestics, they cannot do enough for you. They put you at ease; they give you encouragement. If you are in pain, they relieve it,' she said.

'When I was in hospital a little while ago, I heard people screaming out when they were dying. But since I have been here, two ladies have passed away, but it was all so peaceful. There was someone with them the whole time.'

Mrs Allsopp, aged 45, who is married and has a 20-year-old daughter, is just one of the many patients in Britain who have benefited from hospice treatment, since the movement took off in the late 1960s.

Since 1967, numbers of hospice beds have increased from 120 to nearly 2,000 today.

But the 100 hospice units that now exist, have sprung up haphazardly and unevenly across the country, depending more on the activities of charities and local groups than on the precise needs of the locality.

An attempt to bring order to the system will be made on Tuesday when the Department of Health holds a conference on care for the dying. It will bring together health service planners and voluntary sector workers for the first time.

Prince Charles is opening the 1,100-strong gathering at the Central Hall, Westminster, and the Duchess of Kent will attend as Patron of the National Society for Cancer Relief.

The delegates will consider four main problems:

■ Uneven distribution of services, with black spots in the North-West of England, where 11 out of 19 health districts have no special service at all. The 11 centres include centres of high population like Stockport, Rochdale and Oldham.

■ Lack of co-ordinated planning by health authorities: the West Midlands seems to be the only region with a co-ordinated policy.

■ Shortage of NHS funds to run the services: many hospices are built by charities but have their running costs paid by their health authorities which are now suffering severe financial problems. St Catherine's Hospice, in Crawley, Sussex, for example, had its running costs slashed from £50,000 to £10,000 by its health authority on the day it opened.

■ Poor understanding of the needs of the dying in many general hospitals: many patients still die on busy wards where there is little time to consider individual needs.

Source: *The Observer*, Sunday 1 December 1985.

Group work Your teacher may want you to work in groups for these assignments. Groups of six would be best. When taking part in group work, always elect a group leader who will speak on your behalf, as well as a secretary who will make notes.

Assignment 1 Make a note of all the good things in life that the poet refers to in her poem. Then make a list of the things in life that you enjoy and derive pleasure from.

Assignment 2 Read through the information again. Write down whether the writers are in favour of euthanasia or not, as well as the reasons they give for holding such a view.

Assignment 3 Discuss and make notes of some of the occasions where euthanasia has been used. You do not need to confine your ideas to the information here. You may be able to think of other cases mentioned in the press.

Assignment 4 Make a list of the reasons why groups like LIFE may be opposed to euthanasia. (You can contact them to find out details of their views, see p.102 for their address.) What problems could there be if euthanasia became legal?

Assignment 5   Read the material about the Houghton family. Discuss the reasons the family give for supporting the use of euthanasia. At the end of the discussion take a vote to see how many are in favour of the decision taken by the Houghton family and how many are against.

Now as a group take a vote to see how many are in favour of euthanasia and how many are against.

Is there anybody who is in favour in certain cases but not in others? Why is this? Remember, it is sometimes difficult to come down wholly on one side or the other.

Now listen to the decisions other groups have arrived at and why they did so. This will give the leader of your group the chance to make your ideas known to the class as a whole.

Assignment 6   *Write an essay on the following.*

'If a man comes up to you in the street and shoots you he is guilty of murder. If a doctor decides a patient is not worth saving it is euthanasia.'
Are there differences between these cases? Should anyone have the power of life or death over another human being? Very carefully, examine the above example and its implications as far as the legalising of euthanasia is concerned.

Plan your essay carefully. Make a list of points that you wish to mention and make sure that you give reasons for holding such an opinion.

Your essay will need a good first sentence and a convincing conclusion.

Useful organisations to contact
Organisations opposed to euthanasia
Note: All the following will provide information on the subject for students.

The Medical Director, St Joseph's Hospice, Mare Street, Hackney, London E8.

The Catholic Truth Society, P.O. Box 422, 38-40 Eccleston Square, London SW1V 1PD.

LIFE, National Headquarters, 118-120 Warwick Street, Leamington Spa, Warwickshire CV32 4QY.

Society for the Protection of the Unborn Child, 7 Tufton Street, Westminster, London SW1P 3QN.
(This is an anti-abortion society but it also feels strongly about the way handicapped children, once born, can be allowed to die in certain cases.)

Organisation in favour of legalising euthanasia

The Voluntary Euthanasia Society, 13 Prince of Wales Terrace, London W8 5PG.

Section 6 Animal Experiments

Introduction

Animals are used in large numbers to further the cause of science. Research on animals is often the first step towards a cure for humans. All kidney transplants, heart transplants, and many other types of operation were all performed and perfected on animals before they were tried on humans. Similarly, all the drugs and medicines with which you are familiar – aspirins as well as antibiotics like penicillin – have been tested on animals.

Animal experiments are allowed under an Act of Parliament dated 1876 – over one hundred years ago. Since then the world has changed beyond recognition. When this Act became law there were about 300 animal experiments a year; now there are over 4 million, mostly on products that had not been thought of in 1876.

Many people now question whether it is right to use animals for experiments and if some kinds of research are more justified than others.

Graduation Day

Small, chattering, fearful things;
Each to the other clings,
Pain-dreading, haunted eyes
Watch the Instructor rise,
His hand upon the lever:
'Now observe
How the discharge will jar through every nerve,
Making adrenalin rise -'
(From throbbing throats, wrenching those knife-sharp cries)
'Note how they vocalise!'

Calm now, don't fear,
The larger seems to say
To the small mass of palpitating fur
Burrowing close to her -
But it will come again,
That searing, scorching pain,
And she must hold him tight,
Her strength to calm his fright -

'Now students, we can start
Another observation – tear apart
That closely clinging pair,
And in your notebooks lucidly explain
Their marked response to *solitary* pain.

Later, we'll note reaction when they're blind;
Then, lessons learnt – YOU'RE FIT TO SERVE MANKIND.'

Heather Vineham

EVERY 6 SECONDS AN ANIMAL DIES IN A BRITISH LABORATORY

BUAV AGAINST ALL ANIMAL EXPERIMENTS

BUAV, 143 Charing Cross Road, London WC2H 0EE Telephone: 01-734 2691

By the time you have read this leaflet another 20 animals will have died in British Laboratories.

All over the world millions of sensitive, innocent animals are locked away in cages behind closed laboratory doors and tortured for the supposed benefit of human beings.

How much longer are we going to allow animals to be used as 'scape goats' for our vices and faults?

In this country alone, every year, millions of animals are used in experiments. They are force fed with such noxious substances as weed killers, lipsticks, insecticides, dyes, drugs; they are forced to inhale the noxious fumes of tobaccos and burning plastics; they are used in chemical and germ warfare experiments; they are starved, electrocuted, psychologically disturbed; they are given lung transplants, heart transplants, liver transplants; they undergo specific pain experiments – the list is endless.

The results of these experiments rarely tell us anything which will actually be beneficial to human beings. Animals react differently to us and we often react differently from each other. What is lethal to a mouse may have no effect on a cat but may cause side effects in humans.

Drug companies make a fortune out of the thousands of drugs flooding the market place – many of which are duplications. While drugs are constantly being withdrawn because of their side effects, new 'wonder drugs' replace them. It is a vicious circle and innocent animals are poisoned to death, caught up in the middle of this frantic race for profit and power.

We do not need all the new products which flood the market place nor do we need all the new drugs. The World Health Organisation itself states that out of the 30-40,000 drugs on the market, only 220 are of any real benefit*.

While people receive expensive heart transplants, others die because they are denied basic health treatment. Improved sanitation and housing have played a greater part in the improvement of human health and the fight against disease than all the 'wonder drugs' put together.

We have been brought up to believe that without animal experiments we would die, as medicine would still be in the 'dark ages'. We have minds and consciences of our own – how much longer will your conscience allow you to keep silent about the suffering and misery of millions of defenceless animals that have no voice with which to speak and plead for themselves?

* Ref New Scientist 18th May 1987

Source: BUAV.

Change in law to forbid live animal experiments

by Susannah Kirkman

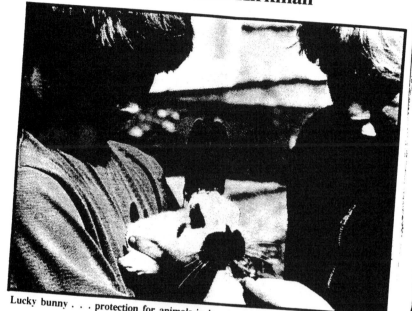

Lucky bunny . . . protection for animals in less tender hands is being stepped up.

Schools throughout the country are having to reconsider the way they teach biology in the wake of new legislation coming into force later this year, banning experiments on live animals.

The legislation, which replaces the Cruelty to Animals Act, has prompted the RSPCA to issue new guidelines to schools, warning them that the use of live animals or insects for experiments will be forbidden and to take greater care of animals kept in schools.

In one common A level experiment, the pithing of frogs, a frog's brain is destroyed while it is still alive to test reflex actions. Another popular experiment was recently demonstrated on a Granada schools' programme, and studies the reactions of a live locust whose legs have been cut off and electrode planted in its thorax.

Source: *Times Educational Supplement,* 18th January 1985.

Source: BUAV.

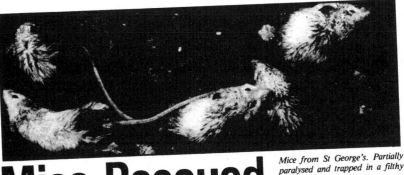

Mice from St George's. Partially paralysed and trapped in a filthy prison.

Mice Rescued from 'Horrific Conditions'

Members of the ALF raided a public health laboratory at St Georges Hospital, South London on 23rd April, St Georges Day. The lab was cleared of its entire stock of 190 mice which were the subject of brain damage, toxicity experiments; some were infected with "toxoplasmosis" which is a type of glandular fever.

The ALF gave an exclusive statement and photographs of the mice to the *Wandsworth and Putney Guardian* which is delivered free to all homes in the area, including that of David Mellor MP. The story took the whole front page. The ALF said: "The mice were in the most appalling conditions, some were blind, others had weeping sores and several appear to have epileptic type fits after being used for brain damage. Some were lying in a quarter of an inch of their own excrement. They are being treated by a vet, a lot will have to be put down. I have taken part in such raids before but I have never seen animals in such atrocious conditions. This the start of a major campaign against St Georges to highlight conditions under which dogs, cats, monkeys, rabbits and mice are kept at the hospital".

The raid was also the subject of the paper's editorial entitled "on the horns of a dilemma" — "On our front page we show the unacceptable face of animal experimentation. No matter how strong your views — or even if you have none — this picture must surely shock. The animals our photographer saw clearly suffered, and suffered badly over a period of time". It went on to say that if it had been dogs, cats or monkeys that had been subjected to these horrific conditions there would have been mass protest, and that the experiments were being carried out at an influential teaching hospital that is supposed to be dedicated to saving lives. The article concluded saying that St Georges must open its laboratory doors to independent witnesses who can confirm it has no other animals in such a pitiful and shameful condition.

The South London Animal Movement is starting its own campaign against St Georges, by producing a leaflet showing photographs of the rescued mice.
WARNING — many animals in laboratories, particularly Public Health labs, are infected with dangerous diseases. Everyone in the animal rights movement should show great responsibility and common sense in this matter.

Source: BUAV.

Warfare Tests Up 13%

A government minister has confirmed the links that exist between animal exploitation and warmongering.

Speaking in the House of Commons, junior defence minister Mr John Lee admitted that last year, for the first time in at least five years, the number of experiments carried out at the Ministry of Defence's research establishment, Porton Down, had increased.

The number of experiments subject to the 1876 Cruelty to Animals Act had risen to 10,900 from 9,500 the year before — an increase of more than 13 per cent.

Mr Lee told MPs the increases of tests on animals "reflects the need to ensure that effective protection and treatment remains available to our forces to meet continuing developments in the threat posed by the Soviet Union's chemical warfare capability."

Source: BUAV.

What are the alternative methods?

'Alternatives' are methods which provide essential information without depending on the use of living animals. Alternatives being developed include:

1. Cell, Tissue & Organ Culture – human and animal cells maintained outside the body can provide information on the effects of chemicals on body tissues.

2. Micro-organisms – tests based on bacteria and yeasts can be simple, rapid and inexpensive.

3. Mathematical Modelling – the effects of chemicals and the body's responses to them can often be predicted.

4. Computerised Data Storage – a great deal of information is already available; computers help scientists gain easy access to it.

5. Audio-visual Aids – a single animal experiment can be recorded on film or tape for repeated use in teaching.

6. Human Studies – more use could be made of human volunteers in drug development, and studies on human populations can provide useful information about disease patterns and environmental hazards.

Source: BUAV.

Note: This information is quite difficult to understand. Ask your science teacher to explain the meaning of some of this data.

Experiments on Animals are Indispensable

For all our sakes –

science still needs animals

- Faced with a severe illness or a critically ill relative, most people do not hesitate to have their doctor prescribe an effective medicine which will have been thoroughly tested, using animals.

- Even ardent anti-vivisectionists do not want to see their pets die if an animal-tested medicine can save their lives, or a vaccine prevent infection.

- Few would refrain from suing a manufacturer whose product disfigured or damaged them.

- At work, trade unionists and safety representatives demand safety data, based on animal studies, on substances they handle.

These are a few examples of the double standards we all apply but prefer to overlook.

However, we must ensure that those animals that *have* to be used are properly safeguarded.

Source: Research Defence Society

How the health service benefits from animal-derived and animal-tested medicines

It can cost over £40 a day to keep a single patient in a NHS hospital. Modern medicines which reduce the length of stay, or permit treatment of the patient at home, are saving the NHS vast sums of money.

Over the past 15 years the number of beds in non-psychiatric hospitals fell by 15% and the average duration of stay fell by nearly one-third, to less than two weeks.

All this is besides the relief of suffering that animal-tested medicines provide.

Children have benefited most. There has been a 90% reduction in the death rate in the one to fourteen age group in the last 40 years. More than half of this was achieved by conquering the killer diseases like pneumonia, tuberculosis, diphtheria, measles and whooping cough. Animal experiment played a vital part in developing the necessary treatments.

Polio vaccines, developed by animal experiment, reduced the number of cases in 1958 from 2,495 (with 150 deaths) to 4 in 1975, with no deaths. (If the anti-vivisectionists had succeeded in halting animal experiments in 1950, for example, hundreds of thousands of people around the world would have died from polio since then, and many more would have been disabled.)

Please remember, animals themselves, at home or on the farm, enjoy better health and an improved survival rate due to animal-tested veterinary medicines, anaesthetics and foods.

We must recognise that scientists are also animal lovers. Wherever possible they avoid using animals where valid non-animal alternatives are feasible and acceptable. *Scientists need your support* if they are to achieve the results society demands for its welfare and that of its animals.

The Facts

80 per cent of all animal experiments in Britain are for medical, dental or veterinary advancement. The remainder are for the protection of consumers or *workers in industry*.

In the past 50 years medical research expenditure has increased, in real terms, 40-fold. In the same period the number of animal experiments had increased only 25-fold.

There has been a *steady decrease in animal experiments* in the last ten years.

We eat more than 400 million animals (cattle, pigs and poultry) each year in Britain – about 7 each.

Over 80% of all experiments involve rats or mice. Dogs account for only 0.25% and cats 0.14% of the total. The RSPCA kills very large numbers of unwanted cats and dogs every year – many times the number used in all UK laboratories.

Source: Research Defence Society.

Examples of diseases greatly reduced, virtually eliminated or the symptoms well controlled in humans:

Acute leukaemia
Acute poliomyelitis
Anti-inflammatory and anti-ulcer treatment
Asthma treatment – *control*
Diabetes – *control*
Diphtheria
Epilepsy – *control*
Heart disease
Herpes infections
Infection following burns – *pseudomonas (by vaccine)*
Leukaemia
Measles
Mental Illness – treatment of neuroses & psychoses – *control*
Parkinsons disease – *control*
Pneumonia
Puerperal fever – *antibiotics*
Smallpox
Treatment for endocrine disorders (Addison's disease in fertility)
Treatment of high blood pressure
Tuberculosis – *TB meningitis*
Whooping cough

Are animal experiments necessary for cosmetic products?

- It is very easy to apply double standards and the issue of animal experiments required by the cosmetics industry is a good example.

- Few people are prepared to suffer damage to their skin, hair, eyes or mouth because soap, shampoo or toothpaste has not been properly tested before being offered for sale.

- Few mothers are prepared to place their children at an unknown risk as a result of swallowing skin preparations.

- Few people would refrain from suing a manufacturer whose products disfigured or seriously damaged them in normal use.

- To ensure safety in use, animal testing is unavoidable for the cosmetics industry at the present time.

However, we must ensure that those animals that do HAVE to be used are properly safeguarded.

A very high proportion of the population owes its health and improved quality of life to pharmaceutical research. Anyone who has undergone surgery or who has been vaccinated or who takes a medicine to combat illness has benefited from such research. Anyone who has administered a veterinary product to farm or pet animals has also benefited from research in animals. Much remains to be done – there are still many challenges for the future in the prevention and cure of disease.

Animals are necessary for the progress that has taken place and in order to enable this research to continue. Nevertheless, the research scientist and animal technicians are fully aware of their obligation to ensure that any animal in their laboratory is properly cared for and protected. This includes the use of alternatives wherever possible and specially bred animals, minimising pain and providing good care of animals before and throughout experiments. The contribution of experimental research in animals to the future health of man and animals is of the utmost importance to us all.

Benefits to animals

Pharmaceutical research has improved the health and well being of animals. A wide range of anti-parasitic and anti-bacterial drugs has greatly reduced the incidence of infective diseases amongst animals and research into other diseases continues. Effective sedatives and anaesthetics are available to relieve pain and fear in animals, to carry out surgical procedures and to facilitate the examination of fractious or exotic animals.

Source: Research Defence Society.

How are they safeguarded?

Animals use for experimental work are safeguarded by the Cruelty to Animals Act 1876. This states that anyone wishing to perform painful experiment on animals has to be licensed by the Home Office. Licences are issued only when the Home Office is satisfied that the person applying has the correct qualifications to carry out such experiments and is correctly supervised. All experiments have to be proven to be necessary and should provide information not available before. Places where experiments are conducted must be registered for such work and Home Office Inspectors can visit such places at any time without notice. If these officers are not happy then the establishment can be closed down immediately.

Assignment 1 Make a list of all the vaccinations you had as a child or could have now as a teenager.
Make a list of all the operations that you can think of that could be performed on a person during his/her life.
Compare notes with a friend.

Assignment 2 Animals are used in laboratories to test a lot of different drugs, cosmetics and household products. Is there a difference between testing drugs and testing cosmetics?
Explain your views on this and say why you feel the way you do.

Assignment 3 Look up the word 'moral' in a dictionary. Many people say we have no moral right to use animals in laboratories – to play at being 'God' as if we have the power of life and death over something.
Do you think we have such a right? Explain your reasons fully?

Assignment 4 Sometimes more embryos than are needed are produced when doctors are involved in the production of a test-tube baby and the government has been discussing the use of human foetuses in experiments.
Is this a step in the wrong direction? Will the benefits to mankind outweigh the drawbacks?
Write your views on this subject.

Discuss this as a class before you begin to develop your own ideas.

Your science or biology department may be able to give you some information on the research issues involved.

How do the class feel about it? Why?

Assignment 5 Are there alternatives to the use of live animals in experiments? Find out as much as you can about any alternatives. Use the science department in your school to help you. What are their views on the use of animals in experiments? Why do they hold such views?
Make notes and then write out your findings giving your own views on the subject.

Assignment 6   *Write an essay on one of the following.*

a) Look around your house at the bottles of disinfectant, deodorants and shampoos, at the bars of soaps, the make-up, the medicines, the pesticides in the garden shed, etc. For each of these items many animals died. Can we really justify such slaughter? Do we need another brand of soap or bottle of perfume that badly?
Explain fully your views on vivisection.

b) 'If it were a choice between my child and my dog I would sacrifice my dog first, wouldn't you? Modern day medicine is here because we experimented on animals in order to save humans. Being an anti-vivisectionist is a luxury we would all like to be able to afford but that no one wants to pay the price for. Human life is just too valuable.'
How do you feel about this writer's point of view? Give your reasons fully.

c) What gives us the right to murder, in the name of science, millions of animals every year? We have no moral right to use animals in this way. How would we feel if the Martians landed tomorrow and decided that *we*, as lesser beings, were to be the laboratory animals?
Explain your views on this subject giving your reasons fully.

Useful organisations to contact
Organisations against animal experimentation

BUAV (British Union for the Abolition of Vivisection), 16a Crane Grove, Islington, London N7 8LB.

FRAME (Fund for the Replacement of Animals in Animal Experimentation), Eastgate House, 34 Stoney Street, Nottingham NG1 1NB.
(FRAME produce a newsletter *Frame News*. They hope to produce a special free newsletter for schools. They will also provide a speaker free of charge who will talk to a class or group about the work of the organisation and the moral and ethical implications of animal experimentation.)

Mobilisation for Laboratory Animals, 51 Harley Street, London W1N 1DD.

TFAR (Teachers for Animal Rights), 29 Lynwood Road, London SW17 8SB.

Animal Aid, 7 Castle Street, Tonbridge, Kent TN9 1BH.

All the above provide a wealth of information about the use made of animals in laboratories and why they are opposed to such experiments.

Organisation which supports animal experimentation
The Research Defence Society, Grosvenor Gardens House, Grosvenor Gardens, London SW1W 0BS.

Part Two

Reading and Responding

General Introduction

Part Two of this book aims to test how well you have understood the content of the written material supplied. It is taken from novels, poems, plays, magazines and newspapers.

After each passage there is some work with questions on what you have read. The number of marks awarded for each answer is given in brackets after the question. The marks are a guide only. If a lot of marks are awarded you should assume that your response needs to be detailed.

At the end of most of the passages you will find longer writing assignments called 'Now let's write'. These aim to extend the ideas expressed in the passages and to help you explore the subject in greater depth. These carry more marks, a maximum of twenty, and you will need to write between 300 and 600 words.

Many of these written assignments could be included in your coursework and therefore they need to be well planned and well presented. Your teacher might ask you to use the topic in a variety of ways – an extended individual piece of work, a group assignment or work towards your oral assessment.

Golden Rules

1 Read the passage carefully before looking at the questions. *Never* look at the questions first.

2 Read the question carefully before you begin to look for information to answer it.

3 Make sure you have answered all parts of each question before moving on.

4 Answer fully; if a question is worth six or more marks it is reasonable to assume that an answer is required containing five or six points.

5 Never begin an answer with the word 'because.'

6 Answer in sentences. It is, after all, an English examination. You are being tested on your ability to write logically and eloquently.

7 Never be tempted to search for the information to answer two questions at once. It is easy to get confused and to answer neither well.

8 Answer in your own words; do not copy out extensive parts of the passage. It is *your* command of English being tested, not the writer's.

9 Attempt all the questions. If you miss out a question you get no marks; if you have a go you may get one or two. In an assessment this could be the difference between one grade and another.

10 Check your work thoroughly before you submit it for marking.

11 Look critically at the tasks set as written assignments. Think carefully about what you are going to write before you choose a topic. Plan your work well so that you keep to the subject given.

Fiction and Autobiography

Section 1 Parents' Day

Simon is a pupil at a boarding school – it is the School Open Day. Bowdon is the school bully and makes a point of watching the behaviour of all the parents, the clothes they wear, the cars they drive and their companions. All this information he will use to tease the other boys later.

Read the passage. Then answer the questions.

Summer Parents' Day. Started all right. Mum had done nothing to shame him. Red hair short and clean, her make-up slight, her skirt a decent length. Her Morris Minor Traveller was nearly ten years old, but clean and shining. She hadn't tried to kiss him, just smiled and said hallo. Not even asked him
5 if he was O.K. Nothing for Bowdon to overhear. Nothing for Bowdon to get his rotten little teeth into.

It was Montgomery's father who spoiled it. Montgomery's father, who used to play tennis for Gloucestershire. Montgomery's father with his lanky legs and bounding stride and crinkly black hair. Montgomery's father had
10 buttonholed Mum. Somebody had cried-off the parents' team who were playing tennis against the staff; would Mum step into the breach? Mum had fallen for it, like a sucker. Even though Simon begged her not to; with his eyes. Begged and *begged*. But Mum was always the willing sucker....

Mum coming onto court, beside Mr Montgomery. In borrowed shorts.
15 Showing her legs. Not that Mum's legs weren't all right. Not fat, with dimpled thighs and varicose veins like some mothers' legs. But when she bent over to pick up a ball, you could see her bottom.

Bowdon, and Bowdon's friend of the moment, and young Montgomery (who smashed anybody Bowdon wanted smashed), sitting on the grass by the
20 umpire's chair. Looking at Mum's bottom as she picked up the balls. Muttering and laughing like they would make themselves sick, so that the Head, who was umpiring and doing his Wimbledon impersonation, turned round and glared at them three times. But they went on muttering and laughing.
25 Simon set his face like a rock – they were watching him too – and turned his mind off. There was a huge privet hedge round the court, because the school couldn't afford proper netting; it was full of the remains of crime. If you had something you wanted to hide, you held it inside your fist, plunged your fist into the hedge, and let go. The hedge was full of the sodden rags of
30 ancient stolen caps, bleached exercise books from the sixties and torn

nuddy-mags. Among which spiders spun and birds built their nests. It was a good place to hide your mind while you kept your face still as a rock, and the Head droned on about forty-love.

But he could still tell from the Head's voice that someone was losing pretty badly. It had to be Mum, because the staff pair were Slogger Newall and the games-master, an Oxford blue. He raised his eyes in desperation above the hedge, to the tall willow trees. There was a hot gusty wind blowing up there, above the airless calm of the court. The trees leaned over, like people at a street accident. They looked as if they were going to fall, fall, as the savage gusts lifted their leaves, showing the pale undersides in waves, like skirts.

'Advantage, Mrs Wood,' announced the Head. In spite of himself, Simon looked.

And there was Mum, up on her toes, spinning a crafty serve that sliced into the very corner. Slogger hit it thunderously into the net.

"Game to Mrs Wood."

People clapping, even the school, as if they really meant it. And Mum standing there, cheeks pink and eyes shining, hair pulled back with an elastic band, looking no older than the sixth-form girls from down the road.

Simon had to watch after that, heart in his mouth with every stroke. Slogger and the games-master and Mr Montgomery all hit the ball hard. But Mum kept sticking her racket out at cunning angles, and the ball would vanish in a puff of chalk. And the school was all on Mum's side, because the games-master was a cocky sod, and even Slogger was still a *teacher*. The waves of applause got bigger and bigger....

"Game, set and match to Mrs Wood and Mr Montgomery!"

Mum was presented with a nickel-plated egg-cup thing. As she took it from the Head she bent one knee and bobbed her head, and just for a moment Simon remembered being very small and watching Mum win at somewhere called Queen's Club, and Dad arriving from the War House, for some reason dressed in khaki and shining leather and moaning he was too late to see Mum win. Then the memory was gone, and Mum passed the egg-cup back to the Head, so it could live in the dusty showcase for another year. Then they all had tea, and then –

Lights out. Whispering.

"I think your mother took *service* rather well," said Bowdon, greasy as a year-old *Playboy*.

For once, nobody sniggered. They were remembering how well Mum had played; they *liked* her. Somebody even said, "Knock it off, Bowdon," in muttered embarrassment.

But Bowdon went on. "She certainly knows how to handle a pair of balls."

The silence was absolute.

"And it was interesting, the way she bent down...."

That was when the devils came.

Simon got out of bed without willing it. Felt the floor cold under his feet, like in a dream. Walked steadily across to Bowdon's bed. He knew he was being insane. Bowdon was twice his size; Bowdon would kill him.

Calmly, he reached for Bowdon in the dark, got hold of his pyjama-coat.

"Hey, what's up wi' you?" said Bowdon querulously.

Simon hit with all his strength.

From *The Scarecrows* by Robert Westall.

1 Look at lines 2-3. In what ways was Simon's mother careful about her appearance? (3)

2 Why do you think his mother didn't kiss him when she arrived? (3)

3 What things suggest that Simon's mother had made a special effort? Do you think it is important for parents to dress and behave carefully for events such as this? (4)

4 Why was Simon's mother asked to play tennis? (2)

5 Explain fully how you think Simon felt about this? (3)

6 Look at paragraph 4. Would you say that Bowdon was afraid of the headmaster? (2)

7 Look at paragraph 5. What could you find in the privet hedge? Why was it a good hiding place? (4)

8 What do you think, 'It was a good place to hide your mind while you kept your face still as a rock' (lines 31-2) means? (3)

9 Why did Simon think it was his mother and Mr Montgomery who would be losing? Explain fully with reasons. (3)

10 What do you think the author meant when he described Simon as having 'his heart in his mouth' (line 49)? (3)

11 If you had been watching the match which side would you have supported? (3)

12 How did Mrs Wood's style of play differ from that of the men? (3)

13 If Mrs Wood were your mother what types of things would please you about her and what would annoy you? Confine your answer to the information found before 'Lights out. Whispering.' (line 64) (6)

14 If Simon were a friend of yours and you had to describe him to another friend, what would you say about him? (8)

Total Marks   50

Now let's write   *Choose one of the following to write about.*

Assignment 1   Very often we can be upset and embarrassed by the things parents and friends say and do. For instance, parents may 'show you up' sometimes when they wear something that you think is outdated. Describe a time when something like this happened to you.

Assignment 2   Bowdon was a bully. Describe an incident where you or a friend of yours was bullied. Were you tempted to fight back? Remember this is an essay. Make sure you give all the details.

Assignment 3   At the end of the extract we are told that Simon hit Bowdon. It was an unusual thing for him to do. Sometimes we may surprise ourselves by our own behaviour or we are surprised by the behaviour of friends. Can you think of a time when this has happened to you?

Section 2 Billycart Hill

Read the passage. Then answer the questions.

After school and at weekends boys come from all over the district to race on
the Sunbeam Avenue footpaths. There would be twenty or thirty carts,
two-thirds of them with ball-races. The noise was indescribable. It sounded
like the battle of Britain going on in somebody's bathroom. There would be
about half an hour's racing before the police came. Residents often took the
law into their own hands, hosing the grim-faced riders as they went shrieking
by. Sunbeam Avenue ran parallel to Margaret Street but it started higher
and lasted longer. Carts racing down the footpath on the far side had a
straight run of about a quarter of a mile all the way to the park. Emitting
shock-waves of sound, the ball-race carts would attain such speeds that it was
impossible for the rider to get off. All he could do was to crash reasonably
gently when he got to the end. Carts racing down the footpath on the near
side could go only half as far, although very nearly as fast, before being faced
with a right-angle turn into Irene Street.

The Irene Street corner was made doubly perilous by Mrs Branthwaite's
poppies. Mrs Branthwaite inhabited the house on the corner. She was a
known witch whom we often persecuted after dark by throwing gravel on her
roof. It was widely believed she poisoned cats. Certainly she was a great
ringer-up of the police. In retrospect I can see that she could hardly be
blamed for this, but her behaviour seemed at the time like irrational hatred
of children. She was a renowned gardener. Her front yard was like the cover
of a seed catalogue. Extending her empire, she had flower beds even on her
two front strips, one on the Sunbeam Avenue side and the other on the Irene
Street side – i.e., on both outside edges of the famous corner. The flower
beds held the area's best collection of poppies. She had been known to phone
the police if even one of these was illicitly picked.

At the time I am talking about, Mrs Branthwaite's poppies were all in
bloom. It was essential to make the turn without hurting a single hair of a
poppy's head, otherwise the old lady would probably drop the telephone and
come out shooting. Usually, when the poppies were in bloom, nobody dared
make the turn. I did – not out of courage, but because in my ponderous cart
there was no real danger of going wrong.

I should have left it at that, but got ambitious. One Saturday afternoon
when there was a particularly large turn-out, I got sick of watching the
ball-race carts howling to glory down the far side. I organised the slower carts
like my own into a train. Every cart except mine was deprived of its front axle
and loosely bolted to the cart in front. The whole assembly was about a dozen
carts long, with a big box cart at the back. This back cart I dubbed the
chuck-wagon, using terminology I had picked up from the Hopalong Cassidy
serial at the pictures. I was the only one alone on his cart. Behind me there
were two or even three to every cart until you got to the chuck-wagon, which
was crammed full of little kids, some of them so small that they were holding
toy koalas and sucking dummies.

From its very first run down the far side, my supercart was a triumph. Even
the adults who had been hosing us called their families out to marvel as we
went steaming by. On the supercart's next run there was still more to admire,

since even the top-flight ball-race riders had demanded to have their vehicles built into it, thereby heightening its tone, swelling its passenger list, and multiplying its already impressive output of decibels. Once again I should have left well alone. The thing was already famous. It had everything but a dining car. Why did I ever suggest that we should transfer it to the near side and try the Irene Street turn?

With so much inertia the supercart started slowly, but it accelerated like a piano falling out of a window. Long before we reached the turn I realised that there had been a serious miscalculation. The miscalculation was all mine, of course. Sir Isaac Newton would have got it right. It was too late to do anything except pray. Leaning into the turn, I skidded my own cart safely around in the usual way. The next few segments followed me, but with each segment describing an arc of slightly larger radius than the one in front. First gradually, then with stunning finality, the monster lashed its enormous tail.

The air was full of flying ball-bearings, bits of wood, big kids, little kids, koalas and dummies. Most disastrously of all, it was also full of poppy petals. Not a bloom escaped the scythe. Those of us who could still run scattered to the winds, dragging our wounded with us. The police spent hours visiting all the parents in the district, warning them that the billycart era was definitely over. It was a police car that took Mrs Branthwaite away. There was no point waiting for the ambulance. She could walk all right. It was just that she couldn't talk. She stared straight ahead, her mouth slightly open.

From *Unreliable Memoirs* by Clive James.

119

Questions

1 Look at paragraph 1. When did most of the racing take place? (2)

2 What perils did the racers face from the public? (2)

3 Look at the lines 8-14. How did the far-side and the near-side runs differ? (4)

4 How did the writer feel about Mrs Branthwaite at the time? (3)

5 Giving your reasons, explain if you would have liked or disliked Mrs Branthwaite. (3)

6 What did the writer mean when he described Mrs Branthwaite as 'a renowned gardener' (line 21)? What evidence is there to support this idea? (4)

7 Describe the construction and the appearance of the first supercart. (4)

8 What suggests that the supercart was a success on its first run? (4)

9 Write down one simile and one metaphor from the passage. Do you think they are striking or powerful? (4)

10 How had the writer miscalculated the effect of the supercart on its second run and what were the results? (6)

11 Give words or phrases similar in meaning to four of the following words as they are used in the passage.

'residents' (line 5),
'parallel' (line 7),
'impossible' (line 11),
'perilous' (line 15),
'ambitious' (line 33),
'miscalculation' (line 54). (4)

12 Imagine that you are an eye-witness and that you are asked to make a statement to the police about the events of the afternoon. Write the statement you would make bearing in mind the following points.

The children were obviously enjoying themselves.
Mrs Branthwaite loved her garden and especially her poppies.
The cart was admired by all the adults.
All the children were riding on it at the time. (10)

Total Marks   50

Now let's write

This poem was written by a child and tells of the guilt the child feels when smoking a cigarette for the first time.

Read the poem. Then choose one of the topics to write about.

Guilty Conscience

I went to the shed for a cigarette. Mind, I was
not allowed to smoke, and if Dad caught me,
there's no telling *what* would happen
I lit it
And puffed.
What's that?
Quick as a flash the cigarette is out and I stand
With beating heart, waiting.
It was only the door, swinging and creaking in the
evening breeze.
I lit up again
And puffed.
The door opened with a push and a clatter, hitting,
storming, searching out the sinner.
Without waiting to think, I dashed out, down the path
round the corner, and indoors.
Safe?
Safe from myself?

Rodney Sivyour

Assignment 1 Write a story that involves children and an accident of some kind. It could be the breaking of a window by children playing football but try to think of some different ideas.

Assignment 2 The children in the extract were obviously going to be in trouble with their parents. Write about a time when you did something wrong and were punished by your parents.

Assignment 3 Imagine you were the parent of one of the children on the supercart and the police visited your home. Write down the conversation you might have with the policeman indicating what sort of action you would take with your child. You could set this out as a play if you wish.

Set the scene by writing a paragraph describing the place where the action takes place.

Look at the play extracts in Chapter 5 to help you set out your work.

If you are going to set this out as a play do not use speech marks. Place the name of the speaker on the left-hand side of the page in the margin.

If you are going to write a conversation use inverted commas. Start a new line for each new speaker.

Section 3 The Theft

Helen Forrester grew up in Liverpool. This story is set in the 1930s and Helen's parents, once wealthy, are now bankrupt. Helen should really be in school but her parents, desperate to find work and earn some money to feed the family, insist she stays home as a full-time baby-sitter.

Read the passage. Then answer the questions.

Each day my mother went out to try and get work and spent most of the morning and afternoon in a fruitless round of offices and shops. Before leaving, she would give me a shilling to buy the day's food. This I laid out to the best of my ability on bread, potatoes, rice, tea, sugar, pennyworths of
5 bacon scraps or margarine and, that dire necessity, a pint of milk for Edward, which cost twopence.

At first, Edward used to cry with hunger, but as he grew a little older, he would lie lethargically in the Chariot, making no sound most of the time. The other children also grew apathetic and the smaller ones tried to take bits of
10 bread when I was not looking. We never heard from the school about their progress nor did my father inquire.

One morning my parents went out quite early, before Edward had been fed. After the children had been given a meagre bowl of porridge each and had been sent to school, there was no food left in the house. I was desperate
15 with hunger. And the usual pint of milk would, I knew, not be enough to last Edward for twenty-four hours. However, clutching the shilling, I wrapped Edward up in his stinking blanket, put on my woollen cardigan, my coat being still in pawn, and went downstairs to buy milk from the first passing milkman.

20 Standing on the doorstep were two pint bottles of milk, presumably delivered for Miss Sinford, the lady with religious mania, and Mrs Hicks, who lived with her unemployed husband in the bowels of the basement. The other tenants patronized a milkman who came later.

I looked at the bottles and then up and down the apparently empty street,
25 hoping that the milkman might still be near by. There was no sign of him, however, and I turned back into the house with the idea of getting out the Chariot and wheeling it round to the dairy to purchase Edward's precious pint.

Edward began to whimper. I look down longingly at the milk bottles.
30 Then, like a fleeing cat, I tore up the stairs, Edward bobbing up and down in my arms. I laid him down gently in the Chariot, took our two cracked cups, ran down to the bathroom and filled one with water, then ran silently down the rest of the stairs to the front door.

I glanced quickly up and down the street. Everyone was apparently
35 sleeping the long hopeless sleep of the unemployed.

Quickly I took the lids off the bottles, filled the empty cup with a little milk from each bottle, topped the bottles up with water, carefully replaced the lids, shook the bottles gently, and then crept upstairs again with my precious prize.

40   I managed to make a feed for Edward before the little fire I made from paper flickered out, and I fed him contentedly, knowing that I could make the pint of milk I would buy stretch further for him. I had no qualms of conscience about my theft – I thought only of Edward – and I was mercifully unaware that the policeman on the beat had quietly watched the whole
45 operation.

    With Edward replete with Miss Sinford's and Mrs Hicks's milk and sleeping quietly in the Chariot, Avril and I went on the usual shopping round.

    The policeman on his beat stopped and chucked Edward under his chin. Edward opened his eyes and managed a small smile. I looked up and smiled
50 too, my morning peccadillo completely forgotten.

    'Nice baby you've got,' he said, putting his hands behind his back and rocking gently on his heels. He beamed at me from under his helmet. 'What's his name?'

    'Edward,' I said. He was a nice-looking young man, neat and clean,
55 despite the acne spots all over his face.

    'And what's your name?'

    'Helen,' I replied promptly.

    (He looked down at the baby again, while the greengrocer peered through the glass of his window, which he had been polishing.)
60   'No Mummy?'

    'Yes, she's looking for work. So's Daddy.'

    He looked surprised, apparently at my clear English, so different from that of the other children round about. It was better English than he spoke himself.
65   'Having a hard time? Got any other brothers and sisters?'

    'Yes,' I said simply, in answer to the first question. 'We are seven. The others are all at school.'

    The wind was getting up and it was beginning to rain. My teeth started to chatter and I wrapped my cardigan closer round me.
70   The policeman stared at me with calm blue eyes and said, 'Humph.' He adjusted the collar of his cape.

    'Goodbye,' I said to the policeman and pushed the pram a bit farther along the street and parked it outside the grocery shop, where Avril watched it while I went inside. The policeman, after a moment's hesitation, went into
75 the greengrocer's shop.

    The following morning a pint of milk was delivered to the top landing of our staircase. When I ran downstairs to catch the milkman and return the bottle to him, he insisted that it was for Edward and was sent by a friend, and not even Father could make him say any more. For two long intolerable
80 years the milkman stolidly climbed the stairs and deposited a pint of milk on our top step. It probably saved Edward's life.

    Many years later, the greengrocer told my mother about the young policeman who had inquired about us from him, and had then gone round to the dairy and ordered a daily pint of milk to be delivered for Edward, and
85 had paid for it out of his own meagre wages.

From *Twopence to Cross the Mersey* by Helen Forrester.

Questions

1 Look at paragraph 1. What type of job was Helen's mother looking for? (2)

2 What food did Helen buy with the shilling? (2)

3 What evidence is there in the first three paragraphs to suggest that the children are starving and poor? (4)

4 Do you think Edward's sister was right not to feel guilty about the theft? Give reasons for your answer. (4)

5 From the passage, what do you learn about the people of the area? (4)

6 What do you think the word 'peccadillo' (line 50) means? Give an example of a pecadillo that you have been involved in. (2)

7 Using information from the passage, do you think Helen could be called responsible? What reasons could you give for your answer? (6)

8 What surprised the policeman about Helen? Do you think this tells you anything about the family and their upbringing? (4)

9 How do you think Helen might describe the policeman to her children many years on? (4)

10 Imagine that you are Helen and you are writing an entry in your diary that night. What types of things might you choose to write about? Although you will need to use information from the passage, you may use your imagination as well. (8)

Total Marks 40

Now let's write

Assignment 1 In the extract someone performs a good deed. Write a story that concentrates on someone's kindness. You might like to write in the form of a newspaper article or a play.

Assignment 2 Describe a day in the life of three different people who live in the area. Choose people from different backgrounds, for example, one may be poor, another rich.

Section 4 Incident

This passage was written by Maya Angelou who is a coloured American. She and her brother Bailey were brought up by their grandmother and her crippled brother, Uncle Willie. They lived in the 'deep south' in the 1920s when it was strictly a white man's world; where the black person was regarded as no better than a slave.

The passage explains why Momma – the grandmother with whom they lived – decided to send them to their mother in California.

Read the passage. Then answer the questions.

Vocabulary

You might find the following words difficult. Here are the meanings of the words as they are used in the passage.

'incident' (line 2)   event
'imitating' (line 3)   copying, pretending to be someone else
'revealed' (line 8)   made known
'tardiness' (line 13)   lateness
'suspected' (line 28)   thought
'delivered' (line 41)   saved
'blaspheming' (line 44)   taking the Lord's name in vain, for example 'Oh my God!'
'calaboose' (line 49)   prison
'inferiority' (line 91)   feeling lower in rank or position
'arrogance' (line 91)   overbearing, proud

Whatever the real reason, The Truth, for taking us to California, I shall always think it lay mostly in an incident in which Bailey had the leading part. Bailey had picked up the habit of imitating Claude Rains, Herbert Marshall and George McCready. I didn't think it at all strange that a thirteen-year-old
5 boy in the unreconstructed Southern town of Stamps spoke with an Englishy accent. His heroes included D'Artagnan and the Count of Monte Cristo and he affected what he thought were their swashbuckling gallantries.

On an afternoon a few weeks before Momma revealed her plan to take us West, Bailey came into the Store shaking. His little face no longer black but
10 a dirty colorless gray. As was our habit upon entering the Store, he walked behind the candy counter and leaned on the cash register. Uncle Willie had sent him on an errand to whitefolks' town and he wanted an explanation for Bailey's tardiness. After a brief moment our uncle could see that something was wrong and, feeling unable to cope, he called Momma from the kitchen.
15 "What's the matter, Bailey Junior?"

He said nothing. I knew when I saw him that it would be useless to ask anything while he was in that state. It meant that he had seen or heard of something so ugly or frightening that he was paralyzed as a result. He explained when we were smaller that when things were very bad his soul just crawled behind his heart and curled up and went to sleep. When it awoke, the fearful thing had gone-away. Ever since we read "The Fall of the House of Usher", we had made a pact that neither of us would allow the other to be buried without making "absolutely, positively sure" (his favourite phrase) that the person was dead. I also had to swear that when his soul was sleeping I would never try to wake it, for the shock might make it go to sleep forever. So I let him be, and after a while Momma had to let him alone too.

I waited on customers, and walked around him or leaned over him and, as I suspected, he didn't respond. When the spell wore off he asked Uncle Willie what colored people had done to white people in the first place. Uncle Willie, who never was one for explaining things because he took after Momma, said little except that "colored people hadn't even bothered a hair on whitefolks' heads." Momma added that some people said that whitefolks had come over to Africa (she made it sound like a hidden valley on the moon) and stole the colored people and made them slaves, but nobody really believed it was true. No way to explain what happened "blows and scores" ago, but right now they had the upper hand. Their time wasn't long, though. Didn't Moses lead the children of Israel out of the bloody hands of Pharaoh and into the Promised Land? Didn't the Lord protect the Hebrew children in the fiery furnace and didn't my Lord deliver Daniel? We only had to wait on the Lord.

Bailey said he saw a man, a colored man, whom nobody had delivered. He was dead. (If the news hadn't been so important, we would have been visited with one of Momma's outbursts and prayers. Bailey was nearly blaspheming.) He said, "The man was dead and rotten. Not stinking but rotten."

Momma ordered, "Ju, watch your tongue."

Uncle Wille asked, "Who, who was it?"

Bailey was just tall enough to clear his face over the cash register. He said, "When I passed the calaboose, some men had just fished him out of the pond. He was wrapped in a sheet, all rolled up like a mummy, then a white man walked over and pulled the sheet off. The man was on his back but the white man stuck his foot under the sheet and rolled him over on the stomach."

He turned to me. "My, he had no color at all. He was bloated like a ball."

(We had had a running argument for months. Bailey said there was no such thing as colorlessness, and I argued that if there was color there also had to be an opposite and now he was admitting that it was possible. But I didn't feel good about my win.)

"The colored men backed off and I did too, but the white man stood there, looking down, and grinned. Uncle Willie, why do they hate us so much?"

Uncle Willie muttered, "They don't really hate us. They don't know us. How can they hate us? They mostly scared."

Momma asked if Bailey had recognised the man, but he was caught in the happening and the event.

"Mr Bubba told me I was too young to see something like that and I oughta hightail it home, but I had to stay. Then the white man called us closer. He said 'O.K., you boys, stretch him out in the calaboose and when the Sheriff comes along he'll notify his people. This here's one nigger nobody got to worry about no more. He ain't going nowhere else.' Then the men picked up corners of the sheet, but since nobody wanted to get close to the man they held the very ends and he nearly rolled out on the ground. The white man called me to come and help too."

Momma exploded. "Who was it?" She made herself clear. "Who was the white man?" Bailey couldn't let go of the horror. "I picked up a side of the sheet and walked right into the calaboose with the men. I walked in the calaboose carrying a rotten dead Negro." His voice was ancient with shock. He was literally bug-eyed.

"The white man played like he was going to lock us all up in there, but Mr Bubba said 'Ow, Mr Jim. We didn't do it. We ain't done nothing wrong.' Then the white man laughed and said we boys couldn't take a joke, and opened the door." He breathed his relief. "Whew, I was glad to get out of there. The calaboose, and the prisoners screaming they didn't want no dead nigger in there with them. That he'd stink up the place. They called the white man 'Boss'. They said, 'Boss surely we ain't done nothing bad enough for you to put another nigger in here with us, and a dead one at that.' Then they laughed. They all laughed like there was something funny."

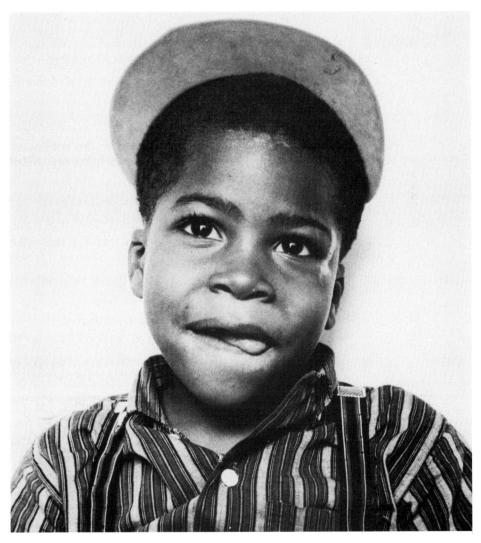

Bailey was talking so fast he forgot to stutter, he forgot to scratch his head and clean his fingernails with his teeth. He was away in a mystery, locked in the enigma that young Southern Black boys start to unravel, start to try unravel, from seven years old to death. The humorless puzzle of inequality
90 and hate. His experience raised the question of worth and values, of aggressive inferiority and aggressive arrogance. Could Uncle Willie, a Black man, Southern, crippled moreover, hope to answer the questions, both asked and unuttered? Would Momma, who knew the ways of the whites and the wiles of the Blacks, try to answer her grandson, whose very life depended
95 on his not truly understanding the enigma? Most assuredly not.

They both responded characteristically. Uncle Willie said something like he didn't know what the world was coming to, and Momma prayed, "God rest his soul, poor man." I'm sure she began piecing together the details of our California trip that night.

From *I Know Why the Caged Bird Sings* by Maya Angelou.

Questions
1 Look at lines 8-14. How could Uncle Willie and the author tell outwardly that something was wrong with Bailey? (2)

2 Look at lines 15-25. Why did the author think Bailey didn't answer at first? (2)

3 What do you learn about Bailey Junior in the first four paragraphs? (4)

4 Look at line 19. What do you think Bailey meant when he said that 'when things were very bad his soul just crawled behind his heart and curled up and went to sleep'? (4)

5 In the fifth paragraph Momma explains to Bailey that they 'only had to wait on the Lord'. What did she expect the Lord to do for them? (3)

6 In as much detail as possible explain what had upset Bailey so much? (6)

7 In paragraph 6 the author says 'Bailey was nearly blaspheming'. Explain fully why she thought this. (3)

8 Look at lines 49-85. Do you think Mr Jim, the only white man there, liked the coloured people? Give reasons for your answer. (5)

9 How do the coloured adults behave towards Mr Jim? Do you feel they treated him as if he were better than they were? (5)

10 Would you say that Bailey had been deeply affected by the whole incident? Give reasons for your answer. (6)

11 After this happened to Bailey, Momma, the children's grandmother, decided to send them to their mother in California. Write the letter that Momma might have written to the children's mother. Explain what has happened and why she has decided to send the children away. (10)

Total Marks   50

Now let's write

Read the poem. Then choose one of the topics to write about.

Incident

Once riding in old Baltimore
Heart-filled, head-filled with glee
I saw a Baltimorean
Keep looking straight at me.

Now I was eight and very small
And he was no whit bigger,
And so I smiled but he poked out
His tongue, and called me, 'Nigger'.

I saw the whole of Baltimore
From May until December;
Of all the things that happened there
That's all that I remember.

Countee Cullen

Assignment 1   The two children you have read about in the above extracts have both had a nasty experience that they have never forgotten. Have you ever been angry or sad about something and reacted violently? Write about a traumatic experience that you yourself have had.

You might like to think about your first experience of death, either of a relative, friend or a pet.

Assignment 2   Write an article for a newspaper that highlights the finding of the body in the extract. You could include interviews in your article, possibly with the white boss and with Bailey Junior.

Remember that a newspaper article has to have a title. It is called a headline and it is normally eye-catching.

If you include an interview, everything said by the boss and Bailey should be direct speech and be enclosed in inverted commas.

Assignment 3   Write a story in which someone is victimised because they are different.

It could be a coloured person, as above, or it could be about a child who is bullied in school for some reason.

Sometimes people are bullied because they behave in a different way from other people.

Drama and Poetry

Section 1 The Visit

Joan and Lyn are the parents of a young Welsh Guard, Barry. He and his
childhood friend, Paul, were killed on the *Sir Galahad* when it was bombed.
Barry was married to Christine who is now expecting their child.

Barry's parents and Christine are on a visit to the Falkland Islands to
attend a memorial service in honour of those who died.

Read the extract. Then answer the questions.

JOAN: It was wicked that feeling, it came over me. I knew it then, I'm not
going to see him again. Remember Christine? She wouldn't let us leave
until the ship was a little dot. You know what she said to me? 'That's it,
we're not going to see him again are we? He's not coming back.' She held
5   on to me for dear life. That's the one time she's ever let me near her. It was
only for a minute then she pushed me away.

LYN: Funny girl.

JOAN: Barry loved her.

LYN: Funny isn't it, the way they used to talk and laugh.

10   JOAN: I don't think she really talks to anyone else. Come on, let's plant
these daffodils I want something to grow on this place, other than grass.

CHRISTINE: I want you to touch me. Put your hands on my stomach and feel
it moving. I pretend y'know, pretend you're still alive. I talk to you…all
the time. I pretend my hands are yours. I tell you if it's moving.

15   *(Barry enters.)*
Come here put your hand on here. It'll move in a minute. It didn't
like the helicopter.
(He puts his hands on her and rests his head.)

BARRY: Takes after me then doesn't it?

20   CHRISTINE: Your mum said I was daft coming all this way, but I
thought I might be premature then I could have the baby here
where you are.

BARRY: I'd love to see it.

CHRISTINE: Everyone wants it to be a boy now you're gone.

25   BARRY: I'd rather it were a girl now. *(pause)* What's it feel like to be
pregnant?

CHRISTINE: Terrible. Full up like. I can't move. Sometimes I like it
though, feeling full. I'm sick of being pregnant but I'm scared of
having it, looking after it. I won't be very good. What if I drop it? I
30   wish I wasn't having it Barry. I don't want it on my own. I don't
want your baby any more, you're no good, you're dead. I don't
want it any more *(pause)* but I want something. I want something of
you I suppose *(pause)*.

Your mum's been making quite a fuss back home, she's been on the
35   tele.

BARRY: On the tele?

CHRISTINE: Demanding an inquiry.

BARRY: Why?

CHRISTINE: Well we want to know what happened, why you were left
40   on the *Sir Galahad* for six hours.

BARRY: And she's making a fuss?

CHRISTINE: Aye.

BARRY: Oh no!

CHRISTINE: What's up.

45 BARRY: Having my mum make a fuss, showing me up.

CHRISTINE: Showing you up?

PAUL: Bloody right there should be an inquiry.

CHRISTINE: Don't let him bully me Paul.

BARRY: What about the lads who survived, they're not going to want
50   it all dragged up, bad enough they have to live with it.

CHRISTINE: I have to live with it too. You joined the army, I didn't. I
    want to know why you died. I want to know why I haven't got a
    husband any more.

PAUL: Sounds like a pretty fundamental sort of question to me Barry.

55 BARRY: We signed up didn't we. I don't want people saying I didn't
    know what I was letting myself in for. I did. I was proud to do it.

PAUL: Same here, but I don't remember signing anything said we'd
    be left stranded in the middle of a war. If there's a mistake I want to
    know how and why.

60 BARRY: It's a risk.

PAUL: Bollocks.

BARRY: I warned you about that before. Trust my mum eh?

CHRISTINE: I'm glad she's got the strength, I haven't.

BARRY: You wouldn't embarrass me though would you?

65 CHRISTINE: It's not weak to want to know how my husband died. Since
    coming here, seeing this place, look, I mean we've got countryside like this
    at home, we don't need it down here as well. I can't help it Barry. I just look
    at it and think…it's been a waste, if this is what you died for you can keep it.

BARRY: No, no, you musn't say that.

70 CHRISTINE: I know, its disrespectful isn't it. A war widow shouldn't say that thing. Well I'm sick of being a widow, being tragic, everybody patting me on the head, being proud of us for making such a 'sacrifice'. I didn't make the sacrifice, I wasn't asked, why not even by you. It wasn't my doing.

75 BARRY: It wasn't my doing either.

CHRISTINE: You took orders! *(pause)* What were you thinking of when you took them? Did you just want a fight? Prove what a hero you were? *(pause)* We've just been used, fools, used to save face back home.

BARRY: Why come here then?

80 CHRISTINE: Why come here? They won't tell us what happened to you. I've come to find out. Feel what it must have been like. I know I can never be on that ship, but I've been close.

From *Taken Out* by Greg Cullen.

Questions

1 Look at lines 1-6. What were the feelings of Joan and Christine when they waved Barry off? (2)

2 Look at lines 2-10. What information is given about Christine? (3)

3 Why did Joan wish to plant flowers? (2)

4 What was Christine's reason for going to the Falklands so close to the birth of the baby? Why is it possible to understand her feelings? (4)

5 Why did everybody want the baby to be a boy but Barry wish for a girl? (4)

6 Using the information that begins 'Terrible. Full up like' to 'you I suppose.' (lines 27-33), explain how you think Christine felt about the birth of the baby? (5)

7 What reasons did Barry give for not wanting an inquiry? (5)

8 How did Christine and Paul feel about the inquiry and why? (5)

9 Sum up how you think Christine felt about Barry's death and how you think it affected her. (5)

10 Imagine you are Christine in ten years' time and that Barry's child has asked about the trip to the Falkland Islands. Explain as clearly as you can what the trip was like and what it meant to you at the time. Think about whether the child was a boy or girl. (15)

Total Marks 50

Now let's write

Assignment 1 Imagine you are left to bring up a child on your own. Write a letter to a friend explaining how you are coping and the things you find particularly difficult to achieve alone.

Assignment 2 'War's a waste of time, all that death and destruction and for nothing!'

'People in the past have been prepared to die for this country. You ought to be grateful to them, mate! Without them you probably wouldn't be here now.'

Which point of view do you agree with? Is war always a waste of time or are some causes worth fighting for?

Section 2 Androcles and the Lion

This play is set at a time when the Romans were rulers of a vast empire. People who believed in a Christian God were in a minority and were despised and persecuted by the Romans who had their own form of religion. It was common for Christians to be captured and tortured or killed. The Romans built large amphitheatres where people went to be entertained. A favourite entertainment was watching the Christians being thrown to the lions.

This extract is reproduced without apostrophes, as written by George Bernard Shaw.

Read the extract. Then answer the questions.

Prologue

Overture: forest sounds, roaring of lions, Christian hymn faintly.

A jungle path. A lions roar, a melancholy suffering roar, comes from the jungle. It is repeated nearer. THE LION *limps from the jungle on three legs, holding up his right forepaw, in which a huge thorn sticks. He sits down and contemplates it. He licks it, He shakes it. He tries to extract it by scraping it along the ground, and hurts himself worse. He roars piteously. He licks it again. Tears drop from his eyes. He limps painfully off the path and lies down under the trees, exhausted with pain. Heaving a long sigh, like wind in a trombone, he goes to sleep.*

ANDROCLES *and his wife* MEGAERA *come along the path. He is a small, thin, ridiculous little man who might be any age from thirty to fifty-five. He has sandy hair, watery compassionate blue eyes, sensitive nostrils, and a very presentable forehead; but his good points go no further: his arms and legs and back, though wiry of their kind, look shrivelled and starved. He carries a big bundle, is very poorly clad, and seems tired and hungry.*

His wife is a rather handsome pampered slattern, well fed and in the prime of life. She has nothing to carry, and has a stout stick to help her along.

MEGAERA *(suddenly throwing down her stick):*   I wont go another step.

ANDROCLES *(pleading wearily):*   Oh, not again, dear. Whats the good of stopping every two miles and saying you wont go another step? We must get on to the next village before night. There are wild beasts in this wood:
5   lions, they say.

MEGAERA: I dont believe a word of it. You are always threatening me with wild beasts to make me walk the very soul out of my body when I can hardly drag one foot before another. We havent seen a single lion yet.

ANDROCLES: Well, dear, do you want to see one?

10   MEGAERA *(tearing the bundle from his back):*   You cruel brute, you dont care how tired I am, or what becomes of me. *(She throws the bundle on the ground.)* Always thinking of yourself. Self! self! self! always yourself! *(She sits down on the bundle.)*

ANDROCLES *(sitting down sadly on the ground with his elbows on his knees and*
15   *his head in his hands):*   We all have to think of ourselves occasionally, dear.

MEGAERA: A man ought to think of his wife sometimes.

ANDROCLES: He cant always help it, dear. You make me think of you a good deal. Not that I blame you.

20 MEGAERA: Blame me! I should think not indeed. Is it my fault that I'm married to you?

ANDROCLES: No, dear: that is my fault.

MEGAERA: Thats a nice thing to say to me. Arent you happy with me?

ANDROCLES: I dont complain, my love.

25 MEGAERA: You ought to be ashamed of yourself.

ANDROCLES: I am, my dear.

MEGAERA: Youre not: you glory in it.

ANDROCLES: In what, darling?

MEGAERA: In everything. In making me a slave, and making yourself a
30 laughing-stock. Its not fair. You get me the name of being a shrew with your meek ways, always talking as if butter wouldnt melt in your mouth. And just because I look a big strong woman, and because I'm goodhearted and a bit hasty, and because youre always driving me to do things I'm sorry for afterwards, people say 'Poor man: what a life his wife leads him!' Oh,
35 if they only knew! And you think I dont know. But I do, I do (screaming) I do.

ANDROCLES: Yes, my dear: I know you do.

MEGAERA: Then why don't you treat me properly and be a good husband to me?

40 ANDROCLES: What can I do, my dear?

MEGAERA: What can you do! You can return to your duty, and come back to your home and your friends, and sacrifice to the gods as all respectable people do, instead of having us hunted out of house and home for being dirty disreputable blaspheming atheists.

45 ANDROCLES: Im not an atheist, dear: I am a Christian.

MEGAERA: Well, isnt that the same thing, only ten times worse? Everybody knows that the Christians are the very lowest of the low.

ANDROCLES: Just like us, dear.

MEGAERA: Speak for yourself. Dont dare to compare me to common
50 people. My father owned his own public-house; sorrowful was the day for me when you first came drinking in our bar.

ANDROCLES: I confess I was addicted to it, dear. But I gave it up when I became a Christian.

MEGAERA: Youd much better have remained a drunkard. I can forgive a
55 man being addicted to drink: its only natural; and I dont deny I like a drop myself sometimes. What I cant stand is your being addicted to Christianity. And whats worse again, your being addicted to animals. How is any woman to keep her house clean when you bring in every stray cat or lost cur and lame duck in the whole countryside? You took the bread
60 out of my mouth to feed them: you know you did: dont attempt to deny it.

134

ANDROCLES: Only when they were hungry and you were getting too stout, dearie.

MEGAERA: Yes: insult me, do. *(Rising.)* Oh! I wont bear it another moment. You used to sit and talk to those dumb brute beasts for hours, when you hadnt a word for me.

ANDROCLES: They never answered back, darling. *(He rises and again shoulders the bundle.)*

MEGAERA: Well, if youre fonder of animals than of your own wife, you can live with them here in the jungle. Ive had enough of them and enough of you. Im going back. Im going home.

ANDROCLES *(barring the way back):*   No, dearie: dont take on like that. We cant go back. Weve sold everything: we should starve; and I should be sent to Rome and thrown to the lions –

MEGAERA: Serve you right! I wish the lions joy of you. *(Screaming.)* Are you going to get out of my way and let me go home?

ANDROCLES: No, dear –

MEGAERA: Then I'll make my way through the forest; and when I'm eaten by the wild beasts youll know what a wife youve lost. *(She dashed into the jungle and nearly falls over the sleeping lion.)* Oh! Oh! Andy! Andy! *(She totters back and collapses into the arms of* ANDROCLES, *who crushed by her weight, falls on his bundle.)*

ANDROCLES *(extracting himself from beneath her and slapping her hands in great anxiety):*   What is it, my precious, my pet? Whats the matter? *(He raises her head. Speechless with terror, she points in the direction of the sleeping lion. He steals cautiously towards the spot indicated by* MAGAERA. *She rises with an effort and totters after him).*

MEGAERA: No, Andy: youll be killed. Come back.
The lion utters a long snoring sigh. ANDROCLES *sees the lion, and recoils fainting into the arms of* MEGAERA. *who falls back on the bundle. They roll apart and lie staring in terror at one another. The lion is heard groaning heavily in the jungle.*

ANDROCLES *(whispering):*   Did you see? A lion.

MEGAERA *(despairing):* The gods have sent him to punish us because youre a Christian. Take me away, Andy. Save me.

95 ANDROCLES *(rising):* Meggy: theres one chance for you. Itll take him pretty nigh twenty minutes to eat me (Im rather stringy and tough) and you can escape in less time than that.

MEGAERA: Oh, dont talk about eating. (THE LION *rises with a great groan and limps towards them.)* Oh! *(She faints.)*

100 ANDROCLES *(quaking, but keeping between the lion and* MEGAERA.) Dont you come near my wife, do you hear? (THE LION *groans.* ANDROCLES *can hardly stand for trembling.)* Meggy: run. Run for your life. If I take my eye off him, it's all up. (THE LION *holds up his wounded paw and flaps it piteously before* ANDROCLES.) Oh, he's lame, poor old chap! He's got a thorn in his 105 paw. A frightfully big thorn. *(Full of sympathy.)* Oh, poor old man! Did um get an awful thorn into um's tootsums wootsums? Has it made um too sick to eat a nice little Christian man for um's breakfast? Oh, a nice little Christian man will get um's thorn out for um; and then um shall eat the nice Christian man and the nice Christian man's nice big tender wifey 110 pifey. (THE LION *responds by moans of self-pity.)* Yes, yes, yes, yes, yes. Now, now *(taking the paw in his hand),* um is not to bite and not to scratch, not even if it hurts a very very little. Now make velvet paws. Thats right. *(He pulls gingerly at the thorn.* THE LION, *with an angry yell of pain, jerks back his paw so abruptly that* ANDROCLES *is thrown on his back.)* Steadeee! 115 Oh, did the nasty cruel little Christian man hurt the sore paw? (THE LION *moans assentingly but apologetically.)* Well, one more little pull and it will be all over. Just one little, little, leetle pull; and then um will live happily ever after. *(He gives the thorn another pull.* THE LION *roars and snaps his jaws with a terrifying clash.)* Oh, mustnt frighten um's good kind doctor, 120 um's affectionate nursey. That didnt hurt at all: not a bit. Just one more. Just to show how the brave big lion can bear pain, not like the little cry-baby Christian man. Oopsh! *(The thorn comes out.* THE LION *yells with pain, and shakes his paw wildly.)* Thats iᵗ! *(Holding up the thorn.)* Now it's out. Now lick um's paw to take away the nasty inflammation. See? *(He 125 licks his own hand.* THE LION *nods intelligently and licks his paw industriously.)* Clever little liony-piony! Understands um's dear old friend Andy Wandy. (THE LION *licks his face.) Yes, kissums Andy Wandy. (THE LION wagging his tail violently, rises on his hind legs, and embraces* ANDROCLES, *who makes a wry face and cries.)* Velvet paws! Velvet paws! 130 (THE LION *draws in his claws.)* Thats right. *(He embraces* THE LION, *who finally takes the end of his tail in one paw, places that tight round* ANDROCLES' *waist, resting it on his hip.* ANDROCLES *takes the other paw in his hand, stretches out his arm, and the two waltz rapturously round and round and finally away through the jungle.)*

135 MEGAERA *(who has revived during the waltz):* Oh, you coward, you havent danced with me for years; and now you go off dancing with a great brute beast that you havent known for ten minutes and that wants to eat your own wife. Coward! Coward! Coward! *(She rushes off after them into the jungle.)*

From *Androcles and the Lion* by George Bernard Shaw.

Questions

1 Why does Androcles want to get out of the wood? (2)

2 Do you think Megaera is right when she says Androcles doesn't care about her? Give your reasons. (2)

3 What might an audience find amusing about the first part of the play (lines 1-26)? (6)

4 Look at lines 29-36. How does Megaera describe herself to Androcles? (4)

5 Look at the descriptions of the characters at the beginning of the extract. What impression was the author trying to create of this couple? Has he succeeded? (4)

6 What does Megaera think is the reason for all their problems? (3)

7 How does Megaera feel about the Christians and Androcles' conversion to this faith? (6)

8 What reason does Androcles give for sometimes preferring animals to his wife? (3)

9 Look at the lines beginning 'Then I'll make my way through the forest' to 'Did you see? A lion.' (lines 77-92). Describe how this scene would look to the audience. (6)

10 How does Androcles suggest he saves Megaera at first? (3)

11 What might a spectator find amusing about the way Androcles speaks to the lion while he is removing the thorn from its paw? Think about the content as well as the tone used. (6)

12 Why does Megaera react in the way she does at the sight of Androcles and the lion waltzing? (5)

Total Marks   50

Now let's write

Assignment 1   Try to imagine how this play will continue and write a few pages about what is likely to happen next.

Where might the next scene take place?

Shaw has given you two well-thought-out characters. Could you introduce another?

What might you find out about Androcles and Megaera as the play continued?

How do husband and wife treat each other? Might this change in some way?

Think about the time this is set in. What happened to Christians at that time?

Assignment 2   Have you ever helped an animal in distress? Write about the incident describing exactly how it came about.

Assignment 3   Write about a modern-day couple whose relationship resembles that of Androcles and Megaera.

Section 3 Russians *and* Communiqué to a Child

These two pieces are about war. The first one is a song about the possiblity of nuclear war.

(Mr Khrushchev was a Russian leader in the 1960s. Oppenheimer was one of the scientists responsible for the development of the nuclear bombs dropped on Japan at the end of the last war. Mr Reagan is currently the American President.)

The second piece is a poem written to a child after he or she has been badly wounded.

Russians

In Europe and America, there's a growing feeling of hysteria
Conditioned to respond to all the threats
In the rhetorical speeches of the Soviets
Mr Khrushchev said we will bury you
5 I don't subscribe to this point of view
It would be such an ignorant thing to do
If the Russians love their children too.

How can I save my little boy from Oppenheimer's deadly toy
There is no monopoly of common sense
10 On either side of the political fence
We share the same ecology
Regardless of ideology
Believe me when I say to you
I hope the Russians love their children too.

15 There is no historical precedent
To put the words in the mouth of the President
There's no such thing as a winnable war
It's a lie we don't believe any more
Mr Reagan says we will protect you
20 I don't subscribe to this point of view
Believe me when I say to you
I hope the Russians love their children too.

We share the same biology
Regardless of ideology
25 What might save us me and you
Is that the Russians love their children too.

Sting

Communiqué to a Child

First of all you must not complain.
The bomb that blew off your left leg,
and tore away one of your eyes,
was placed by some of our volunteers
5 to obtain maximum psychological effect
in the struggle to achieve our demands.
It was not our intention to maim
or kill anyone, and we regret the death
of your mother. However, you must
10 accept that there are no innocents
in a situation such as this.
So, adjust to your present condition,
And do not condemn us. As you
limp into the future your one eye
15 will enable you to see things clearly,
and you will evaluate the event
with the wisdom of age. You will
begin to understand why it happened.
Only an adult can possibly know this,
20 and apply reason to the suffering.

Jim Burns

Question 1   How does the writer of 'Russians' feel about a nuclear war and the countries which might start one? Use evidence from the passage to answer the question. (10)

Read the song by Sting again carefully. What does the writer say about the Russians? What reason does he give for their starting a war?

Is this the same for the Americans?

How does the writer feel about these reasons?

If a war were to break out who would he be concerned for?

Question 2   In 'Communiqué to a Child' who do you think the poet sympathises with – the victim or the bomber? How does he get his feelings across? (10)

Read the poem again carefully.

What has happened to the child in the poem?

Is the writer sorry for the child? How does he get this across?

Is he trying to excuse the bomber's actions? If so, how does he do this?

Look up the word 'sarcasm' in a dictionary. Is this poem sarcastic? Why might this be?

Question 3   What reasons are suggested in the song and poem for wars or violence to take place? (10)

Read the song and the poem again carefully.

According to Sting, why is war likely to occur?

Who is responsible for the violence in the poem? Why are they carrying out such acts?

Can you think of other reasons why countries or organisations resort to war?

Question 4   Study the way in which the two pieces are written. Giving reasons, which one do you prefer? Why do you feel it is better than the other? (10)

How might a song and poem differ? How is the audience different?

Look up the word 'communiqué' in a dictionary. What does it mean?

Does this tell you anything about the style used to write this poem?

Total Marks 40

Assignment 1   Look at a selection of war poems, especially First World War poems. Then look at some that were written before or after that time. Is the message always the same? Have the poems changed in any way?
Choose a poem that you think is particularly good. Write an essay about the poem, explaining what it is about and why you think it is so effective.

Assignment 2   Write your own poem on the subject of war.

Section 4   Tree *and* Going, Going

Read the poems. Then answer the questions.

Tree

They didn't tell us
what it would be like
without trees.

Nobody imagined
5 that the whispering of leaves
would grow silent
or the vibrant jade of spring
pale to grey death.

And now we pile
10 rubbish on rubbish
in this dusty landscape –
struggling to create
a tree

but though the shape is right
15 and the nailed branches
lean upon the wind
and plastic leaves
lend colour to the twigs

we wait in vain
20 for the slow unfurling of buds
and no amount of loving
can stir our weary tree
to singing.

Tina Morris

Going, Going

I thought it would last my time –
The sense that, beyond the town,
There would always be fields and farms,
Where the village louts could climb
Such trees as were not cut down;
I knew there'd be false alarms

In the papers about old streets
And split-level shopping, but some
Have always been left so far;
And when the old part retreats
As the bleak high-risers come
We can always escape in the car.

Things are tougher than we are, just
As earth will always respond
However we mess it about;
Chuck filth in the sea, if you must:
The tides will be clean beyond.
– But what do I feel now? Doubt?

Or age, simply? The crowd
Is young in the M1 café;
Their kids are screaming for more –
More houses, more parking allowed,
More caravan sites, more pay.
On the 'Business Page, a score

Of spectacled grins approve
Some takeover bid that entails
Five per cent profit (and ten
Per cent more in the estuaries): move
Your works to the unspoilt dales
(Grey area grants)! And when

You try to get near the sea
In summer …
                    It seems, just now,
To be happening so very fast;
Despite all the land left free
For the first time I feel somehow
That it isn't going to last,

That before I snuff it, the whole
Boiling will be bricked in
Except for the tourist parts –
First slum of Europe: a role
It won't be so hard to win,
With a cast of crooks and tarts.

And that will be England gone,
45 The shadows, the meadows, the lanes,
The guildhalls, the carved choirs.
There'll be books; it will linger on
In galleries; but all that remains
For us will be concrete and tyres.

50 Most things are never meant.
This won't be, most likely: but greeds
And garbage are too thick-strewn
To be swept up now, or invent
Excuses that make them all needs.
55 I just think it will happen, soon.

Philip Larkin

Questions 1 What is the poet's message in the poem 'Tree'? What is wrong with the tree that has been created? How does it differ from a real tree? (10)

2 Read the poem 'Going, Going' again carefully. According to the poet what will we be able to find in books and galleries that won't exist in real life any more? (Verse 8 will help you to answer this question but you will need to include material from the whole poem.) (15)

3 Why do you think the title of the second poem is 'Going, Going'? What do you think is 'going'? (5)

4 Look at the poem 'Going, Going' verse by verse. In what ways does the poet suggest we are polluting and destroying the environment? Do you agree with him when he says we could win an award for being 'First slum of Europe'? (10)

Total Marks 40

Now let's write

Assignment 1 Between the time you were very small and now you have probably watched changes take place in your area. New houses or factories being built, green fields disappearing as new roads appeared, and so on.
From your own experience would you say these poets were right to be worried about the future of the countryside and the effects of pollution? Are there reasons to be optimistic?

Assignment 2 Write an essay or poem and include this line in it: 'Their kids are screaming for more'.

Paired Passages

Section 1 The Sound of Breaking Glass *and* Leather-Jackets, Bikes and Birds

Read the extract and poem. Then answer the questions.

Passage A   FINCH, the leader of a gang, dislikes another boy named JULIAN. Outside an empty church one evening, his mocking and taunting of JULIAN leads to a game of dares.

JULIAN: If you got me here for a fight – let's fight.
   (Pause.)
FINCH: Or dare?
JULIAN: Just a game then? Me and you?
5   FINCH: Truth and dare.
JULIAN: I'll do what you want – you do what I want. See who's the boss.
   (Pause.)
FINCH: Heads, you say – tails, I say.
JULIAN: All right.
10   *(A coins spins and stops.)*
   Tails. What do you want me to do?
FINCH: Break those coloured windows.
SANDRA: No!
FINCH: All of them.
15   *(Pause.)*
   What are you waiting for?
DAVE: Look, Finch –
FINCH: Scared?
DAVE: Finch –
20   FINCH: Julie-Anne? What are you waiting for, little girl?
JULIAN: I'M LOOKING FOR STONES!
   (Pause.)
FINCH: By your foot. Shine the torch, Sandy. Lots of little stones, see!
JULIAN: What if I don't?
25   FINCH: I'm the boss.
JULIAN: And that's what you want.
FINCH: That's what I want. Scared?
SANDRA: Don't break the windows! They belong to the war! And the names!
   (Pause.)
30   JULIAN: Right!
   (Stones are thrown; some miss, some break glass … Julian breathes hard, moaning slightly as he throws. Some miss, some hit. Then silence.)
   Now do you feel good?
FINCH: *(Awed):* I - I didn't think … you had the guts. You did it!
35   JULIAN: *(Mocking):* Well, I 'had the guts', didn't I!
DAVE: *(Scared):* Somebody must have heard!

SANDRA: They must have done!

FINCH: Come on, let's get away –

JULIAN: Stay here!

40 FINCH: They might've heard.

JULIAN: Who?

FINCH: Coppers, the vicar – I don't know!

JULIAN: Why didn't you think of that before? It's too late now. You've got
to do something for me. Remember? You made an agreement. You do

45 what I say.

FINCH: You're mad!

Passage B *Leather-jackets, Bikes and Birds*

The streets are noisy
with the movement of passing motors.
The coffee bars get fuller.
The leather-jacket groups begin to gather,
5 stand, and listen, pretending they are
looking for trouble.
The juke box plays its continuous
tune, music appreciated by Most.
The aroma of Espresso
10 coffee fills the nostrils and
the night.

Motorbikes pull up.
Riders dismount and join
their friends in the gang.
15 They stand, smoking, swearing,
playing with the girls;
making a teenage row.
They pretend not to notice the drizzle
falling out of the dark,
20 because you've got to be hard to
be a leather-jacket.
A couple
in a corner, snogging,
hope the motor lights will not be
25 dipped too much,
so that the others will see them.
They must all have recognition;
there must always be enough
leather-jackets around them,
30 the same as theirs.
The street lamp on the side
of the street shows the rain
for what it is – wet and cold.
But it does not show their faces
35 for what they are.

Robert Davies

1 Using the information in the passage explain how each person present felt about the dare suggested by Finch. (8)

2 What steps does Finch take to make sure Julian breaks the windows? (4)

3 Look at the information beginning, 'Stones are thrown' to 'Then silence' (lines 31-2). What do you learn about the way Julian felt about throwing the stones? Why did he throw them? (6)

4 What do you think of Julian? Why might an audience's attitude to him change as the incident is acted out? (6)

5 If you had been in Julian's position would you have broken the windows? Give reasons for your answer. Why do you think children like Julian can be made to do such things even though they know it's wrong? (6)

1 Why are the streets noisy? (2)

2 Look at lines 1-12. What are the people in leather jackets doing? (4)

3 How do people in leather jackets give the impression of being tough? Why do you think they do this? Answer in full using evidence from the passage. (6)

4 Choose three examples from the passage that tell you about these people and how they think and behave. Explain what the extract means to you. (6)

5 Explain, giving reasons, the way you think the writer feels about these leather-jacketed people. (6)

What do the people in these passages have in common? How do they differ? How do you feel about the young people described? Would you feel sympathy for any of them? (6)

Total Marks   60

Now let's write

Assignment 1   Write an essay entitled 'The Gang'.

Assignment 2   Imagine you are one of the teenagers mentioned in these extracts. Write an account of your day suitable for putting into a diary.

Assignment 3   Read the first extract again. Write two to three sides continuing the story.

Section 2 The Kestrel and the Classroom *and* Truant

Passage A *Read the extract and poem. Then answer the questions.*

Billy Caspar has been day-dreaming in class. The teacher, Mr Farthing, is annoyed by this and insists he recounts an anecdote.

'Right, now you can do some work for a change. You're going to tell us any story about yourself, the same as Anderson did.'

'I don't know any, Sir.'

'Well you can just stand there until you do.'

5 Mr Farthing began to pace across the space between the board and the desk.

'There's always somebody to spoil it. There's always someone you can't suit, who has to be awkward, who refuses to be interested in anything, someone like you, Casper.'

10 He pivoted round on one foot and thrust an arm out at Billy.

'I'm giving you two minutes to think of something lad, and if you haven't started then, the whole class is coming back at four!'

There was a general stiffening of backs and looking round wide-eyed, accompanied by grumbling and interspersed with eh's and threatening

15 encouragements.

'Come on, Billy.'

''Else tha dies.'

'Say owt.'

'If I've to come back I'll kill him.'

20 Billy tried to blink back the tears shining in his eyes.

'I'm waiting, Casper.'

Mr Farthing sat down and nudged back his jacket sleeve to look at his watch.

'We haven't got all day, Casper.'

25 'Tell him about thi hawk, Billy.'

'If anyone else calls out, it will be the last call he'll make! ... What hawk, Casper? ... Casper, I'm speaking to you.'

Billy continued to show Mr Farthing the top of his head.

'Look this way boy when I'm speaking to you.'

30 Billy looked up slowly.

'And stop sulking just because somebody says a few words to you! ...Now then, what's this about this hawk? What is it, a stuffed one?'

The shout of laughter from the class spilled the first tears on to Billy's face, and left Mr Farthing looking about in surprise at these opposing reactions to

35 his question.

'What's funny about that?'

Tibbut half stood up, placing the weight of his body on the desk top as he shot one arm up.

'Well, Tibbut?'

40 'He's got a hawk, Sir. It's a kestrel. He's mad about it. He never knocks about wi' anybody else now, he just looks after this hawk all t'time. He's crackers wi'it!'

Billy turned on him, the movement releasing a fresh head of tears into wobbly halting motion down his cheeks.

45 'It's better than thee anyday, Tibby!'

'I told you, Sir, he goes daft if you say owt about it.'

'Right, Casper, sit down.'

Billy sat down and wiped his cheeks on the shoulders of his jacket. Mr Farthing rested his elbows on his desk and tapped his teeth with his thumb nails, waiting for Billy to collect himself.

'Now then, Billy, tell me about this hawk. Where did you get it from?'

'Found it.'

'Where?'

'In t'wood.'

'What had happened to it? Was it injured or something?'

'It was a young'un. It must have tumbled from a nest.'

'And how long have you had it?'

'Since last year.'

'All that time? Where do you keep it?'

'In a shed.'

'And what do you feed it on?'

'Beef. Mice. Birds.'

'Isn't it cruel though, keeping it in a shed all the time? Wouldn't it be happier flying free?'

Billy looked at Mr Farthing for the first time since he had told him to sit down.

'I don't keep it in t'shed all t'time. I fly it every day.'

'And doesn't it fly away. I thought hawks were wild birds.'

''Course it don't fly away. I've trained it.'

Billy look round, as though daring anyone to challenge this authority.

'Trained it? I thought you'd to be an expert to train hawks.'

'Well I did it.'

'Was it difficult?'

''Course it was. You've to be right…right patient wi' 'em and take your time.'

'Well tell me how you did it then. I've never met a falconer before, I suppose I must be in select company.'

Billy hutched his chair up and leaned forward over his desk.

'Well what you do is, you train 'em through their stomachs. You can only do owt wi' 'em when they're hungry, so you do all your training at feeding time.

'I started training Kes after I'd had her about a fortnight, when she was hard penned, that means her tail feathers and wing feathers had gone hard at their bases. You have to use a torch at night and keep inspecting 'em. It's easy if you're quiet, you just go up to her as she's roosting, and spread her tail and wings. If t'feathers are blue near t'bottom o' t'shaft, that means there's blood in 'em an' they're still soft, so they're not ready yet. When they're white and hard then they're ready, an' you can start training her then.

'Kes wa' as fat as a pig though at first. All young hawks are when you first start to train 'em, and you can't do much wi' 'em 'til you've got their weight down. You've to be ever so careful though, you don't just starve 'em, you weigh 'em before every meal and gradually cut their food down, 'til you go in one time an' she's keen, an' that's when you start getting somewhere. I could tell wi' Kes, she jumped straight on my glove as I held it towards her. So while she wa' feeding I got hold of her jesses an'…'

'Her what?'

'Jesses.'

'Jesses. How do you spell that?'

Mr Farthing stood up and stepped back to the board.

100   'Er, J-E-S-S-E-S.'

As Billy enunciated each letter, Mr Farthing linked them together on the blackboard.

'Jesses. And what are jesses, Billy?'

They're little leather straps that you fasten round its legs as soon as you get
105   it. She wears these all t'time, and you get hold of 'em when she sits on your glove. You push your swivel through...'

'Whoa! Whoa'

Mr Farthing held up his hands as though Billy were galloping towards him.

'You'd better come out here and give us a demonstration. We're not all
110   experts you know.'

Billy stood up and walked out, taking up position at the side of Mr Farthing's desk. Mr Farthing reared his chair on to its back legs, swivelled it sideways on one leg, then lowered it on to all fours facing Billy.

'Right, off you go.'

From *A Kestrel for a Knave* by Barry Hines

149

Passage B   *Truant*

A truant from the paths of everyday
This boy is wise
Beyond his ten years' learning
His books are blue and green from the world's outside
5 A schoolroom window – there his maps unroll
Beyond the cloth bound limit of a teacher's soul.

With hands in his pockets thoughts deep sunk in
    dreams.
Of taking flight as unpredictable
As thistledown,
10 He sings his vagrant way along the stream.

O sing a song of sunlight,
My pockets full of sky,
A starling's egg for April,
Jay's feathers for July,
15 And here's a thorn bush three bags full
Of drift white wool

They call him dunce and yet he can discern
Each mouse brown bird,
And call its name and whistle back its call,
20 And spy among the fern
Delicate movement of a furred
Fugitive creature hiding from the day.
Ecstatic secrets magnify his play
Into a rare vocation,
25 Laughing at education,
He knows where the redshank hides her nest, perceives
A reed patch tremble where a coat lays seige.

To water territory
One day on winter's fringe he sees
30 A flight of buttercups startling a bank
With spring before the season.

Back in the clasroom he can never find
An answer, and the blackboard, blank and blind
With dusty questions, baffles each reply
35 He stumbles through his sums and cannot see
For his books are printed on the earth and sky.

Phoebe Hesketh

1 Look at lines 1-12. What will happen to the class if Billy can't come up with a story? (2)

2 Look at lines 13-19. Explain how the class reacted to this threat. (3)

3 Why do you think Billy is so upset? (3)

4 How do the class feel about Billy's kestrel? (3)

5 How and where did he find the kestrel? (2)

6 Explain what is meant by the term 'hard penned' (line 83). (2)

7 How do falconers begin to train kestrels? (5)

Questions on passage B

1 Why is the poem called 'Truant'? (3)

2 What do you think the poet means when she says, 'his books are blue and green from the world's outside' (line 4)? What do the two colours represent? (3)

3 Look up the word 'vagrant' (line 11) in a dictionary. Why do you think the poet uses this word to describe the boy's movements? (4)

4 The verse that begins 'O sing a song of sunlight' (line 11) is a parody – that is, a copy of something else. What is the verse copying? (2)

5 In what ways does the poet suggest the boy's cleverness? (6)

Look at both passages

Using information given in the extracts, what do you think these boys have in common? (12)

Total Marks   50

Now let's write

Assignment 1   Write an essay about a child who is interested in some way in animals or nature.

Assignment 2   Why don't schools suit children like those mentioned in the extracts? What could schools do to encourage them?

Assignment 3   Imagine you are Billy in Passage A or the child in Passage B. As an adult you are recounting to a friend your experiences of school and your outdoor activities. What type of things might remain vividly in your memory?

Section 3 Gunner Milligan *and* The Lantern-Floating Festival

Passage A The author of this extract, Spike Milligan, is writing about an incident that took place during the Second World War. Spike Milligan is referred to as 'The Milligan' or 'Gunner Milligan'.

Read the extract and poem. Then answer the questions.

The Milligan had suffered from his legs terribly, during the war in Italy. While his mind was full of great heroisms under shell fire, his legs were carrying the idea, at speed, in the opposite direction. The Battery Major had not understood.

5 'Gunner Milligan? You have acted like a coward!'

'No sir, not true. I'm a hero wid coward's legs. I'm a hero from the waist up.'

'Silence! Why did you leave your post?'

'It had wormwood in it sir; the roof of the trench was falling in.'

10 'Silence! You acted like a coward!'

'I wasn't acting, sir!'

'I could have you shot!'

'Shot? Why didn't they shoot me in peacetime? I was still the same coward.'

15 'Men like you are a waste of time in war. Understand?'

'Oh! Well den, men like you are waste of time in peace.'

'Silence when you speak to an officer,' shouted the Sgt. Major at Milligan's neck.

All his arguments were of no avail in the face of military authority. He was 20 court-martialled, surrounded by clanking top brass who were not cowards and therefore biased.

'I may be a coward, I'm not denying dat, sir,' Milligan told the prosecution. 'But you can't really blame me for being a coward. If I am, then you might as well hold me responsible for the shape of my nose, the colour 25 of me hair and the size of me feet.'

'Gunner Milligan,' Captain Martin stroked a cavalry moustache on an infantry face. 'Gunner Milligan,' he said, 'your personal evaluations of cowardice do not concern the court. To refresh your memory, I will read the precise military defination of the word.' He took a book of King's 30 Regulations, opened a marked page and read 'Cowardice'. Here he paused and gave Milligan a look. He continued:

'Defection in the face of the enemy. Running away.'

'I was not running away, sir. I was retreatin'.'

'The whole of your regiment were advancing, and you decided to retreat?'

35 'Isn't dat what you call personal initiative?'

'Your action might have caused your comrades to panic and retreat.'

'Oh, I see. One man retreating is called running away, but a whole regiment running away is called a retreat! I demand to be tried by cowards.'

A light, commissioned-ranks-only laugh passed round the court. But this 40 was no laughing matter. These lunatics could have him shot.

'Have you anything further to add?' asked Captain Martin.

'Yes,' said Milligan, 'plenty. For one thing I had no desire to partake in

this war. I was dragged in. I warned the medical officer, I told him I was a coward and he marked me A1 for active service. I gave everyone fair
45 warning. I told me Battery Major before it started. I even wrote to Field-Marshall Montgomery. Yes, I warned everybody and now you're all acting surprised?'

Even as Milligan spoke his mind, three non-cowardly judges made a mental note of guilty.

From *Adolf Hitler, My Part in his Downfall* by Spike Milligan

Passage B   The festival described in the poem takes place every year in Japan. The paper lanterns represent the loved ones who died in the nuclear attack on Japan.

The Lantern-Floating Festival

The paper lanterns are sold by old women, little children
at stalls along the willows along the crowded river bank.

Long oblongs of paper – red, green, yellow, dusted with gold,
hastily inscribed with brush and watery Chinese ink –
crammed with the characters of names, prayers, poems and messages.

The papers are fastened round upright struts like cheap chopsticks
that are fixed at the ends of a cross of laths, the lantern's floats.
At the heart of the cross, a small candle stuck on a nail.

The mourners write their poems, light their candles. The lanterns' colours,
ambered by the little flame, delicate and pure.

They are borne carefully, the lanterns for the dead, in both hands,
as if the bearers were holding a precious fluid, a fragile treasure,
or the very soul of someone loved, someone still loved –
borne before them in praying hands, with the respect
that is the only proof of memory, of former life.

Those who are remembering the dead
stand in long lines on the dark shore
and crowd together on the steep steps of unlighted stone, souls
waiting for waftage on the altar and embankment of the grieving river.

The small flames beat like moths, like hearts,
or heave like sighs, like human breath in last release
within the paper shells frail as their bearers.

At the river's quiet verge, whose dark water laps
the steps leading down into its darkening sky,
the summer mourners crouch in blue and white cotton clothes, simple,
thin feet on worn wooden patterns.

One careless virgin flusters her flame, and
the entire lantern flares in an instant,
singeing the sleeves of neighbours.

153

Her loved one's name,
hastily written in gathering darkness
with a wretched brush and weak ink
is obliterated, as he was, by a flash of fire.

Some have inscribed the name of a cat,
a pet rabbit, a tame rat,
a dog who did not come home,
a canary, a grasshopper, a cicada,
a child's summer insect in a bamboo cage, now ash.

All crouch, do not kneel,
but with murmured prayers to Buddha
and sometimes
the chime of a tiny portable gong
gently launch their lighted craft,
wafting them softly away from the bank
with cheap scented paper fans
or hands rippling the water
in beckoning gestures of farewell,
in farewell gestures, beckoning
the dead to the living, that they may return,
if only in a dream,
and speak their peace.

The air fogged with incense
and the surges of dumb temple gongs
shroud us all, shroud
the lanterns that cling to the banks, refuse
to leave the life they could not hate
for what perhaps may be an even deeper misery.

The lanterns cluster stubbornly like set jewels, or
a stiff arrangement of flowers
reflected in the gleaming ripples,
and will not budge.

No breath of wind, no current takes them.
Their unwillingness to go is human, their persistence spectral.
Only two – who are they, who were they? –
for some reason leave the banks and float, lighted still,
downstream, to negotiate the arches of a bridge – but then
founder, flicker, flutter, extinguished on a sudden bend ...

Now whole fleets of lanterns
like battling argosies
lock together, and one,
bursting into flame,
ignites a chain of paper sails –
meaningless reaction, meaningless cause and
meaningless effect: just so does nuclear death
rob death of its one distinction –
a meaning.

No one weeps
and no one smiles.
All are part of Buddha nature,
the Buddha
that neither smiles nor weeps.

But in this festival of ghosts,
who are the apparitions, who
the living?

These survivors,
freaks of destiny,
are they still human?
Do they burn with a flame
of healthy blood?

Or are they also spectres,
floating lighted lanterns
in memory of themselves?

– I pass among them,
a stranger,
outsider,
unnoticed as a ghost.

James Kirkup

Questions on passage A

1 What arguments does Milligan use to defend himself? (10)

2 What do you as the reader find humorous about the passage? (15)

Questions on passage B

1 Explain in your own words exactly what you have learnt about the lantern-floating festival? (10)

2 How does the poet convey the sadness of the ceremony and the people who attend it through the words of the poem? (15)

Look at both passages

Although the Milligan extract is funny on the surface, it has a deeper and more serious meaning. What would you say were the serious comments being made about war in *both* extracts? (10)

Total Marks   60

Now let's write

Assignment 1

The writer of the poem feels strongly about his subject. Choose a subject that you feel strongly about and write a poem or an essay on it.

Assignment 2

Imagine that you were at either Milligan's court martial or the lantern festival and write an article for a newspaper describing the events.

Assignment 3

Write an humorous story about a serious subject, as Spike Milligan has done.

7 Non-Fiction

Section 1   A Chip off the Old Block

Read the extract. Then answer the questions.

A chip off the old block

TEENAGER Paul Patino and pensioner Vic Martin are over half a century apart in age, and might as well be light years apart in outlook. But they share the stigma of belonging to Britain's two forgotten generations.

And now, after being dragged back from their respective corners of the social security net, they share something else: a common pride in reviving a dying skill.

The unlikely pair are part of a unique effort being made in Halewood, Merseyside, to restore the cabinet-making and marquetry, the polishing and carving which were prized skills in Liverpool in the days of the wooden ships.

The experiment is suitably centred in a 16th-century farmhouse, where outbuildings have been converted to workshops in which apprentices stir aromatic glue made from melted-down horse-hooves. Downstairs, craftsmen use old polishing techniques and marquetry cutters burn colours into the 17th and 18th-century reproduction furniture which is the firm's end-product.

For Paul and Vic the enterprise represents rescue from a living death. Paul, 19, faced a lifetime on the dole; now he has proved himself to be an extraordinarily skilled woodcarver and is unlikely ever to be idle. Vic, 67, faced the rest of his life on pension, but has now come out of retirement to pass on his carving skills to boys young enough to be his grandchildren.

Behind the renaissance is David Simpson, a third-generation cabinet-maker who is the boss of Gostins, the firm running the scheme. He exports 80% of his products and has a 14-month waiting-list.

But he was only able to get the firm going by bringing craftsmen out of retirement, and this made him acutely aware of the need to refill Merseyside's pool of skills. And what more logical than that the old should pass on the skills to the wasted generation of school-leavers?

For the last three years, he has taken highly-qualified school-leavers on six-month Youth Opportunity Programme placements. The keenest have been taken on as apprentices.

For years, Simpson has had a vision of a training school offering first-class training in furniture-making skills to 100 young people. That dream will be realised shortly when a disused textile warehouse in Halewood reopens as a workshop.

Chris Tighe

Source: *The Guardian.*

156

1 How large an age difference is there between the two men? (2)

2 Look at paragraph 2. What two things do the two men have in common? (2)

3 Look at paragraph 3. Why have the two men been brought together? (3)

4 Look at paragraphs 3 and 4. What type of skills can people learn on the course? (3)

5 Who set up the project and how has it helped Paul and Vic? (4)

6 Would you say the venture was a successful one? Give reasons for your answer. (4)

7 Choose four of the following and explain their meaning in your own words. (8)

'unlikely pair' (line 14)
'aromatic glue' (line 26)
'reproduction furniture' (line 32)
'third generation cabinet maker' (line 48)
'out of retirement' (line43)
'end-product' (line 33)

8 Give words similar in meaning to four of the following. (4)

'apprentice' (line 68)
'vision' (line 70)
'disused' (line 74)
'unique' (line 15)
'textiles' (line 75)
'skill' (line 13)

9 The article says that Paul and Vic 'are over half a century apart in age, and might as well be light years apart in outlook' (lines 2-5). What do you think the author means by this? (4)

10 Where and how was this project set up? What benefits has it had and will it have for the people in the community?
Give reasons for your answer. (6)

11 Imagine that Paul and Vic are being interviewed on the radio about their work. What do you think they would say about the project itself and how it has benefited them? Consider the way in which old people and young people are involved. (10)

Total Marks   50

Now let's write

Assignment 1   Many people are currently unemployed. What do you think it must feel like not to have a job? Write about this giving reasons for your feelings.

Assignment 2   Write about someone who has special skills like Vic Martin. Show how they might benefit the community.

Assignment 3   Many areas are using schools not only in the day but also in the evening. They are using them as community centres. How could your school be used outside school hours to benefit the area you live in?

Section 2 Nazi Secrets Die with a Spy

This extract mentions the term 'collaborators'. A collaborator is someone who works with someone else on a project. In this case the collaborators were Swedish people who, in spite of their country's neutrality, worked with the Germans during the last war. Some of them turned on their fellow countrymen and in some cases were responsible for their deaths.

Read the extract. Then answer the questions.

Nazi secrets die with a spy

MANY OF the most respectable families in Sweden breathed a lot easier last week when they read in the obituary columns of the death in the South of France of a man called Eric Erickson, at the age of 92.

For he knew secrets that could have toppled business empires and disgraced men
5 still revered in Swedish history books as great political figures.

Erickson was a spy for the allies during the Second World War, the only man in possession of a list of Swedish Nazi collaborators. The list
10 included men who would have run a quisling government had Hitler invaded; the men who used their influence to supply the German munitions industry with Swedish iron ore
15 throughout the war and to allow German Troop and munitions trains to pass through their 'neutral' country en route to occupied Norway.

It was former President
20 Eisenhower who persuaded Erickson not to make his list public. 'Ike said it would do more harm than good,' said Erickson in an interview in 1972, 'and I went along with him.'
25 He was the hero of Alexander Klein's best-selling book *The Counterfeit Traitor*, later made into a film starring William Holden. No one knew more about the grim realities of
30 life as a spy in the Third Reich.

Erickson was born in Brooklyn, New York, of Swedish parents but took Swedish nationality in the 1930s while working in the country as rep-
35 resentative of an American oil company. Most of his business was transacted in Germany and at the outbreak of hostilities he offered his services as an agent to the American Embassy in
40 Stockholm. His cover was that he was a fanatical Nazi.

It enabled him to be on first name terms with Himmler and Goering and to provide U.S. intelligence with the
45 information that pinpointed targets for allied bombing raids which were to cripple the German war effort. The cost to Erickson personally was enormous. At the Moabit prison in
50 Berlin he was forced by a Gestapo officer, who suspected him, to watch the execution of his lover, a girl called Marianne.

'They wanted to get me to reveal
55 myself,' he said. 'But I managed to betray nothing and pretended not to know her. That moment was the bitterest in my life.'

Between 1939 and 1945 he made thirty-one trips to Germany establishing an espionage network bringing back information. Because of his reputation as a Nazi he was able to travel freely and was granted privileges denied to other foreigners. These included a signed letter of introduction from Himmler. 'I loathed fascism and that is why I fought it like I did,' he said, 'there was no adventure in it.'

Towards the end of the war on a train to Leipzig he encountered a man he had known years before, a genuine Nazi fanatic. The man suspected Erickson, always strongly anti-Hitler in their pre-war conversations. When the train arrived the Swede followed his travelling companion who made straight for the nearest phone booth. Erickson killed him with his bare hands as he dialled Gestapo headquarters.

The Counterfeit Traitor himself died a natural death, still the taciturn, soft-spoken guardian of a secret that would have shaken Swedish society to its foundations.

Source: *The Observer*, January 1983.

Questions

1 Look at paragraph 1. Where did Erickson die? (2)

2 Some people 'breathed a lot easier' (line 1) when he died. Why was this so? (2)

3 What information did Erickson have about Nazi collaborators? (3)

4 Give three reasons for Erickson's suitability as a spy for the Americans? (3)

5 How did Erickson get to know the top Nazis? (2)

6 In what ways was Erickson successful and useful as a spy? (5)

7 You are Erickson. Describe, in your own words, the worst moment of your life and your feelings at the time. (5)

8 Using the passage to help you, give the meaning of the following three phrases. (6)

'obituary columns' (line 2)
'establishing an espionage network' (line 60)
'a secret that would have shaken Swedish society to its foundations' (line 85).

9 Would you say that Erickson's life was at risk at any time during the war? Give reasons. (5)

10 This is a newspaper report. Do you think that affects the way it has been written and set out? How has the writer made the article interesting and easy to read? (7)

Total Marks   40

Now let's write

Assignment 1   Write a story set in war-time about a family or a group of people. It could be set in a country that has been taken over by the enemy.

Try to imagine what it is like during a war.

What type of things may be difficult to get?

How does a landscape change?

What does the population look like? Where are the young men?

Assignment 2   Interview someone who was alive during the war about their life in war-time Britain. Imagine that it will be used as part of an interview for TV. Write up the script you would use for the programme.

Look at the interview included as an example on page 211 of Chapter 12.

Assignment 3   The life of a spy is never as glamorous as it is made out to be. Write a story about a real-life spy like Erickson who at some point is in danger of his life. It can be based on fiction or fact.

What qualities does a spy need?

What type of personality does he or she need?

Try to imagine what fear is like. How does it affect you physically and mentally?

Read the poem 'Guilty Conscience' on page 121. It shows you how fear can play on the mind. It makes you imagine things that are not there because every particle of your body is alert to danger.

Section 3 The Royal West Show

Study the diagram and chart. Then answer the questions.

Royal West Show

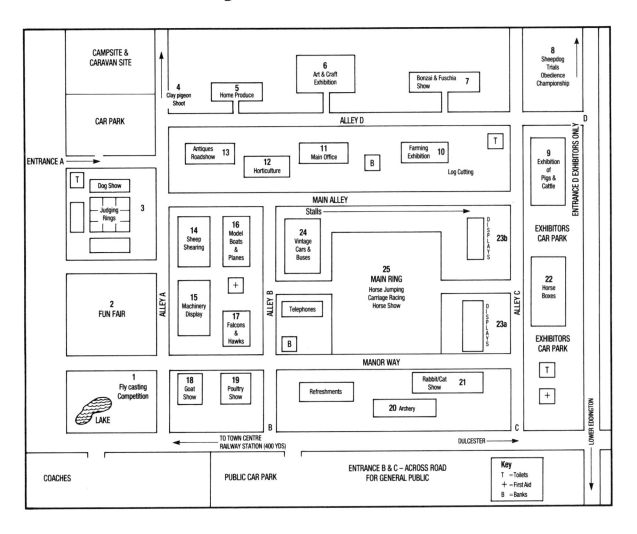

Alphabetical list of events at the Royal West Show

	Thursday	Friday	Saturday
Antiques Road Show	√	√	√
Archery	√ D	√ D	√ D/C
Art and Craft	√ De 12-3.00pm	√ De 12-3.00pm	√ De 12-3.00pm
Bonzais and Fuschias	√ D	√ D	√ De 2-4.00pm
Cat Show	X	X	√
Clay Pigeon	X	X	√ C
Dog Show (Championship)	√ J = all 3 days	√	√
Falcons and Hawks	√ D	√ D	√ D/C
Fly Casting	√ De 1pm	√ D 1pm	√ De 1pm/C
Goat Show	√ D	√ J all day	√ J all day
Home Produce	√ D	√ D	√ C/D
Horses*: Carriage Racing	√	X	X
Jumping	X	√	X
Showing	X	X	√
Horticulture	√ J 9.30am/D	√ D	√ D
Machinery	√ D	√ D	√ D
Obedience Championship	X	X	√ C
Pigs and Cattle	√ J all day	√ J	√ D
Poultry	√ D/J 9.30am	√	√
Rabbits	√ J 9.30am	X	X
Radio Controlled Boats and Planes	√ De all day	√ De all day	√ De all day
Sheepdog Trials	√ J all day	X	X
Sheep Shearing	X	√ C	X
Traditional Farming	X	√ C	√ De 1-3.00pm/D
Vintage Cars and Buses	√	√	√
Special Attractions**			
Fox and Hounds	√ De 3.00pm	√ De 3.00pm	√ De 3.00pm
Falconry Display	X	√ De 4.30pm	√ De 4.30pm
Fun Fair	√	√	√
Parade of Champions	X	X	√ De 4.00pm
Police Dogs/Horses	√ D 4.00pm	√ De 4.00pm	X
Red Devils	√ De 3.30pm	√ De 3.30pm	√ De 3.30pm
Vintage Cars and Buses	√ De 4.30pm	√ De 5.00pm	√ De 5.00pm

KEY:

√	: Present	D	: Display on view
X	: Absent	De	: Demonstration times
J	: Judging time	*	Horse events in main ring till 3.00
C	: Competition in progress	**	Special attractions ALL in main ring

Questions

1 On what days and at what times are the following being judged?

   a) Dogs   c) Goats
   b) Pigs and Cattle   d) Rabbits. (4)

2 At what times and on what days would you be able to see a demonstration of the following.

   a) Art and Craft   b) Fly Casting   c) Bonzais and Fuschias (3)

3 On what days would it be possible to see the Falcons and Carriage Racing? (2)

4 Make an itinerary for the first day so that you would see all the following. (An itinerary is a plan of the places you are going to visit and the times at which you will visit them.)

   Archery; Fly Casting; Carriage Racing; Fox and Hounds; Red Devils; Vintage Cars; Antiques Road Show. (3)

5 Make a list of all the events for which competitors are organised. (3)

6 Make a list of all the events and special attractions not taking place on day 1. (3)

7 Devise an itinerary and map a route for day 3 that would enable you to see all the attractions that provide demonstrations. (6)

8 Devise a route that would enable you to visit the show on the second day and see all of the following at the correct time but wouldn't involve you in too much walking.

   Archery; Goat Show; Sheep Shearing; Show Jumping; the Fun Fair; Red Devils; Vintage Cars; Sheepdog Trials; Home Produce; Horticulture. (6)

9 Design a leaflet publicising the date and venue of the show and its main attractions. (10)

Total Marks   40

Section 4 Channel Link

The following assignments are based on specimen material produced by the Midland Examining Group.

Three different kinds of channel link between England and France have been put forward for consideration. The alternatives are presented below:

Assignment 1 Using these notes and the diagrams write an account of the three proposals which brings out the differences and the similarities between them.

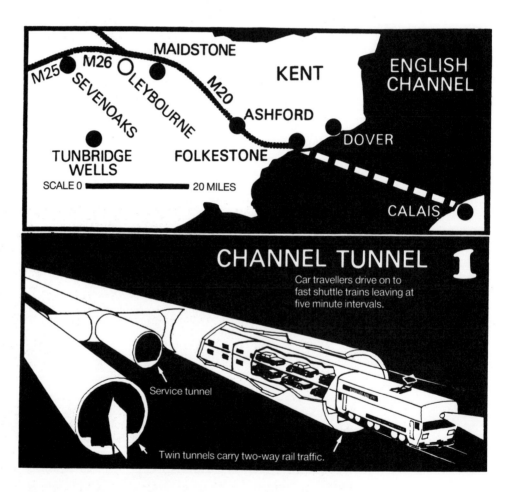

Channel Tunnel: A £2.6 billion twin-bore rail tunnel scheme. British Rail and SNCF trains would share the tunnel with a drive-on/drive-off shuttle service. Backed by Balfour Beatty, Costain, Granada Group, Midland Bank, National Westminster Bank, Tarmac, Taylor Woodrow, and Wimpey.
Due to open in 1992-3.

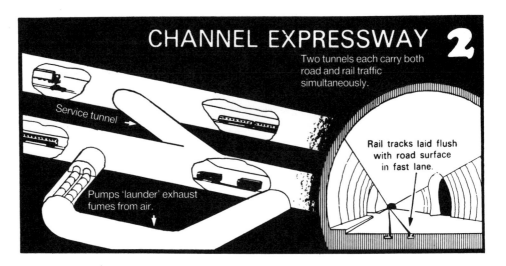

Channel Expressway: £2.5 billion twin-bore tunnels, each of which will carry both road and rail traffic. The project is the brainchild of Mr James Sherwood, who runs Sea Containers which would fund the project with help from Credit du Nord in France and First National Bank of Boston.
Due to open in 1991.

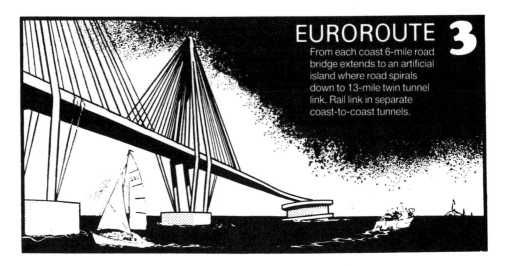

Euroroute: A £5.6 billion bridge and tunnel road and rail scheme, backed by Trafalgar House, British Steel, British Telecom, British Shipbuilders, and Barclays Bank. Motorway bridges from both coasts would connect with a submerged concrete tube tunnel at two man-made islands in the English Channel. Two separate rail tunnels are also on offer.
Roadway due to open 1993.

Source: *The Guardian*

Assignment 2 Study these seven extracts from a newspaper article and decide what you think is a reasonable order.
Then write a brief summary in your own words of the points which the article puts forward and in the order you have chosen. You should aim to write about 150 words.

In 1974 tunnelling work actually began at sites near Dover and Calais, only to be abandoned on environmental grounds after a fierce campaign by Kent villagers. Now, several false starts and mountains of research effort later a Channel link looks certain to be constructed.

Ironically, the one question which has yet to be answered is whether the link will make it cheaper to cross the Channel. Journeys will certainly be quicker – 30 minutes by rail shuttle or driving, against 50 minutes by ferry – with speedier customs facilities. But the rival groups have merely indicated that they will be competitive with ferry fares when a link opens in 1992-3.

The stakes are high. Mr Sherwood, whose Sea Containers group owns the Sealink ferry business, says that the ferry business will be forced to close down if a fixed link is built. 'I've got to win,' he said. 'Otherwise I will be out of business.'

The sudden enthusiasm for a project which has been on the shelf for so long is easily explained. Britain and France are wracked by unemployment which will be a key issue in forthcoming elections in both countries. President Mitterrand has his eye on the French parliamentary elections next March. Mrs Thatcher is already planning for 1987, when she has to go to the polls again.

The idea that a tunnel should link England and France was first suggested by Napoleon nearly two hundred years ago. The proposal was turned down by Britain for security reasons. It was feared that Napoleon would send French troops through the tunnel to invade Britain.

Big business is also champing at the bit to win a slice of the Channel action. The three main contenders to build a link – Channel Expressway, Channel Tunnel Group, and EuroRoute – have already invested tens of millions of pounds in the battle to build the link.

The threat of terrorist attack on a link, the risk of rabies spreading from the Continent, and a welter of other considerations have figured prominently in the debate. But not once has the risk of invasion by French troops been mentioned as a serious option. That, perhaps, is what they call progress.

Source: *The Guardian.*

Assignment 3 Some people are opposed to the building of a fixed channel link. Here are some handwritten notes made by an opponent of the scheme who is worried about the effects which it will have on the environment. Study them carefully and then write ONE of the following.

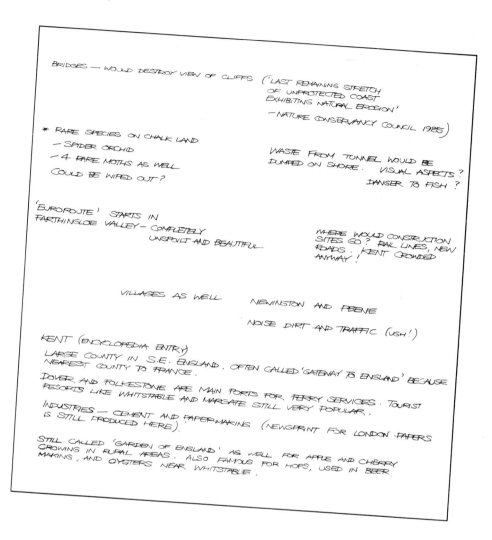

1 A letter to the Editor of *The Dover Gazette* opposing the scheme on environmental grounds.

2 A leaflet to be issued by Friends of the Earth to households in the area, putting these points to local people.

3 A speech to be made at a public inquiry to discuss the proposals.

4 A reply to these arguments suggesting that there are other points to be considered in favour of a fixed link. You can write this as either a speech or a letter to the newspaper.

Part Three

Communication

General Introduction

Communication is the transmission of information. There are various ways in which information may be transmitted – directly from person to person through conversation or indirectly through the medium of radio, television, via satellite, through newspapers, magazines, etc. These various means or ways of communication are known collectively as 'the media' (the plural of medium).

The richness of our language becomes obvious when we think about the different shades of meaning a word can have. Take the word 'smart' for instance. 'That's a smart suit' would indicate one thing but if you were to say 'I always knew he was smart and now he's got a good job to prove it' the meaning would be altogether different.

A word can have various meanings – firstly the meanings found in the dictionary – the standard meanings. Secondly, the meaning that we sometimes give to it, which is dependent on the way we use the word and where we use it – this is called the contextual meaning. For example, 'He looks cool' has two possible meanings. Do you know what they could be?

Not only do words have different shades of meaning but they also have different associations, some good, some not so good. For instance, if someone referred to you as 'slim' you would probably take it as a compliment. However, if they were to call you 'skinny', this would not be as well received. This is because the word 'slim' has pleasant associations for people but the word 'skinny' has not.

The people involved in the media are well aware of the emotive or emotion-arousing power of our language and use it to their best advantage. A headline or an advertisement which fails to catch the eye of a buyer is useless since the newspaper and the product will remain on the shelf.

Look at advertisements and newspaper headlines, read press reports and listen to the news on radio and television and you will have begun to study the art of media communcation. If possible, see how different newspapers cover the same events on the same day. You may also find advertisements for the same product in different newspapers or magazines. Has the advertiser used different language to appeal to a different audience?

Think about the language you use when you communicate directly with people. It is likely that even though you may tell your teacher and your school friends the same story you will use different language to communicate with them. A little more formal communication with your teacher and more informal chat with your friends.

8 Newspapers

Introduction

There are currently three main types of newspaper on sale in Britain today. National, provincial and local newspapers. National newspapers are sold across the nation, provincial newspapers in a large area, possibly covering a few counties, and local newspapers are sold in a district.

Large sums of money are required to keep newspapers in print. They may be financed by advertisers who buy space in order to advertise a product and by the public who buy copies of the newspaper. (Obviously the more people who buy the paper, the more likely it is that an advertiser will wish to use the paper for advertising purposes.)

Not all newspapers are financed in this way – a few are free newspapers. Free newspapers survive on revenue from advertising alone and are distributed free to the public. This can be attractive to advertisers who want as many people as possible to read about their product.

National and local newspapers differ in the type of news they include. Similarly, some of the national newspapers differ in their choice of the news they carry and in the way they present the same event. Discuss as a class why this might be.

Golden Rules

1   Your newspaper reports must be understood, without any problem, by readers.

2   When you write a report for a newspaper include a good headline. It should be eye-catching both to look at and in the language used. The aim is to capture a reader's attention and make him/her want to read the whole story.

3   Headlines sometimes have a double meaning, are witty, or use alliteration to interest a potential reader.

4   Newspaper articles get to the point of the story as quickly and as dramatically as possible.

5   Sometimes photographs are used to good effect in newspapers. Although you may not always be able to include a photograph you might draw a picture to help your report look more realistic.

6   Newspaper stories sometimes include interviews. If you decide to include any, make sure that you use inverted commas to enclose the words *actually* spoken by those interviewed. This is direct speech. Reported speech (indirect speech) is also used in newspapers and this is always written in the past tense. Read some reports and see if you can spot the use of both direct and indirect speech.

Section 1 Local Newspapers

Introduction

Local newspapers are written and produced for a certain area. They may be paid for or free. You possibly know of one that is distributed in your area.

Assignment 1 Make a list of the local newspapers that are circulated in your area. Find out the numbers that are sold or distributed free and how wide an area they circulate in.

Assignment 2 Some local newspapers were established at least a century ago and are famous throughout the country. Find out what you can about some of them.

Group work You will need to be in groups for all the following assignments and to have access to some local newspapers.

Assignment 3 Look at your local newspapers. As a group discuss and write down the type of news that is reported in them.

What sort of news do they carry?

How often are they printed?

Does this affect the news they contain?

Do they have advertisements in them?

Do they include any national news, foreign news, sport, gossip?

Are there any special pages for young people?

Assignment 4 Conduct a survey to find out how many pupils' parents buy a local newspaper. Try to find out why their parents buy it, when they buy it and which members of the household read it. Find out if it is delivered. Find out, at the same time, what national newspaper they buy. Discuss your findings as a class.

Devise a simple questionnaire that people can answer simply by ticking boxes.

Make the questions as straightforward as possible.

Get as much information as you can from the people questioned.

Is there any pattern emerging? Do the people who buy a certain national newspaper also buy the local paper?

Assignment 5 Make a list of any newspapers that are delivered free to your door. How many are there? What type are they? What do they contain? Discuss why the publishers might have decided to distribute them without charge as opposed to selling them.

Section 2 National Newspapers

Introduction

National newspapers are distributed throughout the nation. Some appear on weekdays only; some are also produced on Sundays, though the format for the Sunday newspaper often differs from that of the week-day paper.

If you look at the various newspapers on sale you will find a marked difference between them. This applies not just to the shape of the papers but also to their content.

Group work You will need to be in groups for this work and every group will need to have access to as wide a variety of national newspapers as possible.

Assignment 1 Make a list of all the national newspapers you can think of. Try to find out when they were established and how many copies are sold daily.

Assignment 2 Make a table similar to the one shown. Write the name of a national newspaper (one of the ones you have) above each column.

In groups, study each paper in turn and complete the columns in your table. When you have finished with a paper pass it on to the next group.

National Newspapers, Content and Format

Details of Newspaper	Name of Newspaper			
Price				
Format				
Number of pages				
Number of stories on front page				
Amount of space for home news				
Amount of space for foreign news				
Amount of space for reviews				
Amount of space for TV/radio				
Amount of space for sport				
Number of pages or space for advertisements				
Amount of space for special sections e.g. women's page/horoscopes				
Amount of space for crosswords				
Amount of space for Letters to the Editor				

Assignment 3 Some people feel that the national newspapers can be grouped according to their content. Using the grid to help you, would you say this was true? If so, decide which papers you would group together and why.

Do all the newspapers carry the same kind of news?

Do some concentrate on a particular type of news?

Do some have more news than others?

How does the format of the papers vary? Does a particular format seem to go with a particular style of reporting.

Assignment 4 Conduct a survey in the school asking what newspapers are read by pupils' parents. Find out which paper is the most popular. Why do you think this is so? Discuss the findings of your survey in class.

Assignment 5 Many people complain that newspapers are not always to be trusted in the way they present the news. Look at your daily papers carefully and discuss as a group any stories that you feel may not have been reported accurately. Look for the type of story that is biased in favour of one side against the other.

Can you find two events that are reported in two newspapers in totally different ways?

Why does this happen?

Assignment 6 As a group discuss and make a note of the ways in which local newspapers differ from national newspapers.

Think about why there is a difference. Consider the readership and their needs.

How often do national and local newspapers appear?

Who would read each type of newspaper?

Think about the content of each type of newspaper. What information would you look for in each type?

Section 3   The Front Page

Introduction

Probably the most important part of a newspaper is its front page. Like the cover of a book, it is the first thing people see and it aims to attract their attention through the use of pictures and headlines.

Headlines use simple, hard-hitting language. Long words are generally avoided so that 'negotiations' would probably become 'talks'. Headlines invite curiosity and are intended to whet the reader's appetite for the article or news item which follows.

The headlines are not made up by the journalists who write the news items but by a sub-editor who decides how the pages are going to be laid out and where each item will appear. The sub-editor will decide whether the headline should go across the whole page, across two or three columns or if it should be two lines in one column, for example, and will make up a headline accordingly.

The language used by newspapers may be direct, or matter-of-fact, or it may be emotive and try to arouse an emotional response in the reader. The type of language used will depend on what is being reported. An item about the value of the pound against the dollar will be factual whereas an item about an abandoned baby will generally use 'moving' or emotive language.

Assignment 1   In groups, examine the front pages of four different newspapers published on the same day, then answer the questions in full.

a)   How much room is taken up by the headlines or headline?

b)   Is there only one story on the front page or are others covered or mentioned?

c)   Why have some newspapers got more stories than others on the front page?

d)   Does the front page mention stories that are contained inside? Why would it do this?

e)   How much room is devoted to photographs? Why are they used?

f)   In what ways do the front pages try to arouse the reader's curiosity or feelings?

g)   In what ways do the headlines shock the reader?

h)   List those headlines that rely mainly on their size to attract the reader.

i)   Discuss why the photographs attract attention.

j)   Why do you think the newspapers put these particular stories on the front page?

Assignment 2   Look at the three pictures and write a front page story with a headline to go with *one* of them.

Assignment 3   Look at these headlines and write a front page story to accompany one of them.

Britain's most <u>amazing</u> <u>love story</u>!

FLEEING THE FLAMES OF FURY

Tobacco target

THE YOBBO SEASON

Former champion jockey has cancer operation

Section 4 A School Newspaper

Introduction

Newspapers may be produced by other organisations including companies and schools. The material included is specific to the organisation and will therefore only appeal to a limited audience.

School newspapers include school news – information about school achievements, clubs, societies, community projects, and so on.

Assignment 1

Look at the sections and each page of various newspapers to see what information they contain.

As a class discuss what sections you would include in a school newspaper and make a list. You will need to cater for the interests of all the people who are likely to read it. In addition to general news you could include news about school societies and advertisements for them, perhaps. You could also include sections on sport, pop music, books, films and some reviews, plus crosswords and puzzles. Discuss what illustrations you could use to accompany the various topics.

Make a list of what items would be best together on a page – don't forget that a lot of the front page will be made up of pictures and headlines, information about what is inside, plus a list of contents, perhaps.

Assignment 2

Using your lists from Assignment 1, decide what format your newspaper will be and how many pages it will have. Then make a dummy copy, to actual size, discussing where each article will go, how much space it will occupy and whether there will be any illustrations. Put in provisional headlines for the main news items on each page. Make sure the dummy looks attractive and that it has a good balance of news and diversions.

Assignment 3

Decide which items and illustrations each person will produce. Everyone must contribute in some way to the school newspaper. Write a headline for each article and a caption for any pictures you produce.

There must be a deadline for the copy. That is, the date by which all the material must be complete so that the newspaper can be put together.

Make sure that your article fits the space allowed for it in the dummy copy. Write only on one side of the paper. Don't forget to use the appropriate type of language for the headlines and for the articles you are writing.

Assignment 4

Discuss what the final headlines will be. Then, using the dummy as a guide, make a paste-up of your school newspaper, inserting the articles you have written. Don't forget to add by-lines to the major articles. (A by-line is the name of the person who wrote the article.)

Finally ink in the headlines to make them stand out and draw clear lines to divide up the stories and other items. Make sure that it is obvious which picture goes with which news item and that all pictures have captions.

If the paste-up does not work out exactly it may be necessary to re-write a few stories. This is what newspaper production is all about!

Advertising

Introduction

Advertising is a means of imparting information. It is usually used to advertise a product which is for sale. However, advertising has many other functions. Often it is used to give information to the public. Governments make use of advertising to publicise their own particular politics. Local councils may use advertising to make known the time of elections and so on. You can no doubt think of many more ways in which advertising is used.

Advertisements are to be found in many different places. Think of the main street in your nearest town. Here you will find posters on hoardings, display advertisements in shop windows and advertisements on postcards in newsagents' windows.

Twentieth-century technology has enabled the advertiser to use not only magazines, newspapers and leaflets but also to penetrate directly into most homes through television and commercial radio. These, along with cinema advertising, have created a multi-million pound business.

Technology is advancing all the time and teletext, cable television, satellite television and video recorders will undoubtedly mean more outlets for the advertiser in future.

The income made from selling advertising time or space enables many newspapers, magazines, commercial radio stations and television stations to remain in existence.

Golden Rules

1 When you are designing an advertisement make the item or service you are selling as attractive as possible to the person who will be reading the advertisement.

2 Decide what approach you are going to use to attract a potential buyer. For instance, are you going to appeal to their desire to keep up with everyone else? Look carefully at the different approaches used by advertisers on pages 188-193.

3 Sometimes advertisements use slogans to attract attention. They may also make use of pictures rather than words to convey their messages.

4 The name chosen for a product is important and may affect sales. It is surprising how many times manufacturers change brand names because a product is not selling well. Sales may surge upwards when they hit on a new, popular name; the product they are selling is unchanged!

5 Some advertisements give a lot of information about the product they are selling. This is particularly true when a new product is launched or when a product is 'improved'.

6 Consider who is to buy your product. The age and sex of the buyer will affect the design of the advertisement. If you are trying to sell a product to elderly people, using a pop star to advertise your product may not encourage them to buy.

Section 1 What is Spent?

Newspapers, magazines, journals, TV, cinema and hoarding owners all sell advertising space to companies who wish to advertise their products.

DID YOU KNOW?

The world's biggest advertiser is Sears Roebuck and Co who spent £696 million in 1985 excluding money spent on its catalogue

The most conspicuous advertising sign ever was the electric sign for Citroën on the Eiffel Tower, Paris. It was switched on on 4 July 1925 and could be seen 24 miles away.

The largest 'hoarding' in Britain measures 226ft *68.9m* by 54ft *16.5m* and was produced by Forwardiar Ltd. The site is the roof of the Brentford Football Club stand, at its Griffin Park, Middlesex ground which is on the flight path of London, Heathrow airport. Britain's largest illuminated sign is the name NEI NUCLEAR SYSTEMS LTD extending 170ft 6in *52m* installed at their factory in Gateshead, Tyne and Wear, in June 1983. It can be seen from the air at a distance of 20 miles *32km*.

The highest TV advertising rate has been $550,000 per ½ min *(then £9,166 per sec)* for ABC network prime time during transmission of Super Bowl XIX on 19 Jan 1985.

In Great Britain the peak-time weekday 6o-second spot rate (5.40 – 10.40 pm) for Thames Television is £67,375 + VAT (May '86)

180

Source: *Guinness Book of Records* 1985.

Look at the tables which follow and study them carefully. They give
details of the advertising revenue received by the media from advertisers.

Table 1
Advertising revenue received by the media from the advertisers

	1975		1983	
	£m	%	£m	%
National newspapers	162	16.8	584	16.3
Regional newspapers	283	29.3	817	22.8
Magazines & periodicals	79	8.2	224	6.3
Trade & technical	86	8.9	276	7.7
Other	69	7.2	335	9.4
TOTAL PRESS	679	70.2	2236	62.5
TV	236	24.4	1109	31.0
Poster & transport	35	3.6	137	3.8
Cinema	7	0.7	16	0.4
Radio	10	1.0	81	2.3
TOTAL	967	100	3579	100

Table 2
Advertising expenditure by product type

Product Group	£ millions spent	1975	1983
1 Food		89	313
2 Clothing		12	36
3 Auto		33	185
4 Drink and tobacco		74	247
5 Toiletries and medical		53	157
6 Household and leisure		87	382
7 Publishing		13	52
8 Tourism and entertainment		27	136
TOTAL		387	1508

Assignment 1 As a group discuss the tables. Then answer the questions.

a) In 1975 which media group earned the most from advertising?

b) Did this change in 1983? If so, how?

c) Say why you think any such changes took place.

d) Have there been any other shifts away from one type of advertising to another? If so, describe them.

e) Why are some places more popular for advertising than others?

f) What other places might become popular outlets for advertising in the next ten or twenty years? Why do you think so?

g) Are there any products that have been advertised much more in the 1980s than in the 1970s?

Assignment 2 Discuss the following as a class or group.

a) Are you surprised at any particular products being advertised and at the money involved?

b) Are you in favour of all forms of advertising?

c) Are there any products you feel should or should not be advertised?

Assignment 3 In small groups take a selection of different types of magazine and look at the advertisements. Divide them into categories similar to those in Table 2. Make a list showing which products were advertised the most often in each magazine. Combine your findings into a graph.

Section 2 Who Advertises and Why?

Introduction

Many different types of people advertise and for a lot of different reasons. They also advertise in a variety of places.

Group work You will need to be in groups for this work.

Assignment 1 Make a list of ten items, as varied as possible, and say where you would expect to see them advertised. Give at least three places for each item.

Assignment 2 Study the following table and then answer the questions.

Type of advertiser	Reasons for advertising
Industry and commerce	To sell goods and services; to attract investors; to persuade retailers to stock goods; to recruit staff; to change attitudes or behaviour; to give information about a product.
Organiser of event	To promote sports events; to attract people to the cinema or theatre, exhibitions and displays; to publicise demonstrations or charity events.
Political party, trade union or pressure group	To win support or votes; to lobby government; to attract donations or members.
Educational establishment	To inform about courses in colleges, universities and private schools; to sell evening classes and correspondence or audio-visual courses.
Private individual	To let, rent, sell or buy property; to sell or buy personal goods; to find a job or flatmate; to announce a marriage, birth or death.
Charity	To collect funds, to win sympathy for those in need; to attract voluntary help.
The media	To attract viewers, readers, listeners; to sell advertising space or time.
Government	To give information about new laws and people's rights; to publicise planning enquiries; to give information about local services; to encourage health and safety, to discourage anti-social behaviour.

a) Dealing with each type of advertiser listed in the table, give details of one advertisement you have come across that could have been produced by them.

b) Consider each type of advertiser and give details of where you would expect their advertisements to be placed.
Give reasons for your answers.

Section 3 Advertising Campaigns

Introduction

Advertisers set out to attract a certain type of customer for their product. This is what is called 'the target group'. The target group could be quite specific, that is, young people of 12-16 years. On the other hand the target group could be very wide-ranging and take in most of the population.

Large companies who wish to advertise themselves, or a product, will approach an advertising agency who will plan an advertising campaign for them. The agency may be asked to promote the company rather than its actual product in which case it might concentrate a campaign on how strong the company is in a particular field. This is called promoting the image of the company. Alternatively the agency might be asked to sell a new product, or re-launch an old one so as to make it attractive to a wider group of people. In either of these cases market research is called for.

Market researchers assess the market. They try to find out what the public wants from a product. They will find out things like who is likely to buy a product, how much they would be willing to spend on such a product and their response to the appearance and packaging of the product. If it is an existing product they will try to find out what type of image the product has since the image is important. Think about the following three brand names and the image they project: Yorkie, Zanussi, Heineken.

The information collected by the market researchers enables the advertiser and the agency to decide how best to plan the campaign. They will take account of the following.

Where the product will be sold.
Who will buy it.
Who the target group is going to be.
What approach will reach the target group best.
What type of language and graphics will be used.
How much money they will spend on the campaign.

Assignment 1   Choose ten well-known products. List who the advertiser's target group was likely to have been in each case. Make notes on how you think the advertiser tried to appeal to the target group.

Assignment 2   Imagine that sales of a well-known brand of chocolate have dropped. Set up your own market research campaign to re-launch the product. Design some questions to find out why sales have dropped. In the light of your research, suggest some ways of marketing the product to improve sales.

You will need to find out if the person eats chocolate.

If anyone else in their family eats it.

What brands of chocolate they eat.

How many purchases they make a week.

Do they eat your brand? If not, why not?

What image does your brand project to the buyer?

What image do rival products have?

Section 4   Why Do Advertisements Work?

Use of language

Advertisements attract attention for a variety of reasons. They may use persuasive language or they may use language in the form of a catch-phrase or slogan in the hope that it will remain in the buyer's mind.
It is important to choose the right words for the occasion.

Look at the use of language in these cartoons.

Assignment 1   Write down ten good advertising slogans. Compare your list with others in the class.

Assignment 2   Cut out ten advertisements that rely heavily on the use of language to sell a product. Say how successful you think these advertisements are and suggest ways in which they could be improved upon.

Exploitation of weakness

Advertisements may be aimed at a buyer's weaknesses. They may encourage people to buy for any of the following reasons.

1 Avarice
Products that are sold as bargains or with free gifts. For example, money-saving coupons or the chance of winning a prize.

2 Gluttony
Advertisements that appeal to your greed for food or drink.

3 Envy
Advertisements that suggest you need a product to make you as happy, beautiful, successful or as prosperous as your friends.

4 Pride

These advertisements dwell on how exclusive and superior the product is, and show it in an expensive and 'upper class' setting. (Consider what image this is suggesting to a buyer.)

5 Sloth

Advertisements that offer ease, comfort and plenty of leisuretime.

6 Sex Appeal

This is used frequently in advertisements but often the pretty girl or handsome boy has little or nothing to do with the product.

Assignment 1 Look for one advertisement that attracts a reader to buy in each of the above ways. Make a note of where you found the advertisements and explain why you think they attract in a particular way.

Assignment 2 Choose the advertisement which you think is the best from those you selected for Assignment 1. Explain fully why you think this advertisement is so effective.

Exploitation of people's fears

Advertisements may appeal to people's fears, encouraging them to buy the product lest they 'lose out' in some way.

1 Personal success

A lot of advertisements promise success in love, in friendship, in business and so on if you use a certain product.

2 Conformity

Many people hate to be different and gain pleasure from being the same as everyone else. Advertisements that promise this tend to emphasise the 'thousands of satisfied customers' image.

3 Security

Advertisements of this kind offer a cosy, safe life, secure from disasters. Advertisers for insurance tend to push this aspect.

4 Identification

Advertisers may use a well-known figure in thier advertisements. If the sportsman or film-star approves of the product so will their fans.

5 Respect

Scientists, doctors, nurses, etc, may be used in advertisements to give a product credibility with the public.

6 Maternal/Paternal love

These advertisements suggest that the mother/father who really cares for their child buys this product.

7 Health

These advertisements often show 'before' and 'after' pictures. The create a fear of an illness and then offer a cure.

Assignment 1   Find an advertisement that would fit each of these seven categories. Paste each one in your book with a note of how you think the advertisement fits the category.

Assignment 2   Look at a selection of advertisements and see if you can find any that are guilty of 'sex stereotyping'. Discuss as a class the implications of this type of advertisement.

Appeal to humour

Advertisements may appeal to our sense of humour. Many advertisements, especially those found on TV, do this.

Assignment   Try to think of three television advertisements that appeal to our sense of humour. Describe them and write about how they are humorous. If possible find one in a magazine and paste it into your folder or book with a note of why you have chosen it.

Double meaning

Some advertisements work because they make you stop and think as you read. Often it is because there is some ambiguity or double meaning in the language used. It may make the advertisement amusing or it may add another dimension to the messsage contained in the advertisement.

On a Sea Princess cruise, there's nothing like a few ports after breakfast.

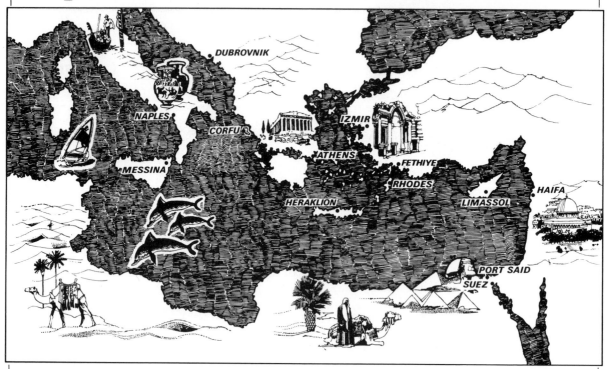

On Monday you visited the colourful port of Naples and saw Pompeii's famous stony-faced inhabitants.

On Tuesday you had an afternoon in Corfu. Just long enough to mingle with the people who'd settled for the same old holiday.

It's now Sunday morning. A good breakfast has set you up for the day and you're looking forward to Luxor and the Valley of the Kings.

Comforted by the thought that after an exhausting day's sightseeing, you'll be returning to civilization as we know it.

British plumbing and the Sea Princess.

With its three swimming pools, gym, sauna, bars, sun terraces and cinema, it offers every creature comfort on your visit to six countries this autumn.

Italy, Greece, Egypt, Jordan, Israel, Turkey, you'll see them all on our 15 night Jerusalem and Valley of the Kings cruise from October 19 to November 3. Or go earlier from September 10 to 23 for 13 nights around the Black Sea and Aegean via Greece, Turkey, Russia, Rumania and Italy.

As an extra attraction on our Pyramids, Athens and Adriatic cruise (September 23 to October 6), Richard Baker and a team of international musicians will be on board to entertain you.

While on the Athens and Holy Land cruise (October 6 to 19), BBC ornithologist Tony Soper will be giving shows for those who are interested in bird watching.

These events, like so many other things on a Sea Princess cruise, such as cabaret shows, feature films, the disco and of course all your meals, are all included in the fare.

P&O

For your 1986 Sea Princess Cruise brochure, call P&O on 01-831 1419 or see your travel agent.

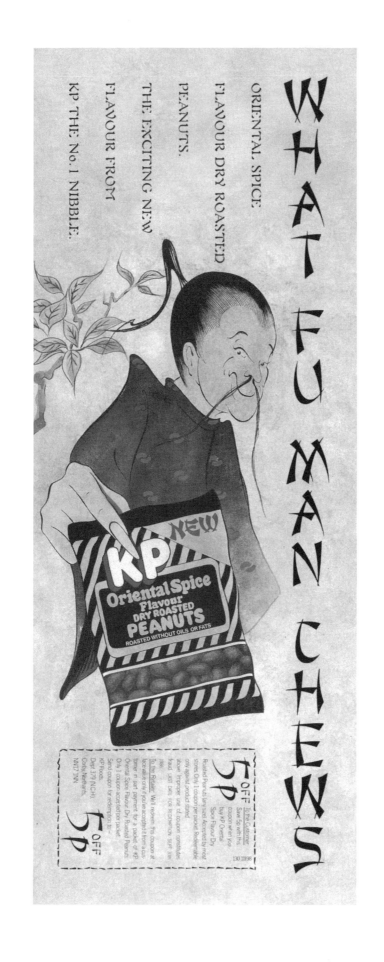

WHAT FU MAN CHEWS

ORIENTAL SPICE

FLAVOUR DRY ROASTED

PEANUTS.

THE EXCITING NEW

FLAVOUR FROM

KP THE No.1 NIBBLE.

189

THE CAT WHO BECAME A TAXPAYER.
(A TRUE STORY)

CLAUDIUS is a ginger tom who lives in West London with his human called Ron. He's a pretty normal sort of puss except for a couple of things. He has his own savings account and he's a bit of a TV star. ❦ Not in Dallas or anything like that, but he recently appeared on a money programme. He was being interviewed about his investments. ❦ It turned out that Claudius's savings account, which Ron had opened for him, was one which had tax taken off his interest automatically. ❦ Now cats don't have to pay income tax. Nor does Ron, because he doesn't earn enough for that. ❦ The trouble is that neither Ron nor Claudius can claim back the tax already paid on the interest. ❦ The experts on the TV programme had a simple but purr-fect solution to Claudius's problem. If Ron opened a National Savings Investment Account for him he would get all his interest in full. Nothing would be taken off for tax. ❦ As a non-taxpaying cat, Claudius would be earning a lot more interest. So would a non-taxpaying human, come to that. ❦ The National Savings Investment Account is currently offering 10.75% a year. And if you are a non-taxpayer, you keep the lot. ❦ Anyone can open a National Savings Investment Account, including children – they are usually non-taxpayers too. But if you are a cat, we have to ask you to open the account in your human's name. (Paw prints aren't valid signatures.) And do remember that if your human is a taxpayer, then the interest earned is taxable. ❦ You can get the details from your local post office. Or call us free on 0800-100-100 (all hours) and we'll send you all you need to know. ❦ Act now, because it's worth real money to you. As Claudius's adviser on the TV programme said: "It's a dog's life paying tax when you shouldn't – even if you're a cat."

Other advertisements

Assignment 1 Dealing with each of the advertisements on pp.191-193 in turn, write down in what publications you would expect to find them and how you feel they appeal to potential buyers.

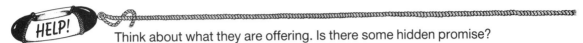

HELP!

Think about what they are offering. Is there some hidden promise?

Who would buy the product advertised?

Why would they buy it?

Quality in an age of change.

Steam Diesel Electric

The glorious past —
The challenging future

Railway Magazine brings the whole world of railways alive

This month: Resignalling around Leicester and also on the Central Wales Line

Railway MAGAZINE

September issue   £1.10
Out now!

Biggest classified section!

Every Mum's Dream.

Mum wants only the best for her baby: That's why she chooses Dreamseat, created by the manufacturer who designs and supplies seatbelts for 60% of all British-made cars.

Because Dreamseat is fitted at just two points it's simplicity itself to lift the seat from the car without waking baby.

And when those little mishaps occur, she can pop the removable cover into her machine for washing.

Dreamseat is available in two subtle shades – brown and blue. See them both at leading stores, garage chains and accessory shops, or write to: A.S.E. UK Ltd, Norfolk Street, Carlisle, CA2 5HX Tel: (0228) 31711.

RECLINER CONTROL

SUBTLY PATTERNED REMOVABLE COVER

SOFT COMFORTABLE HARNESS IN TONING WEBBING

SOFTLY PADDED QUICK RELEASE BUCKLE

INSTANT FITTING AND REMOVAL

OPTIONAL EXTRA IN TOUGH EASYCLEAN PLASTIC

NEW·TRAY

KANGOL Dreamseat

APPROVED BY THE BRITISH SAFETY INSTITUTE AND THE DESIGN COUNCIL

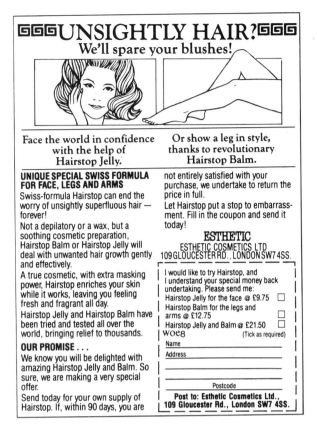

Assignment 2

Now you know how advertising works you should be able to sell anything. Design an advert to sell a new flower that will take over the whole garden or a hair colour that colours your hair and scalp green.

How would you set about doing this?

How would you make it attractive to a buyer?

What would you call it?

Can you think of a suitable slogan?

Could you design a poster for it?

Where would you advertise such a product?

Assignment 3

Soon you will be looking for a job and you will have to sell yourself to a prospective employer. Make notes listing all your good qualities and how you would put them over in the most attractive way. Then write the advertisement.

Decide what information you would want an employer to know about yourself. Qualifications, interests, job experience, aptitude for the prospective job and so on.

Highlight anything that might make you stand out from other candidates.

10 Letter Writing

Introduction

Basically there are two forms of letter that you might need to write.

Formal letters you write to people on business matters or to find out information.

Informal letters you write to friends and relatives.

The language and style you use, which can be called the 'register', will depend upon your reason for writing the letter. Formal letters will be precise, factual language with formal grammar and punctuation while informal letters may be written in the everyday sort of language you may use when speaking to friends. Whatever type of letter you are writing ask yourself the following questions.

Is it a business letter or a letter to a friend?
Do I know the person I'm writing to?
Why am I writing to them?
What register will I need to use?
If you are writing to complain about something you will need to be polite but firm.

Golden Rules

1   There are two main types of letter: the formal business letter and the informal, personal letter. Make sure you use the correct format for the occasion.

2   Letters must be understood by the receiver; make sure you include all the information necessary. For example, if you are arranging to meet someone you must state the day/date, the place and the time.

3   Avoid using a post script (PS) particularly in a formal letter. This tends to indicate that you forgot to plan your letter and left out some information.

4   There are accepted guidelines for the layout of letters, especially formal ones. Use them to help you write a good, well-planned letter.

5   Letters, like all forms of communication, must be well presented and free from spelling errors.

6   Use notepaper that is unlined for writing your letters and make sure that both paper and envelope are clean and neat-looking.

7   Allow for a margin on the left hand side of the page. If your letter is going to be short, try to position it nicely on the page – don't end up with a few lines squeezed at the top and a lot of space at the bottom.

8   Address the envelope clearly and accurately, naming the addressee by name or title. Always include the post code, which enables your letters to arrive safely and quickly at their destination.

Section 1 Why Do We Write Letters?

Assignment 1 Discuss with your family and make a list of the types of letters that are sent to your house over the course of a month. As a class compare lists.

Assignment 2 Answer the following questions.

a) Why have people written to you or your family in each case?

b) What advantages has a letter got over any other form of communication?

c) Why are some letters called formal as opposed to informal?

d) List some differences between these two types of letter.

e) How does the tone of a formal letter differ from that of an informal one?

f) Are all formal letters written in the same way? Is the same type of language or register used?

g) Why might different registers be used?

h) What would be the effect if the wrong register were used?

Section 2 Formal Letters

Beginning the letter

Letters should have the address of the sender in the top right-hand corner. The address of the person to whom the letter is going should appear on the left-hand side as in the diagram. Write the date on the right just below the second address.

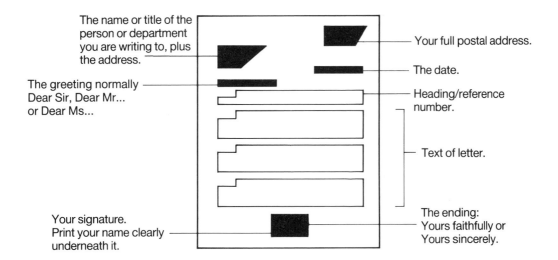

The name or title of the person or department you are writing to, plus the address.

Your full postal address.

The greeting normally Dear Sir, Dear Mr... or Dear Ms...

The date.

Heading/reference number.

Text of letter.

Your signature. Print your name clearly underneath it.

The ending: Yours faithfully or Yours sincerely.

If you know the name of the person to whom you are writing use it. Dear Mr..., Dear Mrs..., Dear Miss..., etc. If you do not know the name of a person, write to whoever you think will be the most appropriate person using 'Dear Sir' or 'Dear Madam'. Put their position in the company on the first line of their address on your letter to them as well as on the envelope. Using a name rather than a position means that your letter goes directly to the person who will deal with it quickly. It will not be passed from one department to another which will take time.

If you are replying to a business letter check whether there is a reference number on the letter you received. It should appear at the top of the letter – 'Our ref:....'. If there is one, quote it as the first line of your reply, like a title, and underline it. This will enable a firm to trace their correspondence with you quickly when they receive your letter.

Assignment Imagine that you are writing a letter to the following. The Features Editor, Dress Sense Magazine, Clayton Road, Bilthwell, Herts BI3 2HE. Placing your own address in the appropriate place, set this information out as you would a business letter. Remember to include the date.

Planning your letter

Planning is important and you need to think carefully about the type of information you wish to include in your letter. People are usually prompted to write formal letters for a reason and you will want to make sure that all vital information has been included. Think also about the order you will put it in; make notes to help you.

The length of the letter may vary a good deal depending upon your reason for writing. The acceptance of an invitation will generally be shorter than a letter asking for a lot of information.

You should divide the text of your letter into three parts.

1 **A beginning** Explain your reason for writing.

2 **A middle** This will contain the main information which should be divided into paragraphs. Make notes before you write to help make your paragraphs as clear as possible.

3 **A conclusion** Possibly explaining what the next step should be, if you expect a reply, or summarising the main purpose of the letter.

4 **Ending** Finish your letter courteously and add something like 'I look forward to hearing from you' or 'I hope to hear from you soon'. Do not forget to add 'Yours faithfully' if you are writing Dear Sir/Dear Madam or 'Yours sincerely' if you are writing to the person by name. Sign your name and print your name clearly below your signature.

Assignment 1 You are Mr Smith. Write a letter taking account of the following.

Mr Smith bought a vacuum cleaner at a shop called Highfield Stores on 6th December. It cost £110 and was guaranteed for six months. At the end of two months it broke down. The shop he bought it from has closed down so he has to write to the manufacturers to ask them to mend it. He writes to them at this address. Mr W Payne; Vac-cleen Inc, Clevedon Industrial Estate, Bartley EC3 6AN.

Assignment 2 Read your local or national newspaper and choose a subject reported on that you feel strongly about. Write to the editor expressing your views.

Assignment 3 You are leaving school soon and would like some information about a training scheme. Write a letter asking for this information.

Section 3 Informal Letters

Informal layout and plan

The informal letter is easier to set out since it only includes the sender's address on the top right-hand side of the page. The use of the word 'dear' in the greeting is a formality but it helps to begin the letter. The choice of ending really depends on how well you know the person you are writing to. 'Yours', 'With best wishes', or 'Love' followed by your name are fairly common endings.

Assignment 1 You are away on holiday and have promised to write to an elderly relative telling them about the good time you are having and the places you are visiting. Write the letter you would send.

Assignment 2 Write to a friend who has moved to a different area inviting them back to stay with you for a few days.

Section 4   Applying for a Job

Many jobs require that you send a formal letter of application. If there is no application form to accompany this letter then you will need to send details about all or some of the following.

age; schools attended with dates; courses followed and qualifications obtained; any posts of responsibility held, for example, prefect, sports captain; previous work experience – Saturday jobs, etc; leisure activities – if you are a member of a team or have any qualifications to do with this, for example, umpire, referee; if you hold any special awards – for example, the Duke of Edinburgh award, life-saving awards, etc.

Since it is difficult to incorporate all this information in a letter you may set out the information about yourself in the form of a 'curriculum vitae' (CV). (Translated, this means a summary of your career.) People who are applying for a lot of jobs often make a standard CV for themselves to enclose with all their letters of application. They are especially useful if an application form is not provided. Look at the outline for a curriculum vitae.

Curriculum Vitae

PERSONAL DETAILS
Name/Address/Date of birth

EDUCATION (Schools attended with dates)
Primary
Secondary

FURTHER EDUCATION

QUALIFICATIONS (With dates)

POSITIONS OF AUTHORITY HELD

MEMBERSHIP OF ANY TEAMS

JOBS HELD (With dates)

NAME OF RECENT EMPLOYER

HOBBIES/INTERESTS

REFEREES

Many firms supply an application form for completion and much of the information on a CV would be useful for this. When you have completed the application form or CV you should write an accompanying letter stating the type of person you think you are and how you feel you would benefit your future employer.

Like all formal letters the text of a letter of application needs to be planned and written in three parts.

1   **A beginning** Why you are writing, for what job and how you came to know about the vacancy.

2   **A middle** This should include any details about qualifications you wish to highlight. Any relevant experience for the job and why you feel you will be suited to the job.

3   **A conclusion** This should contain the usual polite ending and possibly suggest your availability for interview.

Assignment 1   Read this advertisement which was placed in a local paper. Reply to it, in the appropriate manner, applying for one of the positions listed.

FALCON CREST LTD
ARE PROUD TO ANNOUNCE
THE OPENING OF A NEW FACTORY AND SHOP

We are looking for the following staff:

Supervisors
Qualified machinists
Apprentice machinists
Qualified/Apprentice mechanics used to industrial sewing machines
Management trainees
Secretaries (trained and undergoing training)
Shop assistants
Shop manager/manageress
Factory floor workers
Packagers
Night security patrol

Wages are competitive. If you think you are the person we need write a letter of application giving brief details of qualifications and experience and quoting Ref. 2361 to:

Miss Jane Dean, Personnel Manager, P.O. Box 675, Brent SA6 2QZ.

Assignment 2   Read the following letter which appeared in the Letters to the Editor column of a local newspaper. You would like to go on the trip and should write an appropriate reply.

ADVENTURERS REQUIRED!

Dear Editor,
   I am a member of a group of young people, aged between 18 and 35, who are planning a trip to the Rocky Mountains in the USA next summer. We aim to tour that whole region of America and plan to cover a minimum of 500 miles. We will be taking a raft onto the river and sailing about 100 miles downstream. The trip has taken a year to set up and is fully organised. It will last about one month and we anticipate that the overall cost should be around £500.

   We already have twenty people who are committed to going, but would like to take about ten more. Obviously, the people concerned would need to be fit and fond of the outdoor life. There will be no mod cons on the trip! However, we do have a medical team comprising of a doctor and a qualified nurse.
   We would like anybody who is interested to write to me at Honey Ridge Farm, Newtown, Dyfed, giving some information about themselves as well as some indication as to why they would like to join us.

Yours faithfully
Stuart Brown

Include only the important information about yourself.

Tell them your age/sex/hobbies/interests/prior experience of camping, etc., if you have any.

Try to convince them that you are the right type of character for a trip of this kind.

You will be living closely with these people and will need to get on with them well so choose a friendly style.

Assignment 3   Look at job advertisements in the newspaper and choose one that you would like to apply for. Write an appropriate letter.

Section 5 Additional Assignments

Assignment 1 Look in your local newspaper for an advertisement for a holiday. Cut it out and place it in your book. Write an appropriate letter to book such a holiday or to request information about it.

Assignment 2 Your grandmother has invited you to stay but you are going to a party the weekend she has invited you. Write a letter apologising for not being able to go and arranging another time.

Assignment 3 Look at the 'Letters' column in your local newspaper and choose one to reply to. Cut out the letter and paste it in your book then write the reply.

Assignment 4 A month ago a friend of yours moved away from the area. Write them a letter giving them the local news and news of old friends, as well as news about yourself.

Assignment 5 You are writing to a pen-pal for the first time. Write a letter you might send introducing yourself and asking for details about them.

Assignment 6 You are secretary of a local sports team and have been asked to arrange a fixture with another local team. Write the letter you would send.

Assignment 7 You are in charge of organising a fun run for charity and would like the mayor/mayoress to start the race. Write a letter of invitation requesting his/her attendance and give details of the event.

Assignment 8 You have recently bought a new pair of jeans from a local shop and they are falling apart at the seams. You have now moved from the area. Send them back along with a letter of complaint to The Managing Director, Vagabond Jeans Shop, Sleeway Street, Berkely, Kent SW3 1BT.

Part Four

Coursework

General Introduction

For GCSE you will be assessed not just at the end of your two years' study of a subject but throughout the course. In some cases your school's assessment of your ability will be the only assessment you will have; in others it will be coupled with a formal examination of some kind.

You will be assessed on written coursework and on oral coursework. In both cases it is your teacher who will be marking your progress. It is likely that an external moderator will visit the school to check that the marking is in line with that of other schools and that your teacher has not been too hard or too lenient in allocating marks.

Your teacher will take into account the requirements of the syllabus and will decide when coursework should be carried out. Requirements vary between examining groups but the work and assignments in this book will form part of your coursework.

Coursework gives you an opportunity to show your skills more effectively, particularly your practical and oral skills. You are able to attempt work that is more wide-ranging, use videos, films, tapes and theatre performances as the basis of your work. Wider reading may also be incorporated.

More time may be spent in researching and collating material and in planning your coursework. This means you will be able to attempt longer and perhaps more interesting pieces of work than you could in an examination. Coursework also allows you to work more freely in groups; enabling you to tackle larger projects than you would if working alone. Another advantage of coursework is that a poor piece can be replaced with a good one. This is not possible in an examination.

Assessment over two years is intended to work in your favour. It means that everything does not rest on one examination at the end – if you are taking one at all. It is up to you to ensure that the work you produce, whether it be written or oral, is the very best you are capable of. Assessment will benefit you if you are a hard-worker in the classroom but become nervous the moment the word examination is mentioned. Your good work throughout the course will be rewarded and there should be no need to get unduly nervous as the final examination time approaches.

Coursework will prove difficult if you are away from school a lot. You will need to ensure that your attendance record is good or you may fall behind with your work and find it difficult to catch up.

11 Written Coursework

Golden Rules

1   Present your work in a folder of some kind with your name clearly written on it.

2   Make sure all pieces of work are clearly numbered and separated from one another.

3   Include a list of the contents. When you have finished the folder, number the pages.

4   Ensure that all pages look neat and tidy. Creased and dirty pages do not create a good impression.

5   You may illustrate your folder in some way if you wish. This can only improve the overall impression given by the folder and is well worth doing.

6   Where possible, try to use the same pen throughout, or at least the same colour ink. It makes the folder look neater.

7   If you have bad handwriting, space your work out so that it is easier to read.

8   Check all work for spelling and punctuation. Never hand in unchecked work.

9   Underline all headings with a ruler and do not submit work that is full of crossings out.

10 Write an introduction to your folder. Explain why you've included each piece and how you came to write it. If you have a choice of pieces to put into the final folder decide carefully what to include.

Section 1   Coursework Requirements

What types of work might go into a folder?

What to include in your folder will obviously depend on the examining board. Your subject teachers will tell you exactly what is expected of you as far as the board is concerned. However, the following will give you some idea of the type of work that *might* be expected from you.

Writing

This could be descriptive, narrative, factual and informative or argumentative – any of the work suggested in Part One of this book. The writing could be literary and be based on books, poems or plays that you have read. It is likely that the type of essay set for you will vary.

Other assignments you may do as part of your coursework are as follows.

1 Write a diary that might have been kept by a character in a literary text you have read.

2 Take a scene from a novel or from a narrative poem and re-write it in the form of a play.

3 Write an alternative ending to something you've read.

4 Write a letter from one character in a novel to another.

5 Write an imaginary interview between yourself and a character in a book.

6 Write an imaginary conversation between a character from one book or play and that of another.

Testing your reading and understanding of a passage

This involves you in the answering of questions on a passage, poem or extract, as well as assignments which explore the subjects in greater depth. Examples of these can be found in Part Two of this book and may include work on the following.

1 Novels, poems, plays.

2 Passages that are *listened to*, not read.

3 Passages from a wide variety of different sources such as magazines and newspapers.

Work on the media

Assignments for coursework on the media include the following. Examples of these may be found in Part Three of this book.

1 Newspaper reports you write yourself based on real events or on incidents in a text.

2 Advertisements you write and design yourself.

3 Reports you are asked to write.

4 Letters of some kind, either business or personal.

5 Charts, maps and diagrams.

Section 2 Presenting Your Coursework

Making a folder

In the 'Golden Rules' you were told that you must present your coursework well. It is quite easy to make a folder for your work and often a home-made folder is far more impressive than a bought one because it is original.

You can make a folder from two pieces of cardboard taped together along one edge. The cardboard can be obtained from an old cereal packet or the sides of a box. Punch holes in the side of the folder so that the paper can be held with laces. The card is only the basis of the cover and it is easy to decorate it with any of the following.

Left-over wallpaper – tin foil – plain white or coloured paper obtainable from most newsagents.

If you decide to use foil or plain paper you could decorate your folder even further. For instance, if you have included some imaginative essays you might like to design a cover along the lines of a cover for a book. Similarly, if you have included an argumentative essay about a certain topic you might like to look out for a newspaper article that deals with the same subject. You could then cut it out or copy it and use it to decorate the cover.

It is possible to make a collage of a number of relevant items. (A collage is a picture made from an assortment of materials which are cut out and arranged then stuck to the surface with glue.) If you decorate the cover like this protect it by placing a further cover of clear cellophane over the folder.

If you have already bought a folder there is nothing to stop you covering it to suit the information contained within.

Separating pieces of work

It is really up to you how much effort you put into this. You can buy or make dividers of some kind to split up your work. On these you could print neatly in block capitals either horizontally, vertically, or diagonally the title of the next piece of work.

If you wish to spend more time and effort on this, and many pupils do, then you could design dividers specifically for each piece, depending on what it is about. If it is an imaginative essay about space, you could copy or trace a picture of a scene and place this on the divider. Of course, if you are a good artist you could design your own cover to suit the essay. No matter what the subject of the essay is, it is always possible to design a divider that is suitable. How you set out your work is really up to you. You may wish to put work of a similar kind into one section, for example, all imaginative essays together, or you may wish to put the work in the order in which it was done.

Contents list

Although the contents list is to be found at the beginning of the folder, it is best to compile it when your folder is finished. It is only then that you will know what is to be included in the folder. The list should be set out clearly with page numbers if possible.

The introduction

Like the contents list, this has to be done last. It is a chance for you to explain the work in the folder. The way you set about working on it, the time spent on each piece and why you have included the work you have. It is also a chance for you to say how you felt about doing the work, whether you enjoyed compiling it, found it interesting and so on.

Illustrating your work

You might wish to include illustrations within an essay that you have written and this is perfectly acceptable. The more interesting your work is, the better the impression it makes. If you are going to include illustrations they should be mounted or drawn on plain paper so that they stand out.

Logging your work

Keep a record of each piece of work you have done in the front of your folder. This can be very useful when you come to write the introduction; it will tell you exactly when each assignment was done and how long it took you.

You could make a grid similar to the one shown. (One piece of work has been entered as an example.) Underneath the column marked classwork/homework you should write, briefly, details of the discussion work done before an assignment. Sometimes quite a lot of discussion work can go on in class before you actually begin writing. If you use reference books to help you, make a note of them.

Record of English Coursework

ASSIGNMENT TITLE

Key I = Imaginative   A = Argumentative   F = Factual   C = Classwork   H = Homework

Writing	Key	Classwork/Homework/Time	Date	Mark	Reference books
THE HERO	I	C WE SPENT 10 MINUTES DISCUSSING	1.3.87	13/20	—
		WORK. 1 HR. WRITING.			
Comprehension					

Writing	Key	Classwork/Homework/Time	Date	Mark	Reference books
Reports, Speeches, Letters					
Poetry Assignments					
Drama Assignments					
Novel/Short Story Work					

Oral Coursework

Golden Rules

1 Presentation: present your talk or your point of view well. You should be in command of the situation. Look and sound confident in what you are saying. Never try to shout the opposition down, or use slang when an argument gets heated.

2 Diction: make sure everyone can hear you and remember to vary the pitch of your voice. Speak clearly and slowly so that an audience can catch every word you say.

3 Content: whatever you say, whether to a small group or to a class, must be well thought out. The content needs to be interesting and logical. Remember, it is important to listen carefully when taking part in a discussion or debate, as it is to talk.

4 Contact: you cannot talk to someone without looking at them. This is called making eye-contact. A good speaker or communicator is one who maintains eye-contact with the audience. Reading your talk word-for-word from a piece of paper makes this difficult.

5 Timing: watch presenters and interviewers on TV. All these people have what is commonly called timing. If they amuse an audience, as you might try to do whilst giving a talk, they pause and wait for the laughter to die down a little before they continue. You should do this. If you don't, you will be trying to talk over a lot of noise and the audience will miss out on part of your talk. Politicians are also careful about timing in a speech. They might pause in the middle of a sentence to give the audience time to think about what they have said. It is important that you try to develop a sense of timing.

6 Register: make sure you speak in the appropriate register for the situation. Register does not just mean the way you speak to someone; it also means the type of language you use, as well as the way you say it. You do not speak in the same way to your mother, as you would speak to a person who is interviewing you. This is because you have automatically changed to a different register. You use a form of language that is suited to the situation you find yourself in, as well as being appropriate to the people you are with and your relationship with them.

Sometimes a particular register can contain language that is peculiar to it. An extreme example of this is book makers on the race-track who have got a register all of their own; their arm-waving and unusual jargon is all part of the register. A clergyman in the pulpit also has a very individual register.

As a class list other occupations that have a register peculiar to them. Try to describe the register and the type of language used. Discuss the reasons that cause people, including yourselves, to change fluently from one register to another in the course of the day.

Section 1 Oral Communication

Introduction

Oral work has now become a very important part of your English work. Every pupil will be assessed orally and this assessment will probably take place over the two-year course.

Remember that much of your oral work will be done alongside your written work. This can be seen in the argumentative section of this book where you are not just asked to write down your opinion on an issue but to discuss your views with your class or group first.

Communication of the kind you will be involved with can be divided into formal and informal or semi-formal speaking situations.

Formal speaking

A formal situation is one where a pupil or a group of pupils speak to the class in a conventional manner. An extreme example of this would be a debate. In a debate speakers are chosen beforehand. They prepare thoroughly a talk which they will give to the class/group. They will also prepare answers to questions they might be asked. Finally, they will follow the conventional patterns or routines laid down for this kind of speech situation.

Formal speaking situations include the following and assignments based on these situations may be found on p.210.

1 Group discussions where a member of the group will have to report back to the class. There are many examples of this kind of discussion in the chapter on argumentative essays.

2 A prepared talk by one pupil to the whole class, possibly followed by some questions from the audience.

3 An introduction and reading of a prepared passage from a book of your choice.

4 A mock interview between two pupils. Possibly a job interview or something similar to a radio or TV interview.

5 An interview between a pupil and teacher.

Informal or semi-formal speaking

Formal or semi-formal situations do not follow any special conventions or traditions. The pattern that the talk will follow is not set out beforehand which means it can be much more flexible.

Informal speaking situations might include the following and assignments based on these situations may be found on p.210.

1 Group discussions following which there is no report back to the class.

2 Re-telling a story to the class. Similar to that told in written form by Jasper-Carrott on page 32.

3 Describing an event to the class.

4 Discussing your views on a book with other members of the class.

5 Contributing to classroom discussions in general.

6 Taking part in some form of improvised drama in the classroom.

7 Talking with group members on a shared project.

Oral assignments

Assignment 1 *An interview*
You will need to work in pairs. Turn to page 199 and read the advertisement for the jobs carefully. Set up an interview for a prospective employee for one of the jobs listed. Decide who will be the interviewer and who will be the interviewee.

If you are the interviewer devise your questions carefully so that you know exactly what to ask.

If you are the interviewee decide on the type of questions you might be asked and have prepared answers ready.

Assignment 2 *Improvised drama*
You will need to work in groups. Imagine that a few married friends have got together for an evening meal. At the end of the meal one of the male guests begins to clear the dishes and offers to wash up. The host protests saying that that is a woman's job. An argument develops about the role of men and women in the home.
As a group act out the events of the evening putting across your own points of view.

Assignment 3 *Giving and following instructions*
Work in pairs. You will each need a map of the same area. Sit back to back and decide who is to begin. The person beginning chooses a place on the map and then tries to explain to the other person where s/he is without cheating by turning around and pointing. Take it in turns to do this.

Assignment 4 *Narrating a story or giving an account of something*
Tell a friend about your summer holiday and how you spent it.

Assignment 5 *Arguing and persuading*
Choose a subject you feel strongly about and try to talk the class around to your point of view.

Assignment 6 *Explaining*
You will need to be in groups. Each person in the group should demonstrate to the others the way something is done. For example, a group member who can knit or tie a fly can demonstrate the skill to the others. Your success can be measured by whether or not you succeed.

Assignment 7 *Describing*
Bring in an ordinary everyday object from home and keep it hidden from the class. Describe it to them without mentioning what it is. See if they can guess the object.

Assignment 8   *Expressing your personal feelings, opinions or attitudes*
In pairs, have a discussion about a TV programme. Discuss how you feel
about it and whether you would recommend it to someone who hasn't seen
it before.

Assignment 9   *Collaborating*
In a group decide and plan how you would raise money for an item of
equipment for the school.

Section 2   Conducting an Interview

Hints on interviewing

1   If you are an interviewer you should not speak as much as the person
being interviewed. If you do, you are not doing your job well.

2   Read the extract from an interview. The extract is the opening sequence
of a longer piece of work.
   Notice how the interviewer has let the audience know who the 'expert'
is. This is very important since the audience will be looking to that
person for some information.
   Notice also how the interviewer has interrupted the speaker and
asked him to explain the meaning of a difficult word for the audience.
   The interviewer has also tried to keep the talk going by asking
questions that lead the speaker on to a new point or asking questions
that clarify a point for the audience.

*Brian is interviewing Sue about her hobby which is dog showing. The extract is
part of a longer piece of work for which both have prepared thoroughly.*

BRIAN: My name is Brian Evans. Today, on 'Hobby Hour', we are going to
hear from Miss Sue Smith about her unusual hobby. Sue exhibits her prize-
winning beagles....I'm right, they are called that, aren't they?
SUE: Yes, that's right, they are a type of hound.
BRIAN: Sue shows her beagles all over the country. When did you start
showing and how did you become interested, Sue?
SUE: Well, it began about four years ago when my father and mother bought
me a beagle for Christmas. They wanted to buy a pedigree puppy and one
that was registered with the Kennel Club.
BRIAN: Who or what is the, uh, 'Kennel Club'?
SUE: They are the governing body. If your puppy isn't registered with the
Kennel Club then you can't show it. All shows are licensed by the Kennel
Club as well. So the KC are quite important – by the way, they also
organise Crufts every year. It's probably our best-known show. Anyway, I
got my puppy and started training her at a dog training class. You know,
walkies...sssit, all that! Anyway, someone there said she was a lovely
beagle and they thought I should enter her in a local show that was taking
place.
BRIAN: How do you 'enter' a dog for a show?

SUE: Well it seems complicated at first but you get used to it. You send to the show secretary for an entry form which you have to fill in and send back by a certain time. Oh, you also have to pay! If it's a small show it's normally under £1 a class. If it's a championship show then it's as much as £5 to enter one class.

BRIAN: But you can obviously win a lot of prize money.

SUE: Actually, no. It tends to be quite a small amount and always works out less than it cost you to enter! Anyway, we trained both the puppy and me for the show. The person at the training class also had beagles and showed me exactly what to do and how to prepare her. She was super.

BRIAN: Does it take a lot of time to prepare your dog?

SUE: Well it can do. Beagles are supposed to be easy to prepare. They really just need a bath and a groom and, because they have a short coat, it shouldn't take more than a couple of hours. I'm also lucky because she doesn't take a long time to groom daily. Some people have to spend hours every day grooming their dogs just to keep the coat free from tangles. Imagine having Old English Sheepdogs, you know the 'Dulux' dogs!

Assignment 1 Look at interviewers on TV to see how they conduct an interview. Make notes about the following points as you watch.
Do all interviewers talk little and listen a lot?
Are some of them strict with the people they are interviewing? Is this a good thing?
Should the interviewers be sympathetic listeners?

Assignment 2 In pairs set up an interview where one is interviewing the other about a school outing or trip they have been on.

Section 3 A Talk to the Class

How to plan a talk

1 Always plan carefully beforehand all that you intend to say.

2 List the main headings of your talk on a card. A glance at the card every now and then during your talk will help you to keep the talk going. Do not read directly from your notes. You need to be free to look at the audience.

3 To make your talk more interesting you could use visual aids. These could be diagrams used to explain a difficult point or pieces of equipment connected with your subject.

   If your talk involves a pet, ask if it is all right for you to take it to school. Don't just appear with your pet tarantula!

   If you are talking about your interest in pop music and groups you like, you could use album covers, tapes and tee-shirts, as well as programmes from concerts to illustrate your talk.

   Visual aids can help to make your talk more interesting. They can also help to explain something difficult and technical to your audience. There is no easier way to lose an audience's interest than to fail to explain some complicated point well enough for them to be able to understand it.

4 You need to interest the audience. Be enthusiastic or committed to what you are talking about. There is nothing worse than a bored speaker.

Assignment You have been asked to give a talk on your hobby, interest, or on a person of whom you are a fan, possibly from a well-known TV programme.
Prepare the talk you will give and make a list of the types of visual aids you will use to help you.

Make notes but don't read the whole talk out to the class.

Number any visual aids and place them in front of you in the order you will use them in your talk.

Paste or pin pictures or diagrams on a board to hold up at the appropriate time.

Speak clearly and slowly so that the audience can hear what you are saying.

Section 4 Reading Aloud to the Class

Introduction

You might be asked to read a passage from a book to the class. Normally you are free to choose a book that you like and to choose your favourite passage from it. Choose carefully the passage that you intend to read. If there is a conversation in the passage, you will probably have to pretend to be the people involved. This means using different voices so that you get this across to the listeners.

You might also be asked to prepare a short talk on the book, possibly giving your reasons for choosing that passage. This needs to be well thought out as you are expected to talk at length on this.

Hints on reading aloud

1 Read the passage aloud at home so that you are used to reading it out.

2 Remember that commas and full stops require you to pause.

3 If you are reading a conversation aloud and questions are asked, use the correct intonation. Make sure it sounds as if a question is being asked.

4 Be ready to answer questions about the book and the passage in particular. Prepare a brief talk explaining why you chose it.

Assignment You could work in groups for this assignment.
Nearly everyone has a favourite book. Choose a passage from one such book, read it aloud and explain fully why it is your favourite.

Do you like the book because it is the type you enjoy reading, for example, horror, thriller, science fiction?

Is it exciting?

Are there some good descriptions in it?

Do you like or dislike a character in it?

Do you feel sorry for a character for some reason?

Did you learn anything from the book?

Is it true to life?

Section 5   A Debate

What is a debate?

A debate is a formal discussion normally on a contentious issue. A contentious issue is one where people hold different views and can therefore disagree. You have come across issues like this in the argumentative writing section of this book – whether or not we should have field sports will cause disagreement between members of the class and is an example of a contentious issue.
   The 'motion' is the wording of the proposal put forward for discussion. To set up a debate you will need the following.

1 A chairperson who conducts the debate and ensures that an orderly discussion ensues.

2 A speaker for the motion and his/her seconder or supporter. These people are in favour of the motion put forward.

3 A speaker against the motion and his/her seconder. These people are against the motion put forward.

These people put forward their views formally to the audience in turn and then the chairperson will invite questions from the audience. Questions may be invited after each side has spoken or after all the speeches.

Hints on debating

1 You must be well informed on the subject.

2 Gather as much material as possible about the subject before the debate.

3 Use this material as a basis for your talk if you are a speaker or seconder.

4 Don't try to give a talk without prior planning. It is difficult to do and rarely works.

5 Speak clearly. Don't read directly from a sheet of paper.

6 When answering questions from the audience be courteous!

7 Do not try to shout the opposition down. It is not the best form of attack and rarely achieves anything.

8 Be confident in yourself and try not to let nerves get the better of you. After all, the class is made up of people you have known for a long time; they are not strangers.

9 If you are the chairperson you will need to be well informed on the subject. Often the chairperson becomes a referee between sides and ensures that both have a chance to answer questions and air their views.

10 The chairperson needs to ensure that both sides are given an equal number of questions to answer. Do this by encouraging the audience to write down some questions they wish to ask before the speakers give their views. In this way the chairperson can call on those members of the audience to speak.

11 Members of the audience should make sure that they have planned their questions well and that they are easily understood.

Assignment As a class debate the following motion.

'Nuclear war is avoidable only if we dispense with all nuclear weapons and rely solely on conventional arms.'

You will need to find out who supports this motion and who opposes it before you begin. From these people you should be able to elect speakers.

Remember that you have strong views on this subject and need to be able to explain why you feel the way you do.

Try not to use over-emotive language.

Do not get nasty with those who oppose you. They have as much right to their opinion as you do to yours.

Make sure that you are aware of the arguments the opposition will put forward. In this way you can come up with answers to counteract them.

Think about questions you might be asked and plan your answers thoroughly. Nothing is more likely to lose the debate than a speaker being unable to answer a difficult question.

Section 6 Additional Assignments

Individual work

Assignment 1 Give an account of *either* the happiest day in your life, *or* a holiday you have enjoyed.
Explain why they were enjoyable as well as describing them.

Assignment 2 Explain whether you think it is easier to grow up now than it was when your parents were young.
Give reasons for your views.

Work in pairs

Assignment 1 One of you is a child who would like to get a Saturday job; the other is the parent who is opposed to the idea.
Think of the arguments for and against the idea and act out the scene between child and parent.

Assignment 2 One of you has just witnessed an accident involving a dog, a bike and a car. (The witness can choose to be an old woman/man, a middle-aged woman with two young children or a person of about nineteen riding a motor-bike.) The other one of the pair is a member of the police force investigating the accident.
Act out the conversation that might follow the incident.

Work in groups

Assignment 1 In many areas facilities for the old and handicapped could be improved. Discuss what facilities are available in your area and how you think they could be improved.
Plan a campaign designed to improve the facilities and persuade shop-keepers, etc., to take part in your plans.

Assignment 2 You have been asked to organise a disco to raise money for a charity of your choice. Outline in a discussion all the things you would need to do to get such a venture off the ground.

Author's note

Much of the information for the factual and informative writing section of the book was kindly provided by various organisations. Many of these were charities, all sources have been named and the addresses are included should teachers or pupils wish to contact them at any time. I'm sure I need not say how grateful I am to all bodies concerned for their time and invaluable help.

Acknowledgements

The author and publishers would like to thank the following for permission to reproduce copyright material:

Allen & Unwin for the extract from *The Hobbit* by J.R.R. Tolkien; Robert Westall and The Bodley Head for extracts from *The Scarecrows*; Helene Hanff and Andre Deutsch for the extract from *84 Charing Cross Road*; Heinemann Educational Books Ltd for 'My Grandfather' by Tracy Starrett and 'Dilemma' by Gavin Bridge from *Young Writers 26th Year: W H Smith*; Grafton Books, a division of Collins Publishing Group for extracts from *My Family and Other Animals* by Gerald Durrell; The Hogarth Press for the extract from *Cider with Rosie* by Laurie Lee; Arrow and Century Hutchinson for the extract from *A Little Zit on the Side* by Jasper Carrott; Michael Joseph for extracts from *Adolf Hitler – My Part In His Downfall* by Spike Milligan and the extract from *A Kestrel for a Knave* by Barry Hines; Oxford University Press for the extract from *Collision Course* by Nigel Hinton (1983) and 'Leather Jackets, Bikes and Birds' by schoolboy Robert Davies, from *Every Man Will Shout* edited by Roger Mansfield and Isobel Armstrong (1964); Joan Lingard and Hamish Hamilton for the extract from *Across the Barricades*; Helen Forrester and The Bodley Head for the extract from *Twopence to Cross the Mersey*; S.E. Hinton and Victor Gollancz Ltd for the extract from *The Outsider*; Leslie Thomas for 'The Isle of Wight'; James MacGibbon for 'Not Waving but Drowning' by Stevie Smith, from *The Collected Poems of Stevie Smith* (Penguin Modern Classics); Faber and Faber Ltd for 'The Stag' by Ted Hughes, from *Season Songs*; DnA Ltd on behalf of EURYTHMICS for the reproduction of lyrics from 'Sisters' by Ann Lennox and David Stewart; Doris Manning for 'Reply to Euthanasia'; Susannah Kirkman and the Times Educational Supplement, 18 January 1985, for 'Change in Law to Forbid Live Animal Experiments'; Extract from *I Know Why the Caged Bird Sings* by Maya Angelou, published by Virago Press Limited 1984, Copyright (c) 1969 by Maya Angelou; Harper & Row Inc for 'Incident' by Countee Cullen from *Harper and Brothers 1925*; Longman Group UK Ltd for 'Guilty Conscience' by Rodney Sivyour, from *Let the Children Write* by M. Langdon; A.D. Peters and Co Ltd for the extract from *Unreliable Memoirs* by Clive James; Tina Morris for 'Tree'; G.M. Summer for lyrics from 'Russians'; The Society of Authors on behalf of the Bernard Shaw Estate for the extract from *Androcles and the Lion*; James Kirkup for 'The Lantern-Floating Festival' from *No More Hiroshimas: Poems and Translations* (Kyoto Editions) by James Kirkup; Manchester Evening News for the article '100 Year Old Elizabeth Dean looks back on her life as a Suffragette'; Enitharmon Press for Truant by Phoebe Hesketh; Greg Cullen for text from 'Taken Out'.

Thanks to the following for supplying copyright source material:

North Western Regional Health Authority for material from 'Project Smoke Free'; the Health Education Council, London; GASP; Christian Aid; Palm Tree Press; Child Poverty Action Group and Carla Ostra; British Field Sports Society; League Against Cruel Sports; Welsh Joint Examining Board; *Today* and Richard Shears; the *Police Federation*; the Voluntary Euthanasia Society and the *Mail on Sunday*; *Research Defence Society*; the Midland Examining Group and the *Guardian*; the *Observer* (1/12/85); British Union for the Abolition of Vivisection; Princess Voyages; the Director of Savings (c) Crown copyright; KP Foods; Matthew Gloag & Son Limited; the *Railway Magazine*; the *Western Mail*; the National Trust of South Wales; CADW; the Advertising Association; the *Manchester Evening News*; *Which?* and the Consumers' Association.

We would also like to thank the following for supplying copyright photographs:

The Bodley Head p.61.
Hamish Hamilton p.81.
Barnaby's Picture Library p.14. (Ken Lambert); p.15 (Dick Huffman); p.28 (Mark Boulton); p.42 (Ben Green); p.50 top (Max Hunn); p.79; p.127 (D. McLaughlin); p.131; p.141; p.142; p.145; p.149; p.163.
Network Photographers p.19 (Judah Passow); p.92 (Martin Mayer); p.98 (Barry Lewis); p.176 top (John Sturrock); p.176 bottom left (Roger Hutchings);
Popperfoto p.139, p.176 bottom right (Rob Taggart); p.212.
Russell Falkingham pp.114 and 170.
Sally and Richard Greenhill pp.1 and 202.

Illustrations by: Steve Norton and Julie Dodd

Typesetting and artwork by TDR Photoset Ltd Dartford, Kent.
Design and Consultancy by Susie Home

It has not been possible in all cases to contact copyright holders. The publishers would be pleased to hear from any unacknowledged source and full acknowledgement will be made at the first opportunity.